Living with an Architect
and
Finding Myself

I0137395

Living with an Architect
and
Finding Myself

by
Sylvia Coles

Designed and Edited by
Leonard W. Kagelmacher

Copyright © 2012
Sylvia Coles

Front cover image: Morganton, North Carolina bridge 2010, photographed by
Sylvia Coles

Back cover images: (top) Photo of Sylvia Coles by Chuck Terranova
(center) The Coles' home, designed by Robert Coles,
photographed by Len Kagelmacher
(bottom) 'Rose Pavilion, Delaware Park' 1990, photographed
by Sylvia Coles

Buffalo Arts Publishing
Tonawanda, New York

ISBN 978-0-9839170-4-5

Printed in the USA

For all those women who ever played second fiddle
and weren't content to stay there.

Foreword

Sylvia first told me of her book one beautiful day as the two of us hiked in the California Coastal Mountains above Santa Barbara. I now have had the opportunity to read a draft after a number of years, with great interest.

Hers is a story filled with caring for family and friendship, along with her inimitable touches of humor—a little twist here and there that catches one up short. It is by turns graceful and painfully honest.

There are fascinating adventures related here against the backdrop of three important constants: An interracial marriage and its subtle, and sometimes not so subtle, impacts on Bob and Sylvia's life together; her role supporting Bob's cutting-edge architectural firm; Sylvia's engagement in Bob's sustained community leadership advocating the location of a downtown university campus—against hugely powerful local forces—and, later, for a transit system to connect downtown with the university's final suburban location. To Bob's eternal credit, it has now been confirmed by then-Governor Rockefeller's head of the Urban Development Corporation that Rockefeller wanted a downtown campus—as suggested in my book, *Power Failure*.

But the grandest adventure of them all is Sylvia's own story. I call it "high adventure" and it is what each of us must do in our own way. At the onset, she speaks of her mother's values and strengths, which she clearly embraces as wife, business associate and mother—sometimes with mixed outcomes. Then Sylvia takes charge of her own life and does what she needs to do.

Along the way, she and Bob face medical challenges. But Sylvia is determined to discover who she is. She tries "various roles" as she pursues and receives an MBA, which she considers one of the great moments in her life. She has success lecturing on small business development and tries teaching in college settings. Later she attains a Masters Degree in Social Science, having written a thesis on the conflict between Canisius College and the black community surrounding the campus. There is "the most beautiful dig" in Africa and excursions to Papua New Guinea, Germany (her father's birthplace) and Peru. Her passion for photography grows organically over time and today she is recognized as an artist-photographer.

By the book's end one realizes that this is only the beginning of Sylvia Coles' story. But something remains of who she always was.

Diana Dillaway
Author

Acknowledgments

I thank those friends who read portions of or the entire manuscript and offered helpful comments. I also thank the many friends who showed continued interest in the book through its progress. Special thanks to Diana Dillaway, who contributed the Foreword.

Thanks to my sister, Helen Allen, and long-time friends Gerry Evans and Suzanne Taub, who cheered me on in this and other endeavors.

I'm grateful to my editor-publisher, Len Kagelmacher, whose encouragement and expertise made publishing this book easier than I could have imagined.

Lastly, thanks to Susan Morrow, who listened to my stories and whose innocent remark, "Why don't you write a book?" was the impetus I needed to begin.

Contents

List of Photographs 243

Introduction

When I finished writing my memoir, I realized that my mother had served as a perfect example of the woman I aspired to be. Elizabeth Bunge was a women's libber ahead of her time—intelligent, attractive, and musically gifted, she was also fiercely independent. By marrying Claus Meyn, my minister father, when she was 21, she escaped a confining life as the eldest daughter of fourteen children in her Lutheran minister father's household, mothering her younger sisters and brothers while her own mother was busy having babies. Married, she served dutifully as a minister's wife, adapting to new circumstances whenever my father was called to another congregation.

My father went back to Germany for a visit to his relatives in December 1929 as he thought he might be inheriting property there. While he was gone, my mother, my brother, Werner, and my sister, Helen, stayed with my mother's cousin in Pasadena, California; and I was born there on December 24. When my father returned, the property having been deeded to his uncle, he was called to a new congregation in Hildreth, a small town in Nebraska.

My intrepid mother made the perilous trip to Hildreth from Pasadena over the Rocky Mountains, driving their model-T Ford with isinglass curtains, eleven-year old Werner in the passenger seat, and nine-year-old Helen minding me, bundled in a wash basket, in the back seat. My mother's heart must have been in her mouth as she maneuvered the narrow, winding roads over the mountains. Werner remembers they ran into an awful blizzard in New Mexico and joined a long line of cars stuck in the snow. Somehow my mother got through and made the rest of the trip safely to Hildreth.

There was a point in which my father questioned whether he was really called to be a minister; he made several trips back to Germany and debated returning there to try another profession. My mother, however, firmly put her foot down and said she wouldn't go with him, and he was finally forced to abandon the idea. Only a few years later, our country became embroiled in World War II, and my mother's refusal saved our family from whatever fate awaited us in Nazi Germany.

She stuck with my father faithfully through what must have been some very trying years, moving from one congregation to another. And of course there was always the problem of making ends meet, particularly during the depression years. I still remember the bitter arguments they had revolving around money, painful to hear. The best years were the ones in Altenburg, Missouri, where I grew up. Congregants there were mostly supportive, and my parents made good friends among them.

Teaching music to pupils throughout the community not only supplemented my father's modest salary but gave her a degree of independence, as she used the income for extras she couldn't otherwise afford and at the same time expanded her social network; she loved meeting people and making new friends. My father never learned to drive, my mother having told him he was "too nervous." Perhaps, but I think the real reason was that she didn't want to share the car, even though it meant chauffeuring my father all the places he needed to go.

During my father's forty-three years in the ministry, my mother provided her steadfast support. His ministry was characterized by his philosophical quest for truth and a high regard for all people, in all walks of life. Her contribution was to convey to people everywhere she went her zest for living, love of nature, and her legacy of music appreciation. An accomplished musician, she was dedicated to the cause of musical education, and her many music students included Werner, Helen and me; she started me on piano when I was four years old, instilling in me a life-long love of music. I didn't become an accomplished pianist like my brother, but I enjoyed playing, and the piano is still my favorite musical instrument.

My father's last call, in 1947, was to Ellis, a small town in midwest Kansas, where he served a rural congregation with a church five miles out in the country. The parsonage was across the way from the church, and my mother didn't like living there: She felt isolated. So she designed a house, complete with a music room, to be built in Ellis, and did part of the finishing work herself. She and my father moved into their attractive, while modest, new home in 1953. After my father died, in February, 1958, she stayed on, becoming a vital force in the community and teaching music until the last years of her life. Her continual contact with the children and young people who were her students kept her vibrant and youthful, flexible, and able to adapt to changing times.

I like to think that I inherited some of my mother's admirable qualities. However, my mother seemed always to know exactly who she was; I did not possess that confidence. I wonder what she would have thought about my long journey to find myself?

Sylvia Coles
2012

Living with an Architect and Finding Myself

1

A Fateful Night at the Key Club

That evening at the Key Club determined the rest of my life.

I'd come to Minneapolis in October, 1951, leaving Des Moines, Iowa, where I had my first job after graduating from Wartburg College, a small liberal arts college in Waverly, Iowa. I'd been working in Minneapolis for a year as a stenographer, sharing an apartment with four other young women—Doris, Terry, Irma and Cora. Doris was dating Frank, a rising young black musician; and she invited me to come with her one evening to hear him play at the Key Club, near St. Paul, a popular hangout for students attending the University of Minnesota.

This was an adventure for me. I was not in the habit of going out to bars or clubs to meet young men, but I was intrigued with the thought of a possible rendezvous with some interesting new fellow. I had recently broken up with a young man I'd been going with and now wasn't dating anyone. After Doris and I arrived at the Key Club, we sat at one of the tables in one end of the room, near the stage where the band played. We ordered Manhattans and listened as Frank, with his sax, and the band played "Take the A Train" and other jazz favorites. As I sipped my cocktail, I took a look around; there was a small dance floor in the middle of the room, and more tables on the opposite side. I noticed several young black men among the crowd.

Frank was the only black I'd known. I grew up in a small town in southeast Missouri, redneck country, and the consolidated high school I attended wasn't integrated, nor was Southeast Missouri State College, which I had attended two years before transferring to Wartburg College. There were many blacks in St. Louis, where I worked several summers, but I had never known any blacks socially.

As Doris and I sat listening to the music, one of the young black men, tall and nice-looking, neatly dressed, strode purposefully over to our table, fixed me with a charming smile, and asked, "Would you like to dance?"

Thrilled at the invitation, I said, "Yes," and he led me out to the dance floor. As I leaned my head against his shoulder, I caught the pleasant aroma of after-shave. With an athlete's build, he was a graceful dancer, and we glided along, mixing with the other dancing couples. While we danced, he told me his name, Bob, and that he was attending the University. "I'm studying to be an architect," he said.

"You are?" I had just read Ayn Rand's novel, *The Fountainhead*, about the desperate battle waged by architect Howard Roark, "whose integrity was as unyielding as granite." Bob told me he was the only black student in the University's School of Architecture and expected to receive his Bachelor in Architecture degree in 1953. I was impressed: I'd never known anyone in this esoteric profession or with the ambition to enter it.

As the dance ended, we stayed on the dance floor and danced again. Before he brought me back to my table, where Doris sat watching us, he said, "I'd like to see you again." Completely charmed, I suggested we meet the following Friday evening in Loring Park, near my apartment. That turned out to be a perfect summer evening, and we strolled awhile and then sat down in the grass to talk. And then, sheltered from passersby, we kissed. The first kiss was followed by an impassioned kiss; wrapped in his arms, I felt myself falling in love.

After that, we met often in Loring Park, sometimes to play tennis, when I discovered I was a better player than he was. The fact that Bob was black and I was white didn't seem to matter then. We became friends with two other mixed couples, university students and their sweethearts. Bob roomed in Westbank Hall, the men's dormitory, near the University, and some evenings I would meet him for a movie in the neighborhood theatre. Occasionally we went to hear a concert in the University's Northrup Auditorium, and Bob came over a few times to our apartment to see me. But one day the landlady, showing her disapproval, announced a new rule: "Only select guests will be allowed to visit." She didn't need to spell out that this excluded Bob.

One night he invited me to see his room in Westbank Hall, and while I knew having women visitors was against the rules, I went anyway. His room was barely large enough for a cot, desk and chair, and closet. Books and records were piled on the shelves, and Bob had decorated the walls with school banners. After that first visit, I came again, and sometimes I stayed overnight, surreptitiously leaving the dormitory early the next morning and returning to my apartment and my housemates, who knew about my clandestine trysts.

Bob and I were unaware at that time that we were being monitored by the F.B.I. I had been working at their Minneapolis branch office for a year as a stenographer when on the afternoon of October 1 was called into the office of the CEO. This was quite unusual, and I nervously took a seat opposite the head man, not knowing what to expect. He came directly to the point: "Miss Meyn," he said sternly, "you are being dismissed for conduct not in keeping with the standards expected and required of employees of the Bureau. You are to leave this afternoon." I was shocked. I knew I hadn't broken any rules, but I was too intimidated to ask questions. I stumbled out of the office and to my desk in the steno room. Gathering my purse and other belongings, and avoiding the stares of the other stenographers, I hurried out of the building. Back in the apartment, I had a good cry.

After this episode, Bob and I learned that he was considered a student radical, having started the first campus chapter of the NAACP, and was under surveillance by the F.B.I. Our unconventional relationship had led the F.B.I. to conclude that I was providing him with information I'd gained by working in the branch office, where I took dictation from several agents. That was absurd: I kept whatever I heard confidential. But it was the McCarthy era, when many innocent people were being falsely accused, brought to trial, and persecuted. Fortunately, my firing was the last brush Bob or I had with the F.B.I.

But soon after the F.B.I. fired me, I was shocked to discover I was pregnant, a dilemma I had, naively, not anticipated. Bob and I discussed my predicament and the options. We couldn't afford to get married then and have a baby, and in those days it would have been difficult to arrange the adoption of a racially-mixed child. The possibility of having either of our parents raise the child was out of the question. Even though it would be a heart-rending decision, I couldn't see any option other than to have an abortion.

It was years before Roe vs. Wade and the Supreme Court's decision, in 1973, to make abortion legal. Not only were abortions illegal, but they were dangerous. I'd heard horror stories about abortions that had gone grievously wrong. It was also difficult to find a doctor to perform the abortion. But with cash contributed by sympathetic friends added to our meager savings, Bob found a reputable provider. On the afternoon of the appointed day, I lay, frightened, on a cot in the doctor's office while he administered an abortifacient. The kind nurse held one of my hands and Bob held the other. The pregnancy had been in the early stages, and the abortion was successful; there were no after effects, and I recovered quickly. But the profound regret I felt about ending a life would stay with me forever.

I had been worried about getting another good-paying job; luckily, I found another about a month later, with the law firm of Morley, Cant, Taylor, Haverstock and Bailey, where I replaced the secretary who had been with Mr. Cant for fifteen years. My relationship with Bob continued through the winter, although there were times I wondered what I was thinking. We shared an interest in the arts and music—I learned to like jazz; he learned to appreciate the classics—but we disagreed on a number of issues and sometimes got into arguments. We came from such different backgrounds. He was black, a postmaster's son from Buffalo, the second largest city in New York; I was white, a minister's daughter from Altenburg, a small town in southeast Missouri.

Meanwhile, Bob was attending classes and also working part-time. Neither Bob nor I told our parents of our romance. I was concerned that my parents' reaction would be negative. That Christmas Eve my mother came to Minneapolis to visit an aunt of hers, and also, I suspected, to check on me, staying in our apartment. On Christmas Day she and I went to services at Central Lutheran Church, and that evening she went out to dinner with friends.

Later that night I waited until I was sure she was asleep, then got dressed and went over to Westbank Hall. In Bob's room we exchanged presents, opened them; he gave me a pair of red pajamas and silver earrings, and I gave him a green sweater ...and drank Mogen David wine. I returned to the apartment at 3:00 a.m. and, waking Doris, slipped into bed. She had slept there, wearing my blue night-cap in case my mother woke up and missed me. My mother and I went shopping the next day, and she left the day after, none the wiser.

Bob and I continued our affair, and one night in March, we went to see the play, "Point of No Return." After I came home that night, I pondered the message and wondered whether, in fact, Bob and I had reached the point of no return. I phoned Bob and we had a long talk. Finally, I asked, "Bob, were you serious when you said you'd like to marry me?"

Bob hesitated for a moment and then said, "Yes, absolutely." The next day I went over to Westbank Hall and we talked ourselves into getting married. Coincidentally, a room in the apartment building where our recently-married friends, Lucas and Joyce Smith—another mixed-race couple—lived, was available, and we arranged to move in.

We found a friendly Lutheran minister who married us in a private ceremony with a few of our friends attending on Palm Sunday, in his church near the university campus. I wore a new navy blue suit and a beautiful orchid corsage Bob had given me, and he looked dashing in his new black suit. After the minister pronounced us husband and wife, Bob and I engaged in a long kiss. Our friends gathered round and congratulated us.

We celebrated afterwards with dinner at Roadbuddys with Doris, Terry, Lucas and Joyce, Louie (an architect friend of Bob's) and his wife, Fern, and then a party at Maurice and Mary Jo's, other friends. I felt happier than I'd ever been! Afterwards, we went to our new home, which Bob had decorated with a dozen red roses.

I had no idea then how complicated this marriage would be.

Bob and Sylvia, Minneapolis. Summer, 1952

2

Beginning our Marriage

Our home was a furnished room with a bed in the upstairs apartment of a two-story house. We had access to a "sitting room" across the hall, where we could entertain guests, and shared the kitchen and bathroom with Lucas and Joyce and a single black man. Our landlord lived downstairs. He kept the front door unlocked so tenants could come and go as they pleased. The house was in a working-class neighborhood in southeast Minneapolis, and we rode a bus to work and university. We didn't mind that the place was shabby as we weren't home much. The rent was cheap, and we were happy just to be together.

Once we were married, Bob and I both told our parents. However, while I had told my parents that Bob was attending the University of Minnesota, I held off revealing that Bob was black. Her curiosity aroused, my mother decided to pay an impromptu visit to meet her son-in-law. On a Saturday morning, Bob and I were sitting in the kitchen, door closed to the hall, enjoying a leisurely breakfast. Bob and I were both dressed casually, and he was wearing one of my silk stockings to press down his nappy hair. Suddenly I heard someone coming up the wooden stairs, and a cheery "Hoo-hoo," announcing a visitor. The kitchen door opened, and there stood Mrs. Meyn. "Mother!" I exclaimed in surprise.

She stood there for a moment, stunned, and then quickly regained her composure. She certainly had encountered many unexpected and sometimes difficult situations in her experience as a minister's wife. Bob scrambled to his feet, and I made the introductions. I hastily cleaned up the kitchen while Bob and his mother-in-law left for the sitting area; I joined them there in awkward conversation. Bob was on his best behavior, and my mother was as diplomatic as I'd ever seen her. Somehow we managed to get through the afternoon. She returned to her hotel and left Minneapolis the next day, cutting her visit short.

Her visit was followed soon after by one from my father. This time, we knew he was coming. Upon arrival, he waited at the front door while Bob came down to greet him. Thrusting out his arm to shake Bob's hand, he announced. "I'm Rev. Meyn." Bob jumped. He told me later he thought my father had a gun in his hand. But my father, certainly troubled, was as kind as he could possibly have been under the circumstances, and we managed to get through his visit as well.

While they were good people and harbored no racial prejudices, the idea that I might have married a black man never crossed my parents' minds. After all, at that time, inter-racial marriage was against the law in half the forty-eight states. They concluded that Bob had put me under some kind of spell, from which they hoped I'd soon recover.

Last to visit was my sister, Helen Allen. She was especially concerned because she herself had had an unfortunate marriage. As a young working woman, she fell in love with a handsome, charming young man who swept her off her feet; and they married after a brief courtship. What she didn't know until later was that her husband, Tad, was a schizophrenic whose mental problems had already begun while he was in his teens. By the time Helen found out, they had had two young children, and he was trying to hold on to a teaching position. Tragically, he committed suicide one afternoon while she and the children were away, visiting my parents. Helen didn't want me to make the same kind of mistake she did.

While my mother, father and sister all viewed my marriage as a delusion, my brother, Werner, and his wife, Faye, saw it in a positive light. In a note to me, Faye wrote, "You have a right to marry anyone you choose; we're sure Bob is a fine young man." Bob's parents didn't seem to have any problems accepting me. When we met during a belated honeymoon trip to Niagara Falls and Buffalo in September, they welcomed me as their daughter-in-law. Bob's three siblings were all boys, so I imagine his mother was glad to have a female in the family.

After a while, my mother, father and Helen all came around to accepting Bob. They must have been impressed by Bob's ambitious goal—to become an architect—and his progress in achieving that objective. In fact, Bob received his Bachelor of Architecture degree in December, 1953. He was also accepted as a graduate student at M.I.T., beginning in the fall of 1954. That Christmas, my father sent me a note expressing his love for me and sending best wishes to us both. He also expressed his wish to have a heart-to-heart talk with us soon.

In January, 1954, Bob was called to report to the local draft board, as the country was engaged in the Korean war. He came home, exuberant "Great news, I'm 4-F!" He was rejected because of his eyes: He had divergent strabismus, in which each eye focuses separately. While this was not a handicap for Bob, it kept him out of the service and enabled him to continue on his chosen path.

That summer, Bob worked as a waiter in the dining cars on runs the Great Northern Railway made between Minneapolis and Montana. He would come home from each trip with pockets full of money from tips. As Bob emptied his pockets on our bed, we'd count the coin and bills, happy about the extra money.

In September, 1954, we moved to Cambridge and found a second floor apartment on Chilton Street, near Harvard square, and Bob began his graduate studies at M.I.T. On October 31, our son, Darcy Eliot, a healthy 6-lb., 12-oz., was born in Boston Lying-In Hospital. I was overjoyed and Bob was a proud father.

It was a good year. We made friends with other young couples, husbands who were Bob's classmates, and I loved my new role as a mother. Bob was satisfied with his courses and the level of instruction he was receiving, some of his professors renowned architects. His favorite teacher-mentor was Lawrence Anderson, who remained a good friend until he passed away. Successfully completing his studies, Bob was awarded the Master of Architecture degree in 1955.

In addition to achieving the Master's degree, Bob entered the competition for the Rotch Travelling Scholarship. That year's award offered a stipend of $5,000 for a year's travel in Europe. The founder, Benjamin Smith Rotch, and his family believed that travel abroad to become familiar with great works of the past would stimulate a young architectural student's imagination and enrich his cultural knowledge. To that end, the Rotch family created an endowment to enable students to pursue foreign studies and designated the Boston Society of Architects as administrators of the competition.

The Rotch scholar was selected through a two-stage competition, and the winning candidate was then selected among the finalists. Included in the criteria for the winning design were 1) representation of a complete architectural project, and 2) quality, completion, clarity and effectiveness of presentation. The only stipulation was that the Rotch winner was required to write a monthly report and send it to the Rotch Trustees.

Bob busied himself working on a winning design, and I typed the text accompanying the illustrations. The dinner to announce the winner and award the prize was given by the Boston Society of Architects in May, 1955. Bob and I attended, along with other finalists, and sat tensely through the evening, waiting for the announcement. Finally it came.

"The winner..... is Robert Coles." It was almost too good to be true! Flushed with joy, I joined Bob in acknowledging the hearty applause that followed and in the many congratulations he received. More congratulations and good wishes poured in from our families and friends. Bob's dream had become a reality: come fall we would begin the most exciting adventure of our young lives.

3

The Rotch Travels

How does one prepare for a year's travel abroad? Bob's itinerary included England, France, Italy, Spain, Belgium, the Netherlands, Denmark, Sweden and Germany. We obtained passports, immunizations, bought guide books and foreign language dictionaries. Travelling with a year-old baby, we took a folding crib, stroller, toys, clothes and diapers for Darcy, in addition to our own clothes, supplies, and a portable typewriter. To transport our luggage, Bob planned to buy a station wagon in London with part of the Rotch money. After months of preparation, we were finally ready. We left Cambridge and went to New York, from where we would embark for England.

We sailed out of the New York harbor on the luxurious S.S. Ryndam on October 22, 1955, arriving at the port of Southampton, England a week later. From there we took the train to London, where it was disagreeably chilly and damp. There we encountered the first of the few instances of discrimination we experienced during our travels.

Bob had booked a room at one of the hotels, and we spent the first night there. However, the next morning the hotel manager told Bob, "I'm sorry, sir, you'll have to leave." No explanation, but Bob recognized he wasn't welcome in this staid establishment. We packed and left. Luckily, Bob soon found another place, an inexpensive bed and breakfast. I'll never forget the unusual breakfast fare—greasy fried bread, no doubt leftovers from the previous evening's meal—served with syrup and sausages.

The stoic English endured the weather bundled in heavy wool sweaters; we shivered in our hotel room heated only by a gas meter, which we fed with shillings—coins equivalent to U.S. quarters. Bob and Darcy got colds right away, and I went to bed for several days with something like flu. But, once recovered, we did a lot of sightseeing, taking the bus, the underground, or simply walking to such famous places as Picadilly Square, Number 10 Downing Street, the House of Parliament, Westminster Abbey and the Cathedral. Bob and I also visited the British Museum of Art and the Tate Gallery, and heard a concert in Royal Festival Hall.

After three weeks in London we went on to explore the English countryside, traveling in the Ford Squire station wagon Bob bought. He was most interested in England's beautiful cathedrals, so we travelled from one place to another to see some of the most famous, including the Winchester Cathedral, the longest in England. We stopped at Stonehenge, where the dismal weather added to its somber atmosphere. After seeing the medieval cathedral in Canterbury, we ate lunch in the "Old Coffee House" and had the most delicious lemon tarts I've ever eaten. Then it was on through the coastal towns to Dover, where we took a ferry across the English Channel, arriving in Calais, France.

From Calais we drove on to Boulogne, experiencing hair-raising brushes with French drivers: We couldn't understand the French traffic signs. We decided we'd better stop, so we stayed there two days to study our French-English dictionary and French phrase book. While there, Bob also finished his first travel report, which I typed and Bob mailed to Boston. Then, having learned enough French to get by, we continued on a southerly route through the French countryside, staying in comfortable, warm hotels and enjoying the delicious French cuisine. On our last day in France, we drove from Nice to Pegli, on the outskirts of Genoa, Italy. We had a whole day's vista of gorgeous scenery, driving along the Mediterranean coast, roads winding up and down the mountains and down to the sea, crossing the French-Italian border at Grimaldi.

On December 1, we drove over the Bracco Pass, bound for Rome, stopping in Pisa to climb the remarkable Leaning Tower. Once in Rome, we found lodging at La Casa de Tourista, a former monastery. Besides rooms within the main building, the complex included a cluster of motel-like cabins. We settled in one of the cabins, which served as our living room and bedroom. We ate meals in the Casa's dining room and used the toilet and bath facilities in the central building.

In the month we were there, we visited many of the places Rome is famous for, from the Coliseum, the Roman Forum and the Pantheon, to St. Peter's, the Vatican, and the Sistine Chapel. The Trevi fountain was one of the many sparkling fountains we found in the city's delightful piazzas. One of these, the Piazza Navonna, was filled with stalls set up during the Christmas-New Year's season selling toys and trinkets for Epiphany, "the children's Christmas." On Christmas Day, bells pealed all over the city and I could imagine crowds of people attending services. I myself wasn't feeling well and missed going to church somewhere. I did recover sufficiently later to enjoy the grand dinner served in the Casa's dining room that evening—antipasto, pasta, steak and vegetables, and motta for dessert.

We made occasional side trips out of the city; one, particularly memorable, took us to Tivoli. There we saw the ruins of the Roman Emperor Hadrian's Villa and the fabulous Villa D'este with its 1,600 or more fountains, considered the most beautiful in the world. Another day we drove out to see the monumental buildings erected for Mussolini's "Congress Exhibition." In the resort town of Ostia, we saw a 15th century castle and the excavated ruins of what used to be a city.

I felt very much at home in Rome. Once, as I was out exploring by myself, I was even stopped by two Italian women who asked me for directions. Apparently I'd worn off my tourist look. But in mid-January, we left Rome and traveled south, passing through Naples and through desolate, mountainous countryside. At Villa S. Giovanni, we crossed the straits into Sicily and drove along the coast, up the mountains above the sea, arriving in the resort town of Taormina and settling at the Hotel Naumachie. We were the only guests, it being off-season, and received special attention from the friendly staff and the hotel manager.

Situated on the edge of a snow-capped mountain, 800 feet above the sea, Taormina was one of the loveliest places in Europe. The village of one main street, lined with shops, cafes and bars, led to beautiful public gardens, with poinsettia and other exotic flowers in bloom. Bob discovered a Greco-Roman teatro, and one afternoon we sat and watched an Italian movie crew in action there.

While Bob spent a week touring Sicily with an American friend, I stayed behind with Darcy, giving me the opportunity to practice my Italian, as very few people spoke English. My usual routine was to take Darcy in his stroller to the public gardens and let him play there. Invariably, he attracted curious attention, which sometimes proved annoying. During Darcy's naps, I went out to browse in the elegant shops, have coffee at one of the bars, and sometimes converse with friendly people. By chance, I met two Swedish ladies who lived in Taormina in a house down the hillside. I was surprised and pleased when one of the ladies said, "You must come for tea."

"Thank you, yes, we will," I promised. We did go see them one afternoon, and the ladies and I had a delightful conversation while Darcy nibbled on oranges and cookies.

Soon after Bob returned, we left Taormina and headed back to Rome. Crossing at Messina, we took a route through the mountains and were treated to an almost-perfect rainbow, framing the entire mountain range. Driving along the western coast, we experienced much colder weather, with a bit of snow, and spent one frigid night in a hotel with no heat or hot water. At Paestum we stopped to see the three temples and museum, then went on to Naples. From there, we took a side trip to Pompeii, where we had a guided tour of the ruins including the basilica, forum and shops. The remains of paintings and mosaics were still quite beautiful.

In Rome we were welcomed back at the Casa. Bob picked up mail and we spent several days there, seeing friends and partying, before heading out again. Italy was having one of its coldest winters, and it snowed while we were there, enough for a fort which some young men and boys built in the Casa's courtyard. When we left Rome, driving slowly along the snow-covered highway on our way to Florence, we encountered a massive traffic jam: Italians weren't used to driving in the snow. We pulled off the road at a truck stop, joining other motorists for a break before venturing on.

Bob had selected the Pensione Doyle in which to stay in Florence. But we spent a miserably cold night. I went to bed with all my clothes plus overcoat, cap and mittens; and Darcy, with a cold, snuffed and coughed all night. We could hardly wait to leave the next morning, and found a hotel with central heating, toasty warm. In Florence we met students studying at the University, ate meals in the student cafeteria, and partied on Valentine's Day. On my "afternoons out," Bob baby-sitting, I visited the Medici Chapels, the Duomo and Baptistry, Palazzo Vecchio, and the Uffizi Galleries. I also had an unnerving encounter: When I visited the monks' cells at San Marco, with paintings by Fra Angelico, I barely escaped from an impassioned guide with liquor on his breath and devious plans. Florence was a jewel, but I'm sure I would have enjoyed it more had it not been so cold.

Our next stop was Venice, where we stayed only a few days. There we had a comfortable room in the Hotel San Marco, only fifty feet from the magnificent Piazza San Marco, with the Cathedral at one end of the Piazza. Tourists sat at tables lining the Piazza and pigeons flocked, fighting for the bits of food that fell from tables. I took a ride down the canal in one of the vaporetti, and window-shopped along the many interesting little streets and side streets, buying a few things for gifts.

Leaving, we stopped in Padua, on the way to Milan, to see the cathedral. In Milan, the high point for me was the evening Bob and I dressed in our best and saw a performance of two surrealistic ballets at the fabulous La Scala opera house. The low point came when I got lost one chilly afternoon on the way back from the Duomo. By the time I finally found my way back to the hotel, I was freezing and took to bed shaking with severe chills. The hotel provided their equivalent of a hot water bottle, a jug filled with hot water. After a few hours of chills and high fever I woke up, recovered.

In Milan, we encountered the criminal element: Bob went out one morning and found the station wagon gone from its parking space. It turned out that the police had apprehended thieves breaking into the car and had taken the car down to the police station. It was a relief to get the station wagon back and find only a heater stolen.

Now it was March. We had spent three months in Italy and Sicily, and it was time to move on. Leaving Italy, we stopped in Nice and Marseilles on our way to Spain. We crossed the border at La Jungera and drove to Barcelona, where we found a good hotel in the downtown district. We strolled in Antoni Gaudi's playful Park Guell and pondered his unfinished cathedral, the Sagrada Familia. In Barcelona, we adjusted to a slower pace, everyone getting up later going to work later, and dining later.

Leaving Barcelona after a few days, we drove south to Valencia, but the city was crowded with people celebrating festival. Bob said, "Let's get out of here," so we escaped, driving out to the coast and spending an hour in the park there. Then, moving southward along the eastern coast, we stopped for a night in Murcia.

The drive from Murcia to Granada took us through barren country—rocky cliffs and mountains, cactus, and dwellings literally carved out of the hillside. In Granada we found a good hotel and places to buy a few necessities. The main attraction here was the Alhambra, buildings in the Arabic-oriental style, with beautifully-carved walls, arches and ceilings, some executed in a stalactite pattern.

One afternoon I set out on my own, saw the Cathedral and the Albiacin, a former Moorish quarter, and ventured down the road leading out of the city. However, the countryside grew wilder the further I advanced, and after encountering some gypsies, I turned back. Along the way, I met three little girls, begging, and gave one of the girls fifty centos, a few cents.

In Granada, our family attracted quite a bit of attention; and while most people appeared friendly, we detected some hostility. People here had probably never seen a black person before, and Bob became fed up with the many stares he received. From Granada, we traveled on to Seville, where we saw the Alcazar, smaller but perhaps more exquisite than the Alhambra, and then Cordoba before arriving in Toledo, where we settled in for a longer stay, needing a break from continual travelling.

Toledo is noted as the birthplace of the famous painter, El Greco, whose house and museum were open to the public. Toledo is also known for its steel works; and Bob expected it would be a good place to find some inexpensive silver pieces for souvenirs. It turned out to be our most pleasant experience in Spain. We found a good hotel, right off the central plaza, and a room on the first floor, with a warm radiator but no hot water. Fortunately, the weather was warm enough so that wasn't a problem. The hotel staff was friendly, and so were the people we encountered while in Toledo.

We happened to be there during Holy Week, and one night we watched from our hotel balcony as a solemn procession wound its way from the cathedral to the main plaza. In the procession were some two hundred women, young and old, dressed in black and bearing candles; a van bearing a Madonna, fashioned from cloth, lace, silver and flowers; the priest; altar boys; and lastly, the mayor and soldiers. The pageantry was unforgettable.

As tourists, we couldn't resist the opportunity of a lifetime—to see a bullfight, so Bob and I left Darcy with one of the hotel maids one evening and drove to the Plaza del Torres, in a large arena. We sat in sol seats and watched while three skillful toreadors in turn readied six bulls for their final bloody contest against the matadors. As we expected, the bulls were the losers. After each bull's demise, the matadors cut off the tail and other parts and tossed them up to the excited crowd to catch. Totally turned off, I said to Bob, "I never want to see another bullfight!"

During our stay in Taormina, Bob made a side trip to Segovia and Avila. On his return, we celebrated our third wedding anniversary by dressing up and, after Darcy went to sleep, enjoying a delicious meal in the hotel—a manzanilla aperitif, an entrée of stuffed partridge, and a bottle of Chablis. After dinner we left the hotel to stroll about and met a man who invited us for a drink at the El Zoco bar.

On Good Friday we saw the most elaborate procession yet: Nazarones in purple and white, five paseos—Christ crucified, the Virgin, Christ being borne from the cross, the Virgin holding the dead Christ in her arms, and the coffin bearing the body. Horsemen in armor rode by, followed by clerics, and, lastly, the dignitaries. The procession was a long and halting one; Bob and I watched it from the window in a restaurant where we were having dinner, eating our meals at intervals. A friend we'd made treated us to drinks and invited us to his home the next day. It was a rare opportunity, and we were delighted to accept.

Our friend was the owner of the bar where we regularly had our breakfasts of coffee and doughnuts. Driving out, we found our friend's villa, located well out from the city center and overlooking the river below. There was an extensive garden, a flock of chickens, two dogs, and a large bathing pool filled by a fountain. The interior of the house was typical—a living room with a stove and decorated mantle, the parents' bedroom, two children's bedrooms, kitchen, and comedor, where we joined our friend in the noon-day meal. His 14-year old daughter served the señor, one of his two sons, and us a typical Spanish noon-day meal—thick soup, beans and potatoes, fried eggs with tomato sauce and bread—and kept our wine glasses filled. After lunch, our friend excused himself for a siesta. With a "Muchas gracias, señor," we left and drove back to our hotel.

Easter was sunny and warm, and many tourists filled the city. The morning after, we said goodbye to all and drove out of Toledo, stopping at the edge of the city for one last look. From a panoramic view, high on a hill, we spotted our friend's villa, probably the largest in Toledo. That afternoon we arrived in Madrid and found the Hotel Mediodia, centrally located near the railroad station and close to the Prado. Our rooms included a terrace, bedroom hall and bath—quite luxurious. I had my first tub bath since Rome.

The weather in Madrid, sunny and warm, was the most pleasant we'd experienced in months, and facilitated walking about the city. On my afternoon out, I went first to the Prado, where I spent about four hours absorbing the paintings, my favorites being the Goya cartoons. Then I stopped at the Plaza España, where there was a statue of Don Quixote, and walked up to the top of a hill to get a good view of the city. On the way back to the hotel, I strolled along the Avenida José Antonio, the busiest street in Madrid, passing shops, restaurants, bars and movie theatres.

Staying only a couple days in Madrid, we drove on to Burgos, where we crossed the French border. Our first stop in France was in Nantes, to see an apartment building by the famed French architect Le Corbusier. A young man living there was kind enough to show us his apartment and take us up on the roof. Going on to Tours, we stopped there a few days, one day driving out in perfect weather into château country. We visited several fine examples: Villandry, with formal gardens; Azay-le-Rideau, a beautiful castle; Chinon, famous as the place where Joan of Arc met the French king; and Langeais, a fortified castle with a drawbridge.

From Tours we drove to Paris, staying two weeks in a comfortable, fairly-inexpensive hotel on the Left Bank, which provided delicious breakfasts: melt-in-your-mouth croissants served with plenty of butter and jam, and good, strong French coffee. Soon after we arrived, we visited the Champs Elysées, the Arch of Triumph, the Eiffel Tower, and Notre Dame. On one of my afternoons out, I went to the Louvre, where I spent about five hours viewing the paintings, including those by Rivera, Rembrandt, Degas, Toulouse Lautrec, Cezanne and Van Gogh.

While in Paris, we met an American friend who had been studying there and went out together several times to his favorite restaurants and night clubs, one of which featured American entertainers singing English, Irish, American and French songs.

One nice day I took Darcy in the stroller and walked to the Luxembourg Gardens, lovely with many-colored tulips in bloom. We sat near a pool in which children were sailing boats and as Darcy played nearby, I watched the passing parade, mostly mothers with children but also students of all ages, nationalities and colors. One young fellow surreptitiously took pictures of Darcy.

Our friend baby-sat Darcy one evening while Bob and I went to see the Folies Bergiere. There was standing room only, so for tickets at the equivalent of only seventy-five cents each, Bob and I stood during the entire show—two acts and forty tableaux. Most of the numbers were displays of performers in elegant costumes; others were risqué dances by nudes. After the three-and-a-half hour show, we had dinner at a restaurant near Moulin Rouge. Always interested in trying something different—Bob and I had had our first taste of snails, smothered in wine, in France—I had a delicious dish, Lapin Provencale, rabbit stew, yet another example of the savory French cuisine we enjoyed.

During our last day in Paris, we drove out to Versailles, where Bob and I walked quickly through the halls, Darcy running ahead. We left without seeing the gardens as it was a cold and rainy day. Back in Paris, we drove up to Montmarte, where we saw the Sacre-Couer and wandered around the square. There were nice little bars and shops selling pictures and ceramics, and a few sidewalk artists sat at their easels, their paintings observed by passerbys.

Leaving Paris, bound next for Switzerland, we stopped in Rheims to see the cathedral, and again to see another cathedral in Nancy. Then it was on to Ronchamp for a look at LeCorbusier's Chapel. It stands on a hall overlooking Ronchamp and has an odd shape—resembling a Dutch cap, a wooden shoe, or perhaps the prow of a ship. Driving on, we noticed the landscape becoming ever more

Swiss. In the frontier city of Basel, we paused to look at two chapels and also noticed quite a bit of modern architecture.

Our next stop was Zurich, and we spent a night there in a hotel near the railroad station. We found friendly Italian-speaking people in Zurich; and it was a relief to be able to communicate better, even with our limited Italian, than we had trying to speak French. We had an excellent meal at an Italian restaurant in what must have been an Italian section of Zurich. The hotel staff were very nice and gushed over Darcy, giving him candy, cookies and oranges.

Leaving Zurich, we crossed the Swiss-German frontier at Constance and drove to Munich, where we met one of Bob's M.I.T. classmates, Hans von Busso. Munich was crowded with tourists, but we managed to find a hotel, very modern and attractive. Hans took Bob and me and several of his friends to a Bierstube, where we spent three hours eating, drinking beer and having a jolly time. Rather than ending the evening then, Hans took us to another restaurant where we danced to a good, 3-piece orchestra, finally getting home about 3:00 AM.

We woke up hung over the next morning. After recovering, I left Darcy with Bob and went shopping with Hans. Although knowing it would be several years before Darcy could wear them, I bought a pair of Lederhosen, leather shorts. After shopping, Hans took me to see the famous Frauenkirche; we climbed up into the dome and had an excellent view of the city. Afterwards, we had coffee in a modern bar. Dinner with Hans that night was our last visit with him. Saying goodbye, we wished each other good luck.

Now it was May, and the weather was pleasantly warm. Having left Munich, we drove on the Autobahn, stopping at a rest station where we lunched outside in the warm sun. It was a pleasant place, and we lingered while Darcy amused himself, playing with pebbles, going up and down the steps, and petting a friendly dog. Leaving the Autobahn, we drove through Heidelberg, a picturesque town, and then arrived in Frankfurt.

In Frankfurt, Bob had an amusing experience. As the door opened to the first hotel Bob investigated, he tried out one of the few German phrases he knew, "Haben Sie ein Zimmer für zwei?" (Have you a room for two?) The manager was used to having American servicemen bring their German sweethearts there for an assignation. With a curt "We don't open until four," he closed the door. Obviously, it was not the kind of hotel we were looking for, and Bob soon found another one.

There we had good meals and a generally nice, if short, stay. Darcy and I spent most of our days there in a very pleasant park, with Schiller's statue among the blooming tulips. There were pebbles for Darcy to play with and grass to romp on. We met a German woman with her two-year old daughter; and after Darcy overcame his timidity, the little girl and Darcy played together. A German couple took a picture of Darcy.

The beautiful spring weather continued as we drove on to Cologne, stopping briefly in Darmstadt and then at a Jugendheim, orphanage, deep in the woods near Seeheim. In Cologne, we settled in a hotel near the cathedral, which, while damaged, miraculously escaped destruction during the war. Cologne, in fact, was the most bombed of the German cities, and there was still rubble everywhere, a few people living in the ruins of former homes, and new buildings rising on top of the ruins. For whatever reason, we were asked to leave the hotel a day early; and we left, having put the hotel on our blacklist.

During our stay in Hanover, I went first to the bank and the railroad station to inquire about the ferry to Denmark, and then spent the afternoon typing another monthly Rotch letter. Leaving Hanover, we passed through Soltau, where we saw a large building whose sign read "Meyn's Hotel-Restaurant." I should have inquired about possible relatives, as Meyn was my father's name, and he was from the village of Cadenberge, less than one hundred miles away.

From Soltau, we passed through Hamburg on the way to Grosenbrode, staying at a hotel about a mile further out, literally at land's end. We took the ferry from Heiligenhafen to Denmark; after landing, it was a short ride to Copenhagen. We selected a hotel which was right in the center of town and just a couple blocks from the town and railroad station. Our room was cozy, warm, and had hot water. Our first morning there, we had a late breakfast of Danish pastry, bread, butter and jam, and coffee. That evening Bob took Darcy out to Tivoli, a big amusement park; and while he was gone, I gorged myself on a whole sack of those scrumptious Danish pastries. As I might have expected, I paid for it—nauseous the rest of the night, and then temporarily losing my taste for Danish pastries.

In Copenhagen, I caught up on washing. All throughout the trip, I'd been washing Darcy's clothes and diapers as well as our own clothes, usually drying everything on a line strung up in our hotel rooms. Very rarely, we sent the laundry out. This was part of the economizing we did to stretch the travel stipend. As it is, we managed to travel for about $5 per day. My various roles during the trip thus included mother, companion, typist and washerwoman.

On Mother's Day Bob gave me the royal treatment: He got up with Darcy, dressed him, and ordered breakfast while I stayed in bed. Later, he took Darcy out for lunch and returned with a bouquet of yellow roses for me. That afternoon we drove out to see a Danish architect who'd invited us to his home, a traditional house, surrounded by spacious lawn and trees. We met his pregnant wife and four of their six children, blonde, handsome youngsters and took tea together—cheese and crackers, bread, butter and jam, chocolate cake and tea. We chatted for a couple of hours, but when our host said, "Won't you stay and have dinner with us?" we politely declined, with the excuse that Darcy was getting restless.

That evening Bob and I went alone to Tivoli, that fabulous place with all sorts of amusements—beautifully-lit restaurants, several bands, and everything to entertain the crowds strolling through the park. We had the popular smorebrod, open-faced sandwiches, beer and coffee in one of the restaurants. Back at the hotel, Bob wrote letters while I took a bowl bath. It had been a lovely day.

The next afternoon I took off on my own to see Copenhagen, stopping for coffee and pastry and then on downtown. There I browsed in two of the big department stores. Assisted by friendly clerks, I bought a hat for myself and suspenders for Darcy. After shopping, I explored the old section of Copenhagen, stopping for coffee at a sidewalk café. While I was sitting there, a Dutch fellow came to my table to talk, but his three friends dragged him away.

Later that day Bob and I went to tea at the apartment of a young Danish woman, her fiancée, and another couple, all architects. We spent a pleasant evening chatting about architecture, differences between Danish and American life, and other things. One of the young women planned to go to London for the summer and work in an architectural office there.

Our next destination was Stockholm, where our friends, Ken Terriss, another M.I.T. classmate, and his wife Anne lived in an apartment complex. We stayed with them several days, Ken showing Bob some of Stockholm's modern architecture. Together we went to a ballet performance one night and saw "Rite of Spring," "The Three-Cornered -Hat" and "Gaite Parisienne." Anne took me shopping, showing me around in some of the big department stores; and I bought a few gifts. One evening friends of the Terrisses came for dinner and afterwards showed slides of Norway and Finland.

Having left Stockholm, bound for Gothenburg, we ate a picnic lunch at a rest stop halfway there. When we stopped in a small town nearby to look at an interesting building, a photographer appeared, struck up a conversation, and took pictures of us. "I'm going to write an article about you and will publish it, with a photograph, in the local paper. I'll send you a copy," he promised. We were obviously a rarity: Darcy attracted about ten children who came to our car to stare at him. Then, stopping at a couple of gas stations to check the car, we attracted more people, who took photographs. Not only was this attention highly annoying but it was having a negative effect on Darcy, who began shying away from strangers.

Gothenburg was an attractive city, and we spent a pleasant day there before heading back to Copenhagen, and through Germany, on the way to Holland. We thought the Dutch countryside pretty. In Amsterdam, we settled in the Hotel Bon. Gershwin's opera, "Porgy and Bess" was currently playing in Amsterdam, and we found that some of the American cast members were staying at the same hotel. However, we didn't get a chance to meet any of them.

The weather was sunny and warm, so we spent a lot of time outdoors; I took Darcy out to several of the nearby parks. One night Bob and I went to see an American movie, "The Man with the Golden Arm." On our last evening in Amsterdam, Bob and I enjoyed a delicious dinner of steak, potatoes, and vegetables at De Wenteltrap (The Winding Staircase) for only $2.00, not including beer and tax.

We left Amsterdam on May 30th on a rather sour note, as the hotel owner tried to overcharge us. However, after Bob settled the bill, the owner said, "Have a good trip." Driving through Haarlem, we passed by a large park with fields of tulips and stopped for lunch at a roadside restaurant on the Belgian border. We stopped again in Antwerp to let Darcy romp through the park.

We found a hotel in Brussels for only $1.70 per night, about a 15-minute walk from the center of the city. Bob and I walked downtown that night and found a basement café which, the waiter told us, was a meeting place for existentialists. A combo was playing American jazz, and we drank beer and danced for a couple hours, having a wonderful time.

From Brussels we made a side trip to Ghent to see the cathedral, an old fortress and other historic sites. Ghent had a lot of atmosphere, and I was rather sorry we hadn't stayed there rather than Brussels. We dined in an elegant restaurant, La Petite

Auberge, a radio broadcast of modern music playing in the background. Back in Brussels, we checked out of our hotel and sped to Paris. When we got to the hotel we'd stayed in before, we were disappointed to find that no rooms were available. Abandoning the Left Bank, we drove around and finally found a hotel not far from the Eiffel Tower and the Champs Elysees.

During the next couple weeks, we were mainly occupied with selling the station wagon, arranging passage to the U.S., and taking care of other travel details. Also, we completed the last Rotch letter, Bob and I arguing over details, as usual. I did get a haircut, and bought a pair of slacks at the Gallerie Lafayette. Darcy also got a haircut, his first, but it took the barber, another lady and I holding him while Darcy screamed bloody murder. His thirteenth tooth was erupting, and he was getting almost impossible at lunchtime, all over the table and wanting to hold the silverware. It was a good thing we'd soon be back in the States.

On June 14, we left Paris and took the train to LeHavre, arriving on board our ship, a French ocean liner, about 11:00 a.m., and sailed back to America. So ended what had been a most fascinating trip through Europe. Our travels abroad were enriching to us both, Bob gaining a greater appreciation of the architecture of the past, and both of us benefiting from a unique opportunity to see some of Europe's finest art and also experience and appreciate each country's unique culture, landscape and hospitality, all at relatively little cost.

Travelling in Europe heightened our desire to see other parts of the world, and we would do that in years to come. Young, healthy and enthusiastic, we were able to put up with minor inconveniences and adjust to whatever circumstances we found ourselves in. It was one of the best years of our lives.

4

Back to Cambridge

During the end of our travels, we began looking forward to resuming life in the United States. Our plan had been to find a place to live in Boston, after which Bob would look for a job with an architectural firm. But when Bob set out, answering newspaper ads, he was shocked to encounter housing discrimination in the very city called "the cradle of liberty."

Having made an appointment to see an advertised apartment, he would arrive at the address, only to be confronted by the building manager or owner with the news that the apartment was no longer available, or with statements such as "We don't rent to families." His experience shattered the rather idyllic view of America we had entertained when we encountered difficulties in Europe.

Finally giving up this fruitless quest, Bob turned to Cambridge and went back to the neighborhood in which we'd lived previously. We found temporary housing with a family and lived with them for about a month before moving into a duplex on Alpine Street, a block over from our previous residence.

Our neighbors were all young professionals like ourselves, and most with a world view like ours. Another mixed-race couple lived a few doors down from us, and a Chinese family lived across the street. Mr. Chen was an importer of Chinese goods, and his wife, Joyce Chen, opened a restaurant in Cambridge. She eventually became famous, introducing a line of Chinese cookery, a Chinese cookbook, and a chain of Joyce Chen restaurants.

In 1956, Bob began a two-year internship, first with the architectural firm of Perry, Shaw, Hepburn and Dean, and then with Shepley, Bullfinch, Richardson and Abbott, both in Boston. He obtained his Massachusetts license to practice architecture in 1958 and then worked as Custom Design Manager for the firm of Carl Koch and Associates/Techbuilt Homes in Cambridge. Meanwhile, Bob's niece Marion, the daughter of his brother Tom, came to live with us in December, 1957.

This was an unexpected development, and one for which I was quite unprepared. Marion was seven-and-a-half years old, five years older than Darcy. Tom, while serving in the U.S. army and stationed in Germany, had met and fallen in love with Marion's mother, Frances, the widow of a German soldier. Tragically, Tom was killed in an automobile accident on May 8, 1951. Frances subsequently married another American soldier, Glen Eberhardt, white, who adopted Marion; and they had a baby daughter of their own.

Since then, Glen had been transferred from Germany to a post in North Carolina. During the transition period when the Eberhardts moved to the United States, Marion lived for a while with his mother in California. Then, during the Eberhardts' move south, in the fall of 1957, they left Marion with Bob's parents in Buffalo with Glen's promise that they would call for her "as soon as they got settled."

The senior Coles enrolled Marion in the neighborhood school; however, Bob's mother found Marion, an attractive and intelligent child but subjected to chaotic conditions early in life, difficult to handle. In a letter of desperation, she wrote to Bob, telling him about Marion—the first we knew of the circumstances. Bob agreed to have Marion stay with us temporarily and brought her to Cambridge the day before Christmas.

When she learned that Marion was staying with us, Frances wrote me a pleading letter, in German. Fortunately I knew enough German to understand her message. Frances revealed that her husband did not love Marion, and that she felt compelled to choose between a happy marriage with Glen and the new baby, or a possibly difficult life—especially in the South—including Marion. She closed the letter pleading us to adopt Marion.

Under these circumstances, Bob felt committed to assuming a parental role and taking the responsibility of raising Marion. Following temporary guardianship, we adopted Marion in 1960. Although unprepared to be a mother to Marion, I did the best I could. Bob and I both hoped to give her the sense of belonging and security she'd lacked in the last several years.

Marion seemed to fit in well with our family, although her sudden introduction as his older sister did affect Darcy. Before she came, he was used to his status as an only child. He developed a speech problem, having special difficulty enunciating consonants. Although he had been speaking a few words clearly while we were in Europe—one of his first words was "truck"—he was now generally unintelligible except to me. The speech therapist I consulted suggested that the speech problem was a manifestation of his need for attention.

Gradually, Darcy's speech improved. He developed a close friendship with Geoffrey, another boy his age who lived at the other end of Alpine Street, and he had a sympathetic teacher in the nursery school he and Geoffrey attended. In the meantime, we enrolled Marion in a neighborhood school, where she did well; and she, too, found friends on Alpine Street. Her best friend, Meredith Friedman, lived next door, and we were friends as well with her parents, Major, who ran a summer boy's camp, and Anne, a realtor.

One afternoon I watched as a piano was delivered to the Friedmans. The deliverymen tried every which way to get it through the front door, but it wouldn't fit. As the piano, an upright, sat there, it started raining. Anne hit on a solution: "Sylvia, if it fits in your front door, it's yours." It did, and so I acquired a piano, much to my delight. I'd played the piano for years, beginning when I was only four years old, my mother having been my first teacher, and continued through college. I'd never had a piano of my own, so this was a wonderful gift. Now I could get out my favorite piano music and play as much as I liked.

Marion's closest friend was Miriam, the daughter of other friends of ours, Edith and Eric Lenneberg, a psychologist, who lived in Belmont, a few miles away. Friends on Alpine Street besides the Friedmans included an inter-racial couple, Jim Harkless, a lawyer, and his wife, Ann, who lived several doors down from us. Jim and Elaine Young, a black couple, lived at the other end of Alpine Street. Jim had been one of Bob's professors at Hampton Institute, which Bob attended a year before going to Minnesota.

Other good friends in Cambridge were Pat and Bill Hall, Jean and Jerry Voss, and Mer and Ralph Knowles, all young architects and their wives. Pat and Jean had children around Darcy's age, and we spent many happy hours together. Pat and her two boys sometimes joined Marion, Darcy and me on our summer trips to Nahant, a fishing village on the coast, north of Boston. There we waded in the chilly Atlantic water and built sand castles on the beach. I found an unusual black rock at Nahant. Set on edge, it was about 15" high and looked like a sculpted elongated head. It reminded me of primitive African art I'd seen in galleries. I carried it home and still have it, ...my favorite among others in my rock collection.

Alpine Street was conveniently located, within walking distance of Fresh Pond Park, which Darcy and I frequented, and a short bus ride away from Harvard Square. The Square was a bustling, cosmopolitan center for Harvard and M.I.T. students and residents alike, with restaurants, shops, theatres, coffeehouses and a community center, where I took a course in Beginning French. Bob and I frequently saw movies at a theatre which showed art films, and once we heard folk singer Joan Baez, who got her start in Cambridge, in a coffeehouse in the Square. It was easy to get to Boston, taking the subway from Harvard Square. Darcy became fascinated with the trolley buses running in and out of a tunnel in the Square, and some of his first drawings were of trolley buses.

My parents came for a visit in the summer of 1957, staying for a few days and getting to know the children. That was the last time I saw my father, as he died unexpectedly of heart failure on February 27, 1958. I flew to Kansas for the funeral, held in the church where he had served as minister, and spent a few days there visiting with my mother, Helen, and Werner, who had come from his home in Terre Haute, Indiana. Saddened, I was sorry that I'd been too preoccupied with my own family and missed the opportunity to spend more time with my father in recent years.

Bob was not a family man, and spent very little time with either Marion or Darcy, but he did like to travel. So during summer vacations in the next few years, Bob and I and the children travelled, camping while seeing the United States and Canada. The first summer, with tents and all the other necessary equipment, we explored Canada—driving up through Maine to New Brunswick, Nova Scotia, Cape Breton, and Prince Edward Island, coming back through Quebec and Montreal. It was an inexpensive way to tour: Bob and I both enjoyed seeing new places; I loved camping, and the children seemed to have a good time.

Another summer we went cross-country out to the West Coast and back. In California, we visited Frank Gehry (Bob had worked with him briefly in Cambridge) and his family in Los Angeles. Staying a few days in San Francisco, we were captivated by this unique city. In the summer of 1962, we drove through Canada, camping in Glacier Park, stopping in Winnipeg to see our friends, Doug and Donna Jean Gillmor (Bob and Doug had met at M.I.T.), and then going on to Vancouver, where we visited Ken and Anne Terriss. On the return trip we stopped in Seattle to see the Space Needle, and then camped in Yellowstone Park. There we woke up in the middle of the night to find a bear raiding our food box outside our cabin. Luckily, Bob was able to scare it off.

On one trip, we camped on the rim of the majestic Grand Canyon. Bob and I were blown away by the sight, but Marion turned a blind eye to the breathtaking scene and sat in her tent, playing her guitar and longing to be back home with her friends. It was then that Bob and I recognized she was getting too old to travel happily with us, and that was the last of our camping trips.

5

The Move to Buffalo

While he was working at Techbuilt, Bob designed a house for us. His plan was to build it on a lot near Alpine Street and move in as soon as we could. Then, suddenly, he received a call from an engineering firm in Buffalo. DeLeuw, Cather and Brill were looking for an architect to design a recreation center on Buffalo's east-side. Somehow, they found Bob's thesis, which was the design of just such a center, and offered Bob the position. Accepting, Bob began commuting to Buffalo in 1960 to work on the project. During his trips to Buffalo, he'd had second thoughts about living in Cambridge and began looking at vacant land in Buffalo as possible alternative sites for the house.

Buffalo's population then was about 600,000. Although the city had declined in recent years, having lost its prominence as one of the country's great cities, it seemed on the verge of revitalization. The University of Buffalo was expanding, and new faculty, among them some renowned in the arts, music and literature, were moving to Buffalo. Bob reckoned that it would be easier for him to find a niche in a smaller city, facing less competition than he would have in the Cambridge-Boston area, with its surfeit of architects. With this new plan, he redesigned the Cambridge house to fit on a lot he found on Buffalo's east-side and hired a local contractor to build it.

When Bob announced that we would be moving to Buffalo, he met total dismay on my part. "Buff-a-lo! Oh no," I wailed. Bob had grown up in Buffalo and was happy about coming back. I had seen little of Buffalo during the few brief visits to my in-laws, who lived on Florida Street, about a 10-minute walk from our new home. The only positive aspect I could think of was that we would be near Freddie's Donuts, a drive-in-bakery a block from Florida Street. Freddie's made the most delicious doughnuts I'd ever eaten—crullers, peanut sticks, glazed and jelly doughnuts, and we'd always bought a box when in Buffalo. I loved living in Cambridge and hated to leave its cosmopolitan atmosphere, as well as good friends I'd made. Marion and Darcy weren't happy about the move, either, leaving their friends and a familiar environment.

In September, 1961, we moved to Buffalo, Bob having designed a contemporary house, based on the Techbuilt system, which he felt would be "right for the age." Although Bob had shown me the plans before we moved, I couldn't visualize it, and so was quite surprised when I first saw it. Our house and the one next door, ranch style, on the corner of Humboldt Parkway and Loring Avenue, were the only two new homes in a neighborhood of wood frame houses built around 1910. As a contemporary house, ours was unique in the neighborhood, raising the speculation that it might be a public building—perhaps a swimming pool.

The house was sited on a long and narrow lot and, turning its back towards the street, oriented towards the expansive rear yard. Of post-and-beam construction, with a flat roof, the house had four levels—a split entry leading either to the studio/garage, placed at the front as a buffer from the street traffic, or to the upper floor containing the living room, master bedroom and bath, and guest bedroom/study. Set into the ground three feet, the lower level held two children's bedrooms, a bath, workroom, kitchen and dining room opening out to the lower terrace. The fourth and lowest level was designed as the utility room, to hold the furnace, hot water heater, washer and dryer. The feature I would come to appreciate most was the large expanse of floor-to-ceiling glass. It was a delight to be able to look out into the rear yard from the living room, bedroom, or dining room windows and floor-to-ceiling doors and enjoy the view, changing with the seasons.

As our house was not yet habitable, we lived with Bob's parents for a few weeks. While the children were in school, Bob and I would walk over to the house and do the finishing work, including sanding, plastering, painting the walls white, and laying tile and linoleum floors. Once the house was finished, we did the landscaping, setting steps of railroad ties leading from the below-ground terrace up to the yard, set more railroad ties for planting beds; and spread pea gravel over the bare ground between the planting beds to create a Japanese-style garden. Several mature trees shaded the yard: a large elm in the front, another, smaller elm and three large maples in the rear, with a 150-ft. tall cottonwood tree dominating the yard, spreading its branches like a huge umbrella.

Meanwhile, we enrolled Marion and Darcy at School 54, a neighborhood school within walking distance, Marion in seventh grade, Darcy in first. At that point Darcy was still having trouble pronouncing some of the consonants, but, fortunately, he had sympathetic teachers during the years he was a student there. Marion and Darcy found friends in the neighborhood and also among the children of our black professional friends.

Buffalo was then, and still is, considered one of the most segregated cities in the nation; and whites and blacks generally did not mix socially. Bob and I would go to events and affairs in which the audiences and participants would be either mainly white or black. Ours was one of the few mixed marriages in Buffalo at the time, and we were viewed with curiosity as well as with some hostility. But because of Bob's status as an architect, he was accepted in the white professional community. In the black community, I encountered hostility on the part of some of the African-American women I met who, like so many others, viewed mixed marriages—especially white women married to black men—with disfavor. But over the years, hostility gave way to approval, and I became good friends with several black women.

While the neighborhood we lived in had previously been populated, first with Germans, and then with Jews, blacks had gradually moved into the area. The Germans moved out to the suburb of Cheektowaga, and the Jews moved to live with the Italian population in north Buffalo or went further out to the suburbs. Main Street was the dividing line: The population west of Main Street was primarily white, the east, primarily black, and south Buffalo was predominantly Irish. Living in a black neighborhood was an entirely different experience from living in an integrated community in Cambridge. Bob apparently did not feel this was an important factor when he chose to build his house on Humboldt Parkway. In fact, I believe he felt that living where he did demonstrated his commitment to the black community.

Humboldt Parkway was part of a system of parks and parkways within Buffalo designed by Frederick Law Olmsted. The eastern end of Humboldt Parkway led to what became known as Martin Luther King Park, and to the Buffalo Museum of Science. The western section passed by Delaware Park and led to the Albright-Knox Art Gallery and the Buffalo and Erie County Historical Society, the only building remaining from those built for Buffalo's 1901 Pan-American Exposition. We could walk from our house down the tree-lined, grassy center strip all the way to the Science Museum, and often did. Several of our black professional friends lived on the other side of Humboldt Parkway, and we could simply walk across the center strip to visit them. That proximity led to an amusing event.

We had acquired a dog, given to us by friends who could no longer keep him. Duke was a Boxer-Labrador, with a placid temperament and a good companion for walks around the neighborhood, including to our friends across the street. One afternoon we had tethered Duke to the garden hose, thinking that would keep him contained in our yard. But Duke was bent on responding to a female in heat across the street and was on his way across Humboldt Parkway, dragging the garden hose behind him, stopping traffic. When I happened to notice he wasn't in the yard, I called out, "Bob, Duke's gone." Bob rushed out, saw where Duke was headed, and ran out to stop Duke and lead him, still tethered to the hose, back to our yard. From then on, we kept Duke under stricter control.

Sometime in 1962 I made a mistake that would haunt me for years afterward. I had been a pack-a-day smoker since my early twenties and was generally careful about extinguishing cigarette stubs. But one morning, while the children were in school and Bob was on site, supervising construction of the recreation center being built in the Ellicott District, I took Duke and went to Delaware Park for a walk around the ring road and back home. I was gone about forty-five minutes when, as I approached our house, I was horrified to see smoke pouring from the building and firemen busily working to extinguish the flames within, resulting from a cigarette stub I'd thought extinguished, tossed in a wastebasket under the kitchen sink.

In utter dismay, I saw that the kitchen had been completely burned out; the whole house was filled with the nauseating smell of burned wood and smoke. When Marion and Darcy, and then Bob, returned home, they were as shocked as I had been. "What happened?" Bob asked. Shamefaced, I had to tell him the truth. Fortunately, the furniture in the bedrooms and other downstairs rooms was undamaged, so these rooms were still habitable, although the smoke aroma was most unpleasant. I set up the portable, two-burner camping stove, and that served us until the kitchen was re-built and a new oven installed. The sickening smell of smoke lingered for weeks, and for years afterwards I was gripped with fear any time I smelled smoke, anywhere.

Had I not been a confirmed smoker, I might have given up cigarettes then and there; but at least I'd learned a lesson, the hard way. Bob, who stopped smoking years before I did, never let me forget that unfortunate incident. Long after, whenever we got into an argument involving my failings, he used it as a perfect example of carelessness.

6

Settling In

In 1963, with the recreation center completed, Bob opened his own office, in our home, just as he had planned, and began receiving commissions for projects in Buffalo. As seemed perfectly natural at the time, I fell into the role of secretary and bookkeeper. We already had a typewriter, and I set it up in the study upstairs, where I typed letters and other correspondence. His first projects included designing a new elementary school and a block of housing for the elderly, both in Buffalo.

Meanwhile, Buffalo was experiencing an outburst of artistic expression, bringing Buffalo to the forefront of the national cultural scene. The University of Buffalo, which had been a private institution, became a part of the State University of New York in 1962. The expanding university attracted musicians, including Allen Sapp, who helped create a high profile music department. Sapp, a composer of contemporary music and professor of composition at Harvard, was well-connected to the intellectual network comprising the cutting edge of music. Lukas Foss, creative composer, pianist and conductor, arrived in Buffalo in 1963, to become director of the Buffalo Philharmonic Orchestra. He and Sapp formed the Creative Associates and turned Buffalo into an outstanding new music center.

Writers who joined the English Department, which became the most innovative in the country at that time, included such well-known figures as poet John Creeley and novelists John Barth and John Coetzee.

Eager to become part of the artistic community, we joined the Albright-Knox Art Gallery, which had some of the best collections of contemporary art in the country, thanks to collector Seymour Knox. In 1962, a new wing, built to house the expanding art collection, opened to rave reviews. According to Buffalo historian Mark Goldman, the opening of the stunning new wing designed by Buffalo architect Gordon Bunschaft, "attracted people from all over: there were more than 725,000 visitors that year." The Gallery was one of the venues for a festival held in 1965, a mix of visual art, music, dance, film and theatre. The Buffalo Festival of the Arts was such a success that a second festival was held in March 1968.

In his book, *City on the Edge*, Goldman described the Second Festival of the Arts:

> "Among the vast and varied programs that took place during these two weeks in March were readings by John Barth, Charles Olsen, Louis Zukofsky, and Allen Ginsberg; three programs of dances by the Merce Cunningham Company; concerts by the Buffalo Philharmonic Orchestra and the Creative Associates; as well as recitals by John Cage, Yannis Xanakis, and Lukas Foss; lectures by architectural city planners R. Buckminster Fuller and Constantin Doxiadis; a panel on playwriting with Edward Albee, Richard Bart, and Alan Schneider; a new film by Jonas Mekas called New York Diaries; and the world premieres at the Studio Arena Theatre of Edward Albee's *Box* and quotations for Chairman Mao."

As critics, cameramen, musicians, dancers, artists and writers came from around the country, *Life Magazine* called it "bigger and hipper than anything ever held in New York and Paris." It was Buffalo's shining hour, and Bob and I were both excited by the Festival and delighted to be part of the audience for the programs. We went to most of the events; probably the most memorable was the piece in which the Merce Cunningham dancers performed in the nude, shocking staid members of the audience.

Through the Gallery, we met a number of artists, some of whom were teaching at the University of Buffalo and among whom we made lifelong friends, among them Sheldon Berlyn and his wife, Diane. We acquired two of Berlyn's paintings as well as works by other artists, and hung them in our living room. Through Sheldon, we met his brother Gerry and his wife Lynn; and Bob designed a house for them in Worcester, Massachusetts, built in 1965.

As members of the Buffalo World Hospitality Association, we hosted foreign visitors for several years. We usually took them to see Niagara Falls and then brought them back to our home for dinner. I remember a few guests who fell asleep in the car on the way back from the Falls. With an apologetic "I'm so sorry, I've had too much sight-seeing, I guess," they would decline dinner.

Through the Association we met Suzanne Taub and her husband, Harry, a violinist in the Buffalo Philharmonic Orchestra. They, too, became lifelong friends, and we began attending concerts. We loved the exciting programs introducing new music, during which some disgruntled patrons, used to Bach, Brahms and Beethoven, walked out in the middle of a performance. We held season tickets annually until Lukas Foss left Buffalo in 1970.

Besides attending Philharmonic concerts, Bob and I enjoyed other entertainment. For several years in the 1960s, the Albright-Knox Gallery held an annual masquerade ball. Suzanne and Harry, Bob and I, and some of our mutual friends attended several of these—great fun. One year Harry came as Nero, fiddling away on his violin, and Suzanne dressed as a Grecian lady. Bob and I were hits as Othello and Desdemona.

Usually the balls were preceded by dinners at the homes of hosting couples. One year I disguised myself as a young black woman, applying just the right amount of color to my face, hands and arms. At the dinner before the ball, one lady, making conversation, said to me, "You people are great dancers!" I smothered a laugh and thanked her for the compliment. Bob and I did dance well together, and took every opportunity we could to dance. Bob and I were sorry when the balls ended. They were great ice-breakers and a good way to meet new people.

In 1962, I joined the downtown YWCA as a member and until 1965 took classes offered there in copper enameling and ceramics. I crafted slab pieces and also learned how to throw pieces on the pottery wheel. Allentown, Buffalo's hippie neighborhood, held its first annual Arts Festival in 1963, and I joined other artists, both local and out-of-town in displaying our art. No one bought any of my pieces, but it was fun to be there, part of the lively scene. I still have some of those pieces—a copper bracelet, copper-enameled platter, vases and more. Sometime after 1965, I joined a friend, Jill Solomon, in creating pieces which we fired in her basement kiln.

In 1964 Bob met a man who had a major impact on his life. He was Richard Prosser, a Presbyterian minister, then director of the Friendship House, a community center in Lackawanna, on the outskirts of Buffalo and the site of the Bethlehem Steel mills. Bob was selected to design a new building, and in the process he and Prosser became close friends. Prosser was himself a community organizer, and he influenced Bob to also become an activist, concerned with problems in Buffalo's black community.

In the period from 1964 to 1968, Bob also completed a number of commissions for residences and house additions, assisted by intern architect Charles Rush, Jr., then a student at the University of Buffalo. Among these projects was a weekend house in Attica, New York for Lydia Wright. We had become friends with Lydia and her husband, Frank Evans, both practicing black physicians. The weekend house proved to be an ideal collaboration between client and architect, and served as a welcome retreat for Lydia and Frank as well as ideal for entertaining their weekend guests.

A different kind of project was the Sample Memorial Playground, designed jointly by Bob and sculptor friend Jack Solomon, Jill's husband, at Chautauqua Institution, in Chautauqua, New York. The playground, built in 1966, was commissioned by Miriam Reading, of the Sample family, among the Institution's founders. Miriam and her family spent their summers at Chautauqua, and Bob and I usually drove down once or twice during the season to see the Readings and also take in a concert. Had it not been for our friendship with the Readings, Bob and I probably would not have gone, as Chautauqua was then—and still is—a largely white enclave, and Bob felt out of his element there.

Besides his architectural practice, Bob was also engaged in another area, chairing a committee in 1966 which sought to have the new campus for the University of Buffalo's expanding student population located on Buffalo's waterfront. There had been preliminary plans to locate the campus in suburban Amherst, but the committee hoped to forestall a final decision. In the end, however, the committee's actions failed. In years to come, in conversations about "what's wrong with Buffalo," most everyone agreed that a downtown location for the new campus would have done more to revitalize the city and stop its continuing decline than any other project on a planner's drawing board.

7

Cruising the Grecian Isles

In the midst of Bob's activities, we took advantage of an unusual opportunity in 1965 to travel to the Middle East through a tour sponsored by the Albright-Knox Art Gallery. We arranged to travel to Europe, first with the tour, and then set off on our own. Consulting a travel agent, we settled on a cruise touring the Grecian Islands, the travel brochure picturing a luxurious ocean liner. We travelled with the tour group for the first part of the trip, then left them and headed to Venice, where we would meet our cruise ship.

After a delightful day in Venice, we were ready for a new adventure. In the harbor, waiting for the cruise ship to arrive, we joined a crowd of other passengers, among them a German tour group. As the cruise ship motored into the harbor, we couldn't believe our eyes: Instead of the luxurious liner we expected was a smaller vessel that hardly looked seaworthy. The German tourists were outraged. "We want our money back!" they cried, and threatened to leave en masse. In the end, however, there was nothing to do but board the ship, and we all did. We learned later that this ship, a freighter, had been used as a ferry boat in Canada and was a last-minute replacement for the one pictured in the travel brochure.

Once aboard and our ship underway, our expectations gave way to the reality of accommodations aboard a much smaller ship than the one originally scheduled. Our sleeping quarters the first night were separate—Bob in a cabin on the lowest deck, next to the engine room, with nine other men, and I in another cabin with eight other women. The next day, Bob found the captain and held out a generous tip. "We're honeymooners," he explained, "we'd like to stay together." With a knowing wink, the captain promised he'd find a cabin for us, and so he did.

Gradually, all the passengers, even the Germans, adjusted to the conditions. The tux and gown the couple from Chicago had brought to wear for elegant affairs remained unpacked. The swimming pool pictured in the travel brochure diminished to an 8' x 8' tank, just large enough for a quick dip.

But the captain and Greek crew were courteous and capable, and, most importantly, the ship was truly seaworthy, weathering the strong winds and turbulent waves we encountered during our voyage. Our accommodations, if minimal, were adequate; the Greek food was delicious and the Greek wine, retsina, flowed freely; the views were fabulous; and we soon adapted to the role of seafarers.

Bob and Sylvia, Baalbek, Syria, 1965

Our ship sailed on, in the Tyrrhenian Sea, through the narrow Straits of Messina at the tip of Italy's boot, and into the

Ionian Sea to Piraeus, the port of Athens. In Athens we spent a day visiting its famous temples and also absorbing a bit of the busy street life. After Athens, we toured several of the Greek islands, disembarking for the day and returning to the ship in the evening. In that way we visited Crete, where we explored the Minatour's cave; Rhodes; Mykonos, a tiny, sun-swept island often pictured in travel brochures with its windmills; and Cyprus.

From Cyprus we sailed to Lebanon, docking at the city of Beirut, then one of the most beautiful cities in the world, where we spent a day. From Beirut, our tour took us inland and via bus to Damascus, where we visited the ruins of Baalbek, on the site of the ancient city of Heliopolis, and wandered through the bazaars. Returning to Beirut, we sailed from there to the busy port of Alexandria. While we waited on the ship's deck for a passenger boat to take us to Cairo, a magician on the dock below entertained us with his magic tricks.

Cairo, teeming with a multitude of people of all races, revealed a fascinating new world to us. It was our first experience in the vast continent of Africa and left both of us open to further travel in that part of the world. In Cairo we visited the famous Sphinx and the Pyramids, where I had a camel ride. We took a cruise down the Nile, passing villages and meeting fishing boats and sailboats. After Cairo, we returned to Alexandria, and then back to Venice. Our voyage was uneventful except that, as our ship passed through stormy seas, most of the passengers became seasick, and few showed up for meals. Bob and I, two of the lucky ones, continued to dine well and enjoy the retsina with our meals.

Eventually we returned to Venice, having fully enjoyed the cruise. Before returning to the States, we took a side trip to Vienna and then to Geneva, where we visited friends. Finally back in Buffalo, we returned to ordinary life.

8

Involved in the Community

In his initial experience as an architect-activist, Bob joined Richard Prosser, several churchmen and other community leaders, both black and white, in forming the East Side Community Organization (ESCO), which succeeded in raising the funds to bring Saul Alinsky to Buffalo in 1967 to organize the black community. That led to the formation of the action organization BUILD, an acronym for "Build Unity, Independence, Liberty and Dignity," a coalition of black civic, religious, business, labor, social, youth and other groups. BUILD's effort to improve East Side schools led to the creation of the BUILD Academy, Buffalo's first magnet school, still in operation.

While Bob was active in ESCO, he didn't let me sit on the sidelines: he pressed me into service as its Executive Secretary. I held that position during 1966-67 and also unofficially served as its Treasurer, keeping the books until the organization dissolved. I didn't realize then Bob would take for granted my continued, unquestioning cooperation in his various pursuits.

Meanwhile, I was active on my own in other areas. As a member of the Science Museum, I joined the Women's Committee, headed by Miriam Reading, whose goal was to establish a Children's Room, devoted to children's activities, within the Museum. As part of the committee during 1966-67, I contacted other museums throughout the country to see what they offered in the way of children's activities, and compiled the results of my research in a packet which was used by the committee. My efforts helped to establish the first Children's Room in the Museum. While a member of the committee, I also helped organize the first Galaxy Ball, a fundraiser held annually for a number of years.

In the same period, I opened a nursery school in our neighborhood, for children between the ages of three and five. The Northland Nursery School had a room in the Masten Boys Club and in 1966-67 was open five mornings a week. As its director and sole instructor, with eight to ten children attending each day, I provided games, stories, songs and mid-morning snacks. I enjoyed my charges, the youngsters had fun, and their parents were appreciative. I closed the school when Pre-K schools opened in Buffalo.

Buffalo at that time was embroiled in the struggle to end segregation in its public schools. Our friend, Lydia Wright, was serving as the first black member of the Buffalo Board of Education. She faced bitter opposition from another board member, Alfreda Slominsky, who came from the Polish community. Dr. Wright argued for the creation of "magnet" schools, which she believed would attract students from all over the city and, at the same time, allow inner-city students to be bused out of their neighborhood to attend schools of their choice. Both Wright and Slominski had strong support, Slominski's primarily in the Polish and other ethnic communities, Wright's from the black community as well as white civil activists.

In my own small way, in 1966, I contributed to the effort, organizing a small group of those eager to join the causes of desegregation, forming Citizens for Quality Integrated Education. I created a newsletter, which had a small circulation, and also spoke on several occasions to various groups. I was also a member of the Citizen's Advisory Committee to the Buffalo Board of Education, which was attempting to comply with the requirements set forth by the officials overseeing the desegregation efforts.

While not on a scale as others throughout the nation, riots broke out in Buffalo's black community in the summer of 1967. Beginning on the afternoon of June 27, the riots were limited to several streets and ultimately dispelled by an augmented police force, with damage mainly to both black and white-owned stores in the community. The Mayor and the Police Commissioner blamed "outside agitators," and civil rights leaders blamed the system and Buffalo's "broken promises." Although no one was killed, forty people were treated for injuries and forty-six teenage boys arrested. Sadly, the school desegregation ordered that year by Federal District Judge John Curtin contributed to the exodus of many white families, who left for newer, nicer and "whiter" schools in the suburbs, leading to the creation of a public school system with an increasing majority of black students.

How did the school situation affect our own children? After Darcy attended the first few grades at School 54, we enrolled him in Campus School, a school for selected students administered by Buffalo State College, and he continued there through high school. His classmates were primarily white, and while he did have several friends among them, he felt uncomfortable because, as he told me, "I'm not black enough to fit in with the black crowd but too black for the white crowd." As other mixed-race youth, he probably would have felt an outsider in whatever school he attended. Nevertheless, he received a good education there, which prepared him for college and graduate school.

Bob and Sylvia, with children Darcy and Marion, and their dog Duke posing in their home. Buffalo, 1968

Marion completed grades 8 and 9 in Fillmore Junior High School, within walking distance of our home, with a mostly black student enrollment. Although her grades were high initially, they soon fell. Fillmore may have been a good school, but Marion, basically very bright, made the wrong kind of friends there, and their negative influence limited her academic achievement. Her association with the wrong crowd also encouraged Marion's rebellion against us, violating the rules Bob and I set, and frequently engaging in delinquent behavior throughout her teens.

Thinking that a school geared toward scholastic achievement would stimulate her, Bob had Marion enroll in Park School, in suburban Snyder, in September, 1964. Marion attended Park for several weeks but then withdrew, explaining, "I feel outclassed." She may very well have felt, like Darcy, an outsider among her mostly white classmates. She then attended Bennett High School for several terms, with frequent absences. Since Marion's ultimate wish was to leave home and become independent, Bob promised, "If and when you earn your high school diploma, you're free to go." That was the incentive she needed.

Marion earned her diploma in 1967, moved out, and early in 1968, at eighteen, married Christian (Chris) Schillke, a young man she'd been dating for a couple of years. John Buerk, a friend of ours and a Lutheran pastor, married Marion and Chris in a brief ceremony in our house. We had a little celebration afterwards: Together with Chris's parents, we toasted the couple with champagne served in our dining room. The senior Schillkes, conservative Lutherans, may have had as many misgivings as we did about the marriage; nevertheless, we all wished them well. Marion and Chris left Buffalo soon afterwards, bound for San Francisco with the dream of becoming established artists there.

Deciding to further my own education, in 1967, I enrolled in the University of Buffalo's Millard Fillmore College, taking courses in Sociology, Research Methods, and Statistics. My undergraduate major had been Sociology, and my interest in that field had continued. For the Sociology course I wrote a paper entitled, "The Entry of the Negro into the Architectural Profession." Being married to Bob, I was well aware of the particular difficulties blacks encountered in becoming architects.

The Swedish economist, Gunnar Myrdal, had stated in his 1962 book, *The American Dilemma*, "the white economy does not want Negroes" in the position of architects. In my paper, I hypothesized that black entry into architecture was contingent on fundamental change in national policy, enforcing regulations that would increase available opportunities. Based on 1960 New York State statistics, I concluded that the few black architects in New York were mostly employed by federal and state governments. As an example, Bob was then the only black practicing architect in the Buffalo/Western New York area. My prediction was that increasing black political power would increase the opportunities open to black architects.

9

Travel to the Far East

In August 1970, we took advantage of a rare opportunity: travel to the Far East for a Japanese-American Symposium on Architecture and Urban Design. Bob, Darcy and I joined over two hundred architects and their wives and children, travelling to Tokyo, Hong Kong, and Bangkok for professional visits and conferences from August 14-29. The symposium sessions, held in Tokyo on August 17 and Hong Kong on August 24, were conducted by American faculty, members of the American Institute of Architects, and prominent Tokyo and Hong Kong architects.

The two one-day sessions left plenty of time to sightsee and relax. In Tokyo we stayed at The New Otani, a luxurious hotel with a beautiful Japanese garden. The first day there we took a sight-seeing tour, visiting the Sonsoji Temple, one of the oldest temples, and that night were entertained at a geisha party. The next day we took a day trip to Kamakura, Mt. Fuji, and Lake Hakone. In Kamakura, we visited the Sanjusangendo Temple, its hundreds of statues plated with gold leaves. At a quiet inn overlooking a placid lake, we had a distant view of magnificent Mt. Fuji, with its snow-covered peak. At another site, we marveled at a gigantic Buddha, weighing 121 tons.

The last day in Tokyo, Bob and Darcy went to see the Tokyo Tower; then Bob and I went to the Cultural Center, the Museum of Western Art, and the Ginza district, where we strolled through the stalls filled with everything from pungent dried fish to souvenir Buddhas. That evening we all dined on Japanese food at the Chinzan-So Restaurant.

Leaving Tokyo, we took the Bullet Train to Osaka to visit the World's Fair. It was hot and humid there, with temperatures well over a hundred; nevertheless, we joined the throngs—mostly Orientals but a few foreigners like us—moving through the fair grounds. We visited many of the 91 pavilions representing countries from all over the world, the United States' pavilion being one of the largest, and were blown away by the spectacular sculptures created for the fair by Japanese artists.

From Osaka we took the train to Kyoto, for a brief visit, and then to Hong Kong, "the Pearl of the Orient," certainly one of the world's beautiful cities. The city was teeming with activity, the main roads filled with traffic, side streets filled with shops, markets and pedestrians. Victoria Harbor, ranked with San Francisco and Rio de Janeiro as one of the three most perfect harbors in the world, was equally busy, with watercraft of every type, including the picturesque Chinese junks, fishing boats with colorful sails. A street artist, Robert Lo, was selling paintings of these boats. "How much?" I asked, pointing to the one I liked best—two junks with orange sails moving through a golden sea, the sun an outsize disk shining through a hazy orange-yellow sky. When he named a very reasonable price, I bought it, a perfect memento. I brought the painting home, and it hangs on the wall in my office.

Staying at the Hilton Hotel, we took a cruise to Aberdeen, across the harbor, after Bob finished the seminar. The next day we took a train ride through the city and then a ferry ride to Kowloon, on the mainland of Red China. In Kowloon, we took a bus tour through the city and the New Territories, leased from China in 1898 for ninety-nine years. That evening Bob and I attended a cocktail party and afterwards ate Chinese food at the Golden Lotus with an American architect we knew, originally from Hong Kong.

Leaving Hong Kong, we flew to Bangkok, Thailand and checked in at the Dusi Thani Hotel. The next day, Bob, Darcy and I took a motor launch tour down the Chao-Phya River and canals running through Bangkok. As we motored along the canals, we met many "floating markets," boats filled with produce, seafood and other goods. And we observed activities of the families living on the river banks—women washing clothes and small children splashing in the muddy river. Although we were in no danger of getting swamped, the possibility of a dip kept me nervous through the boat ride. As part of the tour, we visited the Dawn Temple, famed for its porcelain decorations, and the Silk Factory, where I bought a yard of beautiful Thai silk to fashion into a gown. We dined that evening at the Pinam Restaurant, savoring the delicious Thai food.

The next morning we went to the Emerald Buddha Temple, with row upon row of marvelous golden statues. That afternoon Darcy and I stayed at the hotel while Bob went off by himself to see more Thai architecture, taking a taxi to the outskirts of the city. While he was looking around, he was approached by several sinister-looking men, one of whom said to Bob, "Do you want to see a beautiful temple? We can take you there." Bob sensed, by their furtive glances, that he was the target of a devious plot. "No thanks," he told them, and made a hasty exit. When he got back to our hotel, Bob told us about his narrow escape. That evening we left to return once more to Hong Kong.

On our last day in Hong Kong, we took a tour around Hong Kong Island, and then a tram up to Victoria Peak, at 1,089 feet, where we had a breathtaking view of Hong Kong, Victoria Harbor, Kowloon, and the surrounding areas. Hong Kong's wealthiest citizens lived in the residential area on the peak, with the less well-off further down the hillside, and squatters' shacks clinging to the steep sides even further below. We left on August 30, having had a fabulous trip.

10

Change

Destructive as the 1967 riots had been, another form of destruction had been underway for some time. To eliminate traffic congestion on the roadways leading into Buffalo's downtown, the State decided to replace tree-lined Humboldt Parkway with the Scajaquada Expressway. This six-lane expressway would bisect Delaware Park and connect to the Kensington Expressway, which brought traffic in from the suburbs. What appears incomprehensible is that public officials could have conceived of a plan that would destroy the beauty of one of Frederick Law Olmsted's parkways and turn Humboldt Parkway into a massive traffic feeder. But the contractor carrying out the necessary excavation had been working since 1958 and in 1968 was ready to begin work on the Expressway.

Bob had been aware of the plans for the Expressway and, knowing what would happen to Humboldt Parkway, sited his house oriented to the rear. Lydia Wright and her husband, longtime Humboldt Parkway residents, tried to stop the project by organizing neighbors and lobbying officials in Albany, with no response. There was little they could have done, as with many other road-building schemes throughout the country, this one had broad support from within the power structure of the community.

While the Expressway was being built, traffic heading downtown was funneled onto narrow lanes on Humboldt Parkway. It was virtually impossible for Humboldt Parkway residents to pull out of their driveways during rush hours. I put on my community activist hat, appealing to authorities, and succeeded in having a traffic light installed at the corner near our house, which alleviated the problem for us and our neighbors.

Meanwhile, plans were proceeding for the construction of the new University of Buffalo's campus in Amherst. After a master plan for the campus was finalized, a number of firms were selected to design and construct facilities for the various departments. Most likely due to the efforts of black New York State Assemblyman Arthur O. Eve to ensure that minorities were involved, Bob received the commission for the Health, Physical Education and Recreation Complex (H.P.E.R.). Originally, he was partnered with the Cambridge firm of Buckminster Fuller and Shoji Sadoa. Fuller had become famous for his futuristic geodesic dome; but when the University rejected his initial plan, he and Sadao bowed out.

Because Bob needed to staff up for this project, he hired Mel Alston, a young black architectural student, as an intern in 1968. In addition, Bob convinced Ed Norris, a black architect he had known in Cambridge, to move to Buffalo and join Bob. The H.P.E.R. project was unexpectedly halted soon after Bob began working on it, but he had contracts for other projects: low-income housing in Buffalo and Rochester, New York; renovating offices in one of the buildings on the Buffalo State Campus; new neighborhood health centers in Buffalo and Rochester; and a new public school. Acting according to our attorney's advice, the firm was incorporated as a Professional Corporation (P.C.) in February, 1971, with Bob as the sole shareholder, its President and Treasurer, and with me as Secretary. We put ourselves on the payroll and started drawing salaries along with the office staff.

Bob added more staff in 1969, including William Hall, who came to Buffalo from Cambridge to work temporarily, and Alan McTaggart, who worked with Bob before establishing his own firm. Between 1970 and 1972, the office staff increased, numbering between fifteen and twenty at any one time. As office manager/bookkeeper, I generally supervised the clerical staff and did the daily bookkeeping, banking, payroll, quarterly reports, and billing. To accommodate the personnel, including architects, draftsmen and student interns, office equipment and furniture, Bob leased a building at 1160 Main Street, occupying both the lower and upper floors, with parking in the rear.

A staff photo taken during that time showed quite a cosmopolitan group: Along with early staff members Charles Rush, Mel Alston and Ed Norris, were Ali Ell-Tobgy from Egypt; Casimir Acholonu, from Nigeria; Ho Kim, Chinese-American; Estonian Viestarts Racenis; Stanley Przyborowski, Jon Gochmanovsky and Ike Kryzwinski, Polish-Americans; Van Johnson and Warren Ansley, black; Gene Holzerland and Robert West, white; secretaries Weanette James and Sharon Jackson, black; and typist Bettye Kaufman, white. Bob and I were also in the photo, as was Sam Fenston, our Jewish accountant.

However, the burst of activity sustaining that size staff didn't last. With the nation in a recession, the volume of work diminished after 1972 to the point that the only employee Bob retained was Ed Norris. We sold the office furniture and equipment and moved back to Humboldt Parkway.

11

Bob Travels to Africa

Richard Prosser, Bob's activist friend, had left his position as Friendship House Director and was currently living with his wife and two sons in Kinshasha, the capital of Zaire (now the Republic of Congo). There he worked with an African community as an advisor, helping them to improve their living conditions. Richard and Bob stayed in contact, and in 1971, in one of his letters to Bob, Richard wrote, "Bob, come out to Zaire for a visit and see some African architecture." Bob jumped at the opportunity, flying to Kinshasha and spending three weeks with Richard, his wife, Janet, and their two sons, Brian and Alan.

Richard took Bob to see various public facilities including a hospital, and Bob accompanied Richard on his daily rounds. Frequently this included driving out into the countryside, visiting families living there, and Richard's suggesting ways in which the farmers among them could improve their crops. Bob and Richard's usual routine was to get up early while it was still relatively cool, have lunch and a long siesta, and then go back to work until late. It was hot in Kinshasha, and one afternoon they all went off for a swim. When Bob saw the muddy water in which they would swim, harboring who knows what, he shook his head; "You go ahead," he said, "I'll watch."

Bob unwittingly had a brush with the local authorities one day. He had gone out on his own, photographing architecture he found particularly interesting. At one point, he was stopped by an armed soldier. Gesturing threateningly with his rifle, the soldier said, "You can't take photographs here!" Bob was unaware that the facility he'd been photographing was a military installation. Assuming he was a spy, the soldier took his passport and camera, handcuffed Bob and took him to the local jail. After Bob spent an uneasy night there, Richard came to the rescue, attesting to Bob's innocence, ignorant of the local rules. Convinced, the authorities released Bob and returned his passport and camera, to Bob's great relief.

He returned to Buffalo with rolls of film and a large bag of souvenirs—a rug and an assortment of ebony figures carved by local artists, and a better appreciation of life in Africa. Bob had also learned that, rather than being accepted by Africans as a soul brother, he was just another American tourist. Long after his trip, Bob entertained friends with his slides and stories of his African experience. Richard and his family came back to Buffalo after several years in Kinshasha. He stayed active in the community and a close friend of Bob's until his death, from cancer, in June, 1984.

12

Sailing

In an editorial written by editor John Dixon for the Progressive Architecture magazine, he observed that "architecture tends to consume an inordinate proportion of its practitioner's total working hours." This was certainly true of Bob who, when not practicing architecture, was involved in one way or another in activities related to architecture. He knew he needed an escape and hit upon sailing as a sufficiently engaging hobby. He had learned to sail from an architectural friend. So, in 1964, Bob bought a Snipe, a small sailboat, and started sailing out of the Small Boat Harbor near the Bethlehem Steel Plant. I went out with Bob on the Snipe a few times and knew what a challenge sailing this fast little boat could be.

One summer day Bob took Richard (Dick) Prosser out for a sail. At one point Bob executed a sudden turn-about; but Dick, caught off guard, missed Bob's cue. Bob yelled, "Dick, we're going overrrrrrr!" Indeed, the Snipe capsized and they went overboard. Fortunately, they were near the harbor, and they swam back to the shore, observed by nearby boaters. The next day an article appeared in the Buffalo News about the dunking of two prominent Buffalo citizens—to the amusement of Bob and Dick and those who knew them.

Bob knew he needed a larger, safer, sailboat, so in 1970 he bought a Columbia 22, with a cabin below deck. Bob could sail it single-handedly, which he most often did, taking it out of the harbor and into Lake Erie. Out on the lake, with the Buffalo skyline in the distance, he could spend a few hours away from the stress of architecture, concentrated on mastering wind and water.

We had heard about the pristine waters still found in the West Indies Virgin Islands, and, in 1972, we decided to try sailing there, Bob confident of his sailing skills. "Mac" Macdowell, an architect living in St. Thomas, made arrangements with the Antilles Yachting Services in St. Thomas to charter a sailboat for us for the week of April 3-10. We were to stay in the apartment of one of Mac's friends until we picked up the boat. The friend, Bill, expected to be away while we were there.

On April 1, Bob, Darcy and I flew from Buffalo to San Juan, Puerto Rico, and then took an air taxi to St. Thomas, a tiny island in the Bahamas. After a hair-rising taxi ride from the airport up the steep mountainside, we arrived at Bill's apartment, which we would share with Evelyn, another of Bill's friends. The next day we borrowed Bill's Toyota and toured the island, stopping at a public beach. There we found the water just right, and we swam and sunned for a few hours. Returning to the apartment that evening, we enjoyed the panoramic view from the veranda.

We had planned to decide, after Bob tried out the boat, whether Darcy and I would stay in the apartment while Bob sailed, or go with him. That afternoon we went into town, found the yacht club, and Bob completed charter arrangements. We went for a short sail, Bob practicing maneuvering in and out of the harbor—tricky— and "getting the feel" of the water by sailing to another harbor and back.

In the meantime, Bill had returned unexpectedly, gone off to work, and—most importantly—the water supply had run out, a common problem in St. Thomas as in other islands with very little rain. When Evelyn told us they were depending on a fresh supply being delivered by truck, I decided I'd rather be on the sailboat and trust that Bob was up to the challenge. Darcy, then a junior in high school, wasn't too happy: "I should've stayed home. I could have finished my English paper by now."

But, as it was, on Tuesday Evelyn drove us with our baggage to St. Thomas, to a grocery store, where we loaded up on food and ice, and then to the yacht club to get the boat. After we'd loaded everything on board, Bob set sail for the nearest harbor, Christmas Cove, where we'd been the day before. We dropped anchor in the harbor and Darcy and I swam ashore while Bob tried out the dinghy which came with the sailboat. Unfortunately, when Darcy set a foot down a few feet from the shore, he yelped with pain: He'd stepped on a sea urchin. Found everywhere in that part of the world, these spiny creatures cling like barnacles to rocks and sandy bottoms. Though I tried, the poisonous barbs were impossible to remove, but they did disintegrate in a few days.

Despite his painful foot, Darcy joined Bob and me in trying out our snorkeling equipment, and we had a fine time exploring the marvelous underwater world we'd never seen before. By evening, several other sailboats had anchored in the harbor. I tried out our barbeque grill, suspended off the boat, and we had delicious grilled steaks for dinner. Dusk came early, around 7:00 PM, and not too long afterwards we settled in our berths for a good night's sleep.

The next day we sailed out from Christmas Cove past some little islands. Then, sailing close to Jost Van Dyke in choppy waters, Bob executed a quick turn-about. I was steering the rudder and

Darcy was manning the ropes when, in the confusion of changing directions, his glasses were swept overboard. Darcy, extremely upset, was about to jump in, but Bob restrained him.

We had still another mishap that day. Having sailed to Caneel Bay, we anchored in the harbor and then took the dinghy to shore. Real landlubbers, we upset the dinghy when I, seated in the front, got off first. Bob and Darcy, seated in the back, sank in the water, Bob's camera still around his neck. They scrambled on to the dock, and, with the help from bystanders, righted the dinghy. Since we were ashore, we took a look around and bought a pair of sunglasses for Darcy, but we figured that Bob's camera and film were damaged beyond repair. Back at our boat, we swam and snorkeled.

The third day out, we hoped we'd experienced the worst. We sailed from Caneel Bay out in the ocean and then to Trunk Bay, a national park with an underwater snorkeling trail, for lunch and a walk around. From there we sailed on to Francis Bay, anchoring there for the night. It was the first night we'd been the only boat in the harbor, and we spent an eerie night in this relatively isolated place. We may have been the only humans, but we were surrounded by other creatures. Immediately after I tossed some spoiled hamburger overboard, the water churned with fish, large and small. For the first time since we set sail, we were bothered with mosquitoes, which may have been the reason we were alone. Cockroaches, hidden until then, also made their unwelcome appearance. The next morning, Darcy said he hadn't slept much: "I heard wild animals calling to each other, all night long."

Our destination the fourth day was Norman Island. As soon as we sailed out of Francis Bay, we realized it was going to be a difficult sailing day: We were heading from west to east, while the wind blew in a north-south direction. As we each concentrated on our respective jobs, my greatest misgiving (and I'm sure Darcy's as well) was what we'd do if something happened to our captain. Fortunately, all went well, and we finally did reach the island, famous for its supposedly being the setting for Robert Louis Stevenson's classic, *Treasure Island*. Motoring out the next morning, we saw caves, conjuring up visions of fierce pirates, cutlasses in their teeth, raiding the ships that sailed by.

Having anchored in Norman Island's harbor about 3:00 p.m., we were all set for a peaceful afternoon swimming and snorkeling. But suddenly the sky grew dark, the wind shifted and turned the boat right around so that it was dangerously near the shore. As we sat there pondering what to do, a sailor from another boat rowed over. "You'd better motor out and put down two anchors," he cautioned. Thanking him, Bob and Darcy lost no time in responding to his advice. Then, as suddenly as it had started, the storm ended. There was still enough time to do some great snorkeling. That evening we watched as the "wild animals"—a few cows, goats and donkeys—came down to the water to drink. We thought this curious, as animals don't usually drink salt water. Perhaps all the fresh water had dried up.

On our last day of sailing, we left Norman Island and headed to St. Thomas. Lacking enough wind to get us to the Antilles Yacht Club, check in the boat and equipment, and make the connection to a flight out of San Juan that evening, Bob turned on the engine to help speed us along. Our last adventure—which could well have been a disaster—occurred as we were coming around a rocky cliff into what Bob thought was the harbor. Just as I noticed rocks beneath the surface of the clear water, we heard a crrunncchh. Darcy and I both yelled, STOP!!! Bob turned the boat around, just in time: Another few feet and we would have been grounded. A look at the navigation chart afterward showed that we had been headed straight towards the breakers over a line of coral reefs. But we managed to maneuver safely into the harbor and set foot on terra firma, relieved to be on solid ground again.

We managed to fly out of St. Thomas on schedule but couldn't fly to the USA that evening. Fortunately, Bob managed to reserve rooms at the Caribbe Hilton. Can you, the reader, imagine what a treat it was for three sunburned (the first time for Bob), bite-ridden, salty seafarers to spend a night in air-conditioned luxury? I washed my hair for the first time in over a week, Darcy got a good look at the rash that had spread all over his arms and legs, and Bob debated whether to shave off his grizzled sailor's beard. After getting thoroughly cleaned up and dressed in proper attire, we went down to the hotel terrace, where we had a delicious dinner, enjoying the view of San Juan's cityscape.

Sunday and Monday we toured San Juan, taking a city tour and seeing historic sites, and again dining well and sleeping soundly. We left San Juan Monday evening, flying back to the USA in first-class accommodations—a last bit of luxury before returning to Buffalo.

A year later, Bob, Darcy and I were back in the West Indies, this time for a week's sail in the British Virgin Islands, near the American Virgin Islands, where we'd sailed the previous year. Bob had chartered a Pearson 35, a larger sailboat with more equipment, easier to manage than the 26 ft. sailboat we had before. We flew to the island of Tortola, landing in Road Town, the capital, with about 8,000, mostly black, inhabitants. Arriving on Friday afternoon, we stayed in a rented apartment until we picked up the boat on Sunday. The apartment was delightful—spacious, airy, and right on the waterfront with a view of the harbor and all its activity.

Having experienced only dry weather during our previous year, we were disconcerted when it rained Friday night, Saturday night, and again on Sunday. This was a side of the Virgin Islands we hadn't expected. Nevertheless, with groceries and other supplies purchased, we were anxious to get going. So on Sunday afternoon we set sail, headed for the island of Virgin Gorda. During the 4-hour sail, the winds were brisk and the water choppy. Bob enthused, "It's a great sailing day!" Darcy, on the edge of being sick, retreated to the cabin below deck. I stuck it out, trying not to become too concerned, but I was greatly relieved when we reached the harbor, crowded with boats. We learned from other sailors who'd gone further north that the weather there had been even stormier.

The anchorage included docks, a shore-side restaurant and bar, washroom and shower facilities, even a store. Later that evening Bob and I went ashore and walked into Spanishtown. There the locals were celebrating festival, the highlight of the night being the choosing of a beauty queen. We didn't get to see the finals as it suddenly began to pour, and we all scrambled for shelter. The rain, coming after a long dry spell, must have been welcomed by the island's inhabitants.

The next day we set out for Drake's Anchorage, further north and between Mosquito Island and Virgin Gorda. On the way, we stopped to see the Baths, rock formations along the southern tip of the island, with boulders as large as small houses. Anchoring about one hundred yards from shore, we debated whether to take the dinghy ashore to explore. Just in time we noticed that the dinghy had become unfastened and was drifting away from us. Bob stripped down to his shorts immediately and dived after it. As he swam further and further away, both Darcy and I were thinking, "What if something happens to him out there?" Fortunately, Bob finally caught up with the dinghy, got in, and motored close to shore to see whether it was feasible to go ashore. We had heard that if a northerly surf was running, it would be next to impossible to get off, once onshore.

Bob said, "No problem," so we took the dinghy and went ashore, propelled by a huge wave and landing with a crash. Then we knew we were in a fix. Putting aside any thought of exploring, our pressing concern now was getting off. Having watched our futile attempts from a distance, a couple came over to help. With all of us pushing and shoving, we finally managed to get beyond the surf and back to our sailboat. Experience is the best teacher, they say, and we had learned another lesson.

That evening, back in the harbor, we were surprised to see a Buffalo couple anchored near us. Bob knew the Schreiners, as they also sailed out of the Small Boat Harbor. I cooked steaks on the grill, and we had just finished eating when it rained again. It didn't last long, though, and we sat outside on the deck for a while watching the spectacular lightning illuminating the sky

Tuesday morning we sailed to Mosquito Island, went ashore and took a walk around. Having stopped at a restaurant, we learned that an M.I.T. professor owned the island, including the restaurant and the few apartments on the island. We spent the day sailing around the nearby islands and coming in for the evening near Saba Rock. The next day we headed to Marina Cay. With favorable winds, we had a good sail—just brisk enough for Bob but not too much for Darcy and me. We anchored at Marina Cay off Great Camanoe Island and there had the best snorkeling yet; the reefs off the island were teeming with fish and other sea creatures. That night I woke about 3:00 a.m. to find Bob up on deck, trying to determine whether or not we had drifted away from the anchorage and into the channel.

The next morning we found that we hadn't drifted but that the boat had changed direction. Our destination that day was Jost Van Dyke. With very little wind, we motored all the way to the island, about a 3-hour trip. Arriving, we found this little island, a row of palm trees along the shore, so picturesque one could easily imagine Van Gogh painting there. Taking the dinghy to shore, Bob and I talked with some of the natives and debated whether we should come back that evening for dinner at Foxy's, which we'd heard was a good place to have lobster.

After taking a look in Foxy's kitchen, Bob decided we'd better have dinner on our boat. But we went back later to listen to the native band. As we sat in the open-air restaurant, we watched enviously as nearby diners were served what appeared to be an utterly delectable meal of lobster, corn-on-the-cob, salad, rolls, coffee and an elegant dessert. But the musicians were very good, and Bob and I stayed until late, drinking the local beverage, a mix of rum and pineapple juice.

Friday morning we discovered that our supply of ice had run out and two of our intended meat dinners had gone bad. It was time for a quick sail back to Roadtown. That we did, quickly secured ice and food, and set out for Norman Island, hoping to anchor there before dark. Fortunately, the winds were favorable and we did get there in time.

The next morning we found that we had drifted about one hundred yards from where we had anchored. Fortunately, we were still in sheltered water and away from any reefs. We spent the morning exploring the pirate caves and snorkeling. Then we sailed to Peter Island and the harbor there for our last night out. This was another "great sail" for Bob. Darcy and I were relieved it wasn't as frightening as the Virgin Gorda sail. We reached the harbor about 6:30, just in time to broil and eat dinner, then watch a gorgeous sunset.

Saturday morning we were up early, ready to head into Tortola and the end of sailing. Having checked in the sailboat, we left Tortola and flew to San Juan. Waiting for our flight later that evening, we started out sightseeing, but found we were too tired. Instead, we spent several hours simply sitting in one of the hotels. Watching crowds of people passing by, we knew we were back in civilization. Sailing in the Virgin Islands, hair-raising episodes and all, certainly met our expectations. Although we didn't know it then, it was the last sailing trip or vacation Bob, Darcy and I would spend together.

Bob and I did take one more sailing trip, in March, 1981,this time in the Abacos Islands. These are a group of islands and cays in the Sea of Abacos, about 180 miles east of Fort Lauderdale. We had chosen the low-lying Abacos to try something new, and Bob had chartered a sailboat from the Bahama Yachting Service. While we would have preferred a smaller vessel, easier to manage, the only one available for the time was a 37-ft. Endeavor, large enough to accommodate six people. Arriving in Marsh Harbor, the port of entry to the Bahamas, we went through customs and then took a taxi to the yachting service, where our sailboat was waiting for us.

After a thorough briefing, we motored out from the dock and anchored in the harbor, taking the dinghy to come ashore for dinner in one of the restaurants that night. The next morning, after a charting lesson from BYS, we bought provisions for the next week's breakfasts , lunches and snacks. Then we set sail, and from then on it was one new sailing experience after another. Sailing in shallow waters was entirely different from the deep water sailing we had done in the Virgin Islands, and we were ever cautious.

In fact, our most harrowing experience came the second day. Sailing from Guana Cay to Green Turtle Cay, we attempted a tricky maneuver, completely miscalculating the critical passage through two landmarks. As we watched the depth finder fall to an alarming four feet, we were suddenly swept over a hidden reef by a giant wave. I held on for dear life! I thought we were going to be swamped, but we actually rode the crest right over the unseen reef into deep ocean water. Crashing into the reef would have been a disaster: a damaged boat and an expensive and untimely end to our sailing.

Sailing from one port to another and anchoring out in the bays, we explored the little villages (with their 18th century flavor, the inhabitants mostly descendants of the Loyalists who separated from England), and ate dinner in one of the restaurants. On our March 28th anniversary, we enjoyed a delicious meal of grouper, rice and beans, and coleslaw, and drank the local "goombay squash," a potent combination of rum, pineapple juice and coconut.

It wasn't as warm as we'd expected. We'd brought swim suits, but the chilly water wasn't inviting either for swimming or snorkeling in the crystal-clear water. We met only a few people from the States, and usually struck up conversations with the friendly people who served tourists. Our last day out, we faced one more navigational challenge—returning to our port by the ocean passage, the island passage being too shallow to navigate. It was a stormy day, and the wind blew at 20-30 knots. As we maneuvered through the choppy water, my heart was in my mouth. At one point, the boat turned completely around. Under normal conditions, I could have handled the steering while Bob managed the sails; but I was not a sailor, and I cowered flat on the deck while Bob got the boat under control.

Motoring part of the way back to port, we managed the tricky passage we'd missed the other day, now recognizing where we'd gone wrong. We did arrive safely at Man-O-War Key, and sailed on the next day to Hope Town, our last anchorage. On April 1, we sailed to Marsh Harbor and returned the sailboat, relieved to be back on terra firma once again, and flew back to Buffalo.

13

The AIA Conventions

As a member of the national association, the American Institute of Architects, Bob began attending the national conventions in 1968, held in Portland, Oregon. During the convention, Bob listened intently as the keynote speaker, black civil rights leader Whitney M. Young, Jr., blamed white architects for helping "to tighten the white noose around the central city," and challenged the Institute to do something about the urban crisis. One of only a handful of black architects attending the convention, Bob vowed to attend every single convention from then on in order to add a black presence, and to remind white architects of their responsibility to increase opportunities for black architects.

After the 1968 convention, Bob became increasingly involved in professional affairs on a national as well as on a local level. He was a member of the national AIA Housing Committee from 1969-1972, member of the National AIA Urban Design Committee from 1971-73, and a member of the national AIA Community Services Advisory Council from 1973-74. Early in his career he had thought of himself as an architect who was black; now he saw himself as a black architect, an advocate for minorities.

I attended many of the conventions with Bob, including my first, the AIA 1973 convention held in San Francisco in May. The newly-formed National Organization of Minority Architects (NOMA) also met there, their sessions having ended before the AIA's began. I attended some of their sessions with Bob, one of NOMA's founding members, and heard a rousing speech by Willie Brown, then a San Francisco councilman, who later became mayor. Perhaps because NOMA was a new organization, only about twenty members attended, in contrast to the estimated 5,000-6,000 AIA convention attendees. Another reason could have been that coming to San Francisco and attending the convention was simply too expensive for most.

Highlights of the AIA convention were the Dodge Party, with free food, drinks, and entertainment; a tour of BART (Bay Area Rapid Transit) including a ride on the train; the AIA President's Reception at the San Francisco Art Museum; speeches on "The Challenge of Growth and Change"; and the Host Chapter Party, beginning at the Oakland Museum and progressing to the Berkeley

Art Museum. Besides the convention events, we went sightseeing on our own, visiting such interesting architecture as the new Transamerica Bank Building and a new Hyatt Hotel with its four "indoor-outdoor" elevators affording breathtaking views.

This convention, like others Bob attended, was an excellent way for him to network with old friends and meet new people. At a private party given by friends Ellen and Bob Marquis in their San Francisco home, we were part of a crowd that included Moshe Safde, renowned for his radical housing complex, Habitat, but missed seeing him. We also ran into people we knew—John Eberhard, then head of the Department of Architecture at the University of Buffalo; architect Mallory Lash, from Boston; and black architect LeRoy Tuckett and his girlfriend from New York City. We had dinner with them one evening at Bernstein's Fish Grotto, one of San Francisco's best seafood restaurants.

We also reconnected with Marion, now divorced and living with her boy-friend, Kenny, in Oakland. One afternoon we went for a drive with them to Sausalito, stopping to see Frank Lloyd Wright's Civic Center in Marin, and wound up having dinner at the Trident, a popular waterfront restaurant with great views of the San Francisco Bay, nearby islands, and San Francisco's skyline. On the way back, we dropped in at the Dodge party, where Marion and Kenny salvaged some of the decorations to take home. We saw them once again, as they met us at the Berkeley Art Museum to attend a party given by the black architectural students attending both conventions.

After the AIA convention, we flew to Vancouver to spend two days with Ken and Anne Terriss. Their house, designed by Ken and completed in 1970, fronted on English Bay, affording excellent views across the Bay of downtown Vancouver and distant mountains. Their two adopted sons, Peter and Matthew, then 11 and 9 years old, were lively youngsters. We met two of Ken and Anne's friends, Peter and Mineka, both Dutch, while we were there. Peter was working as the Vancouver City Architect, and Mineka, a weaver, ran a crafts shop and gave weaving lessons.

We made one more stop, in Minneapolis, before coming back to Buffalo, seeing some of the friends we'd made while living there— Joyce and Lucas Smith, Alpha Adkins, Chan and Katie McWatt, and Jay and Cynthia Tyson. Downtown, we stopped to see the new IDS Tower, then the tallest structure between Chicago and San Francisco. One evening we were invited to have dinner with Helen and Jim Stageberg, Jim having been Bob's competitor for the Rotch Scholarship. During dinner, Jim brought up the subject of the

Rotch, and Bob guessed that Jim had never forgotten Bob's beating him, even though he won it the following year.

Finally, we returned to Buffalo. Darcy had taken good care of the house and our German Shepherd, Mies, the dog we acquired after Duke's demise (he got into a fatal dogfight one day). Darcy spent that summer with us and then went to Boston in the fall to begin his freshman year at Boston University.

In 1974, Bob was selected by the Institute to serve as its first Deputy Vice President for Minority Affairs. In this position, he served on the national headquarters staff as developer and administrator of minority programs. He served in that position until 1976, renting an apartment in Washington and flying back to Buffalo periodically.

In his position, Bob attended other meetings besides the national conventions. One meeting was held in Miami in January, 1975, and another, two months later, in New Orleans. The AIA paid his travel expenses and I accompanied him on both trips. While in Miami we walked along Miami Beach, and I noted the predominantly older, all-white population. It was not a place I'd want to retire to, or even re-visit. New Orleans, though, was a different matter.

Unique among American cities, we found it indeed as described in a brochure: "America's European Masterpiece." In one of the several days we were there, Bob and I cruised the Mississippi River onboard the Cotton Blossom, entertained by a swinging jazz band. Another day he and I boarded a bus for "a complete tour of New Orleans Past, Present and Future," taking us through the city, featuring every important section and landmark, past the Lafayette Cemetery with its unique above-ground burial ground, down to the waterfront, out to Lake Pontchartrain and along Bayou St. John past the Pitot Plantation House. We sampled delicious French food, the beignets at the Café du Monde, Holmesmade pralines, and gumbo at Le Bon Creole. Our stay wouldn't have been complete without spending a night listening to jazz in one of the French Quarter clubs.

While Bob was in meetings, I went out exploring on my own. I took a walking tour of the French Quarter, with its Old World shops and buildings, including the restored Gallier House and courtyard, with its exquisite iron grillwork, and the St. Louis Cathedral, the largest in the United States. I stopped at a couple of the little shops that sold voodoo charms and bought a few souvenirs. In a kite shop, I found an unusual kite, in the shape of a large insect, with beady eyes, wings, and a segmented tail. I brought it home and it still hovers, faded and fragile, from the ceiling in my sewing room.

I could have spent much more time in New Orleans, but thoroughly enjoyed every minute I was there.

In May of 1975, we attended the national AIA convention, held that year in Atlanta, staying in a Hyatt Hotel in downtown Atlanta near the Civic Center, where most of the convention events were held. Attending a function in the suburbs, miles away from the center, we became aware that most Atlantans, including blacks, lived in the suburbs. There was nothing in that city that appealed to me.

In one more trip that year, I accompanied Bob as he attended a week of meetings of the AIA Executive Staff and Board of Directors held in Mexico City, in September. We'd visited Mexico City briefly with Marion and Darcy about eight years before; and I had been especially impressed with the brilliant murals painted by Mexican artists, including Diego Rivera, decorating both the interior and exterior of many buildings. I was delighted to be back in Mexico City and looked forward to revisiting some of the places we'd been before. We stayed near Chapultepec Park, in the Camino Real, a new luxury hotel, which looked like a fortress and indeed operated as one: a 4-walled structure with interior courts kept undesirables out. About sixty architects and their wives were there, most of them, like us, staying at the Camino Real.

The first afternoon Bob and I took a walk along the Paseo Reforma, the city's most beautiful avenue, divided with a park-like green strip. Along the boulevard were many circles containing monuments to Mexico's heroes. We stopped in one of the city's fine and abundant parks, filled with people. As we strolled through the park, Bob photographing some of the most interesting types, we found ourselves the object of stares, very few blacks living here.

That evening we attended the first of several social functions arranged for our group: a reception hosted by the American ambassador to Mexico, Joseph John Jova and his wife, held in their home in the wealthy San Lomas district. Also attending the reception were other Mexican dignitaries, other architects and their wives. The Jovas' home was an elegant villa with a beautiful garden, typical of the residences in the district, populated mainly by dignitaries like the ambassador.

The next day, with husbands in all-day meetings, I was invited by several of the architects' wives to go shopping with them in nearby Taxco and Cuernavaca, Taxco being noted for its silver, and Cuernavaca famous as a resort. However, I declined and went by myself back to Chapultepec Park, filled with much of interest to a tourist, including a castle, a zoo and the famous Museum of

Anthropology. It was closed Monday afternoon, but I visited it the next day with Bob during a tour arranged for the group.

At the Museum, our guide explained the symbolism of the huge, umbrella-shaped sculpture topping a cascading fountain of rain. Rain, as one of the elements, and sun as another, figured predominantly in ancient cultures; and the sculpture stands as a contemporary monument to the ancient Rain God. Our guide went on to explain some of the exhibits, including the famous Aztec Stone Calendar; and we looked at a model of Mexico City before its invasion by the Spaniards.

Another day we took an all-day bus tour to the Pyramids of Teotihuacan, about 20 miles north of the city, lunch at the San Angelo Inn, and a view of the University of Mexico. That day was cloudy, threatening rain, and I observed that the extraordinary brilliant colors I had observed when we were here before must have been due to the beautiful weather at that time. The colors in the murals, parks, and buildings were still there, but they were now shadowed by rain and clouds.

We had a 40-minute limit to visit the ruins of the Sun and Moon Pyramids, and the plazas and remains of buildings between the two. I recalled how, when we were here before, we all made the vertiginous climb up the steep steps of the Pyramids to the top—where we had a panoramic view—and then the frightening descent. As if to mock us, several youngsters literally ran up and down the stairs. I certainly had no desire to attempt that climb again. Instead, I followed our guide as we walked around the site, he pointing out details that gave us insight into this ancient culture. New on the site since we were there was a museum with a restaurant on the second floor and a cluster of souvenir stands, accommodating the increasing number of tourists.

On the return trip, we went through the central city to the south district for lunch at the San Angelo Inn and a glimpse of the University of New Mexico. After a late lunch at the Inn, we went on to the University. Its population of 100,000 had already exceeded the maximum its facilities could accommodate, and some of the students attended classes in branches located elsewhere. Mexico City's population had continued to increase, augmented by people who moved in from the country. We saw beggars everywhere, and squatters had penetrated the better residential areas. As we drove through Lava Hills, a lower-upper class area, our guide pointed out that many of the homes were fenced in mainly to prevent squatters from camping on the grounds.

The day after our tour out to Teotihuacan, Bob had meetings all day. Having consulted my travel guide, I went out to the Pink Zone to look for bargains and souvenirs. I saw many beautiful things—Girasols had lovely dresses, shirts and gowns, all with exquisite Mexican embroidery. At another shop I saw a beautiful silver bracelet but resisted buying it. I did purchase a few small gifts and a little souvenir for myself—a white cotton apron with a golden sun across its front. Having left the Pink Zone, I stopped in the Museum of Modern Art in Chapultepec Park to see its collection of paintings and sculpture by Mexican artists.

That evening we went to a cocktail party given by the AIA President and his wife. At the party, Bob was pleased to learn that his address that afternoon regarding concern over the future of minorities in the profession had been well received. Leaving the party, we tried the Estoril for dinner, and there I had an unusual meal. The hotel guide listed the crepes de huitlacoche "a must." Always ready to try new food, I ordered the crepes, very delicate tortillas filled with a dark mushroom fungus that grows on corn; although it didn't sound very appetizing, it was delicious.

The last social event was a "Fiesta Luncheon" at the home of the Webbs. Peter, an American architect, and his writer wife, who had inherited their house, spent several months here during the year. It was indeed a festive luncheon, with musicians serenading us and waiters hurrying back and forth with cocktails and platter upon platter of roast pork, tortillas, tacos, and enchiladas, which they set on the tables. Throwing caution to the wind, I decided to indulge myself and tasted morsel after morsel, finally stopping when I realized the main course was still coming. That turned out to be Chicken Mole, accompanied by other Mexican dishes, fresh fruit for dessert, and rich Mexican coffee. Sitting together at a table, we conversed with the Webb's pretty daughter. She told us she was a sophomore at Georgetown University and would be leaving soon for school. Her complaint that "there's nothing to do here" sounded all too familiar.

After that fiesta lunch, the only thing to do was to take a long siesta in the hotel, and we did. Waking up about 10:00 p.m., we decided to try the hotel discotheque, the Cero Cero. Once again, Bob was a standout in the crowd. One friendly young Mexican came over and told us how much he liked black people. On the dance floor much of the time, we hardly noticed the time, and it was 2:30 a.m. before we left.

Our last adventure in Mexico City was on the day before we left. We took a subway ride to the Insurgente Station and then walked down the Insurgente, a long avenue running from north of the city to the city center and then further south. Our first stop was at the Polyforum, a fascinating building in the shape of a duodecagon, like a multi-colored diamond, its twelve faces painted with sculptured murals, each expressing a theme. Inside were an art gallery, a circular theatre, a forum exhibiting Mexican handicrafts, and the principal forum, containing a circular stage with seating.

Leaving the Polyforum, we went to see the new Hotel de Mexico, adjacent to the Polyforum, still under construction. We had read that both the Polyforum and the Hotel were planned as focal points to attract new enterprises to the area. I had also heard that the revolving bar-restaurant at the hotel top, 44 stories up, was open for business. We noted that there were no other people around—not even workmen, which felt odd. But there was someone in the ticket booth, so we decided to pay the entrance fee and take the elevator up to the top.

After we got on the elevator with the operator, he pressed the button; the elevator moved a few feet and then stopped. Now we could see that the elevator's exposed side was open to the bare stone wall of the elevator shaft. Again the operator pressed the button, and still nothing happened. Bob asked, "How often does this happen?" The answer, "All the time," heightened our apprehension. Imagining being trapped in the elevator anywhere on the way to the top, we immediately abandoned our plan and asked the operator to return to the main floor. After he repeatedly pushed buttons, the elevator finally descended, and we rushed out. To top it off, when we left the hotel, Bob discovered he'd lost one of his camera lenses. Although we went back and searched the area, we didn't find it.

Our last dinner in Mexico City was a bust. Rather than return to the Estoril, we decided to try another restaurant, the Fonda del Refugio, which had won "renowned for the best Mexican haute cuisine in Mexico City ...serving the best steak anywhere." Imagine our disappointment when our food arrived. Bob's carne asada turned out to be an extraordinarily tough piece of beef and my roast pork a perfectly ordinary pair of pork chops. Not everyone had strong stomachs like ours. We watched as one of the patrons at the table next to us literally turned green as she consumed her meal. The young lady's companion hurried out of the room and returned with a brown paper bag containing a remedy for nausea. She swallowed the remedy and then, encouraged by all the diners, managed to get to her feet. The couple paid the bill and left abruptly, without finishing their meals.

Well, it had been a week to remember. Looking back, I'm glad we were there long before the problems of poverty, crime, traffic congestion and air pollution dimmed the luster of this beautiful city.

In December, 1980, we flew to Washington, D.C. to celebrate R. Randall (Randy) Vosbeck's Inauguration as the 57th President of the AIA. Bob and Randy had met while they were both attending the University of Minnesota and had remained good friends since. After his inauguration, Randy asked Bob to be the chairman for the 1981 national convention. At Randy's request and without Bob's knowledge, I had written a four-page paper in September detailing Bob's continuing advocacy for minorities. The paper supported Randy's nomination of Bob to receive the prestigious Whitney M. Young, Jr. award commemorating the civil rights and urban leader and recognizing significant contributions of an architect in meeting the profession's responsibility to social issues. Bob was selected by the AIA and would be receiving the award during the 1981 convention, held that year in Minneapolis.

The next year, in May, 1981, Bob and I flew to Minneapolis for the AIA Convention, one we would long remember. The high point of the convention for us came during the ceremony in which Bob was presented with the Whitney Young Award. I was pleased for him and proud of the role I had played in that award, one that he richly deserved. In another ceremony, he was, along with a dozen other architects, elevated to Fellow, the highest rank an architect can attain. To celebrate, we hosted an Open House in our hotel suite that Friday evening. The next night, we had dinner with Marion and Michael Ongerth, her new boy-friend, who had flown from Berkeley to attend some of the convention events with us. While in Minneapolis, I revisited the neighborhood in which I had lived and worked and found it changed almost beyond recognition.

Bob and Sylvia, at the Minneapolis AIA Convention. May, 1981

14

A New Era

While Bob was working at the AIA in Washington, I began to seriously re-examine my own status. I imagined that many another architect's wife, like me, assumed a subordinate role in marriage. In an article in the Buffalo News, I was described as one who "worked behind the scenes on various community committees." From the time we married, I had accepted the role of supporting Bob in whatever he was involved. I knew Bob needed a particularly strong ego to be successful as a minority in a predominantly white profession. And naturally, every award, every honor served to feed Bob's ego, but it did nothing for mine. I was unhappy with my current role and realized I needed a change.

Having finished college with an undergraduate degree in sociology, I lacked the qualifications for a position in that field. Then, I hadn't considered a career of my own, expecting, instead, that I'd get married and be simply a wife and mother. Now, years later, I decided that a positive step would be to go back to school for an MBA degree. I reasoned that the degree would be beneficial to me as well as Bob: It would give me the added skills I needed to manage the financial end of an architectural practice, Bob having no interest in that aspect himself.

Peggy Nevin, a guidance counselor in the Adult Advisement Center at U.B., gave me the encouragement I needed as did others, including Will Clarkson, head of Graphic Controls, a Buffalo corporation, and John Boot, a professor in U.B.'s School of Management. In a note to me in 1975, Will wrote that, in his view, "the business world needs as many competent and enlightened managers as possible, particularly women as well as men." So, I applied and was admitted to U.B.'s Graduate Management Program (GMP) beginning in the fall of 1976.

That September I began the program, working full-time during the day and attending classes at night. I joined other students, including a few women, three of whom became good friends of mine. The courses I took during those four years ranged from Strategic Management to Statistics, to Organizational Behavior. For that course, I wrote a paper titled "Job Satisfaction Among Architectural Employees." In the paper I posited that an architectural graduate's job satisfaction was dependent on his or her expectations and how well the individual's goals and purposes matched the firm's. If these were on a higher level than the actual work situation, the graduate would most likely leave the position, apply for another job, or even leave the field entirely. My professor gave me an "A" for the paper, with the note that I should examine possible sources for publishing it in an architectural journal. Perhaps I should have, but Bob did not encourage me, so I never did.

In the midst of office work and the MBA courses, I received the sad news in September, 1977 that my mother, who had recently been in ill health, was diagnosed with inoperable colon cancer, and could expect only a few more months to live. I flew to Ellis during Christmas break, staying with Helen, who lived a block from my mother's house. The night I arrived, I walked over to my mother's house and found her lying on the living room couch, waiting for me. As I kissed her, I noticed she'd dressed nicely, had fixed her hair and put on lipstick, wanting to present the best image possible, just as she always had.

The next day, I spent most of it visiting with her. It was touching to see she'd made the effort to decorate the house with Christmas ornaments—her collection of treasures—to celebrate Christmas one last time. I was glad that in the years since marrying Bob, I'd kept in fairly close contact with her. She came to Buffalo twice to visit us; but after that I regularly went to Kansas to see both her and Helen. She had mellowed a lot in those years, becoming ever more liberal in her views. However, she decided against ever inviting Bob, fearing the negative reaction from her neighbors and friends in small town Ellis, where one rarely saw a black face. Helen told me later that my mother had agonized over this decision.

That evening, New Year's Eve, Helen and I played my mother's favorite card game, Rook, with her. After playing several sets and then having a few bites of Helen's delicious lemon pie, which Helen had made especially for her, my mother said she was tired and went to bed. Helen and I left, but Helen returned later that night to look in on her. She found my mother unconscious, most likely dehydrated. Alarmed, she called an ambulance and my mother was rushed to the nearest hospital.

I went to sit with her there every afternoon until it was time for me to get back to Buffalo. It hurt to see her—the women who'd been so active most of her life—tethered by the various tubes connected to her body, barely able to move, with very little to say. I believe she planned to die peacefully in her own bed that New Year's Eve, not in a hospital. Unfortunately, she failed to communicate her wish to Helen, who was her primary caregiver, and her doctor. I hoped then to never find myself in that position.

My mother died on January 20, 1978. Werner, who'd come from Indiana with Faye, Helen, and I paid tribute to her during the services held for her in St. John's Lutheran Church, where she'd been a member. As special music before the service began, Werner played several pieces including Bach's lovely "Jesu, Joy of Man's Desiring." During the service, Helen sang several of my mother's favorites, and I read the "Eulogy to My Mother" I'd written. Afterwards, we sat together in my mother's living room, exchanging stories of how she'd affected each of our lives. The next day, Werner and Faye left for Indiana, I left for Buffalo, and eventually the house was sold.

May, 1980 marked a milestone for me: successfully completing the MBA program and receiving my degree. After the commencement, held at the University's Amherst campus, Bob and I celebrated with a big party at our house. Many of our best friends came, and out-of-town friends sent cards. I compiled a large scrapbook containing all the cards and memorabilia of the party. I look at it now and then, and remember how elated I was at that time.

Achieving that degree, uncommon for women at that time, was one of the high points of my life. Of my three friends who also obtained the MBA degree, one, Janet LeVan, ascended up the corporate ladder to become a top executive at AT & T. The other two and I simply resumed our regular jobs, Marion LaVigne continuing to teach high school English, and Kathy Dohn working in an administrative position at the University. Nevertheless, we all felt that the knowledge we had gained in the MBA program was very useful. Sadly, Janet succumbed to cancer in her late sixties.

In November, 1980, on the day after Thanksgiving, Bob and I, assisted by staff, moved the office from our home to rooms on the seventh floor of the historic Ellicott Square Building in downtown Buffalo. With an office force of ten utilizing every room in our house except the master bedroom, it had been high time for a move. It was an especially welcome change for me as I, unlike Bob, preferred a strict separation between work and home life. Bob loved the prestigious Ellicott Square Building address.

Active projects now included major commissions such as Phase I of the Health, Physical Education and Recreation Complex, at the University's Amherst campus; the Lindbergh Center in Atlanta; and the Providence Railroad Station in Rhode Island. Bob's firm formed associations with engineering and other architectural firms to complete these contracts.

Bob and I shared a room in the office, and I liked looking out the window next to my desk for a view extending as far as the old Central Railroad Terminal in East Buffalo. Since receiving my MBA degree, I assumed the title of Controller/Business Manager, responsible for managing all the financial aspects of the firm including payroll, cash management, accounting, and filing state and federal employment returns. Our accountant prepared annual tax returns and financial statements based on the information I provided. I took my job very seriously, intent in running my end of the practice as smoothly as possible. That year I attended a seminar, "Financial Planning for the Closely-Held Corporation" (such as ours) sponsored by the New York University, and also a course in Time Management, sponsored by the University at Buffalo.

Besides the Buffalo office, Bob had an office in Washington, with a staff of five. His firm and Randy Vosbeck's firm associated to design a library in Washington, but the project was dropped because land for the library was never acquired. However, Bob and Randy joined with the Washington firm of Devrouax and Purnell, black partners, to design and build the District of Columbia (D.C.) Municipal Office Building. Bob had kept an apartment near DuPont Plaza since his AIA position, and he and several of the Buffalo staff stayed there while working on the D.C. project. On my occasional trips to Washington, I stayed in the apartment and enjoyed strolling around the Plaza and nearby streets, browsing in the elegant shops and dining with Bob in our favorite restaurants.

Shortly after the beginning of 1981, I was invited by the Grosvenor Society of the Buffalo and Erie County Library to present a book review at the Central branch in downtown Buffalo in March. Interviewed by Buffalo News columnist Karen Brady for an article encouraging attendance at the book review and describing my background, I was quoted as saying, "One choice I have made is to remain in the business with Bob (after completing the MBA Degree), and I love it." Only a few years later, I questioned that decision.

The book I reviewed was J. Patrick Wright's *On a Clear Day You Can See General Motors*. It was an expose by insider John DeLorean of the auto industry, including horrendous product decisions and serious management blunders. Reading this controversial, fascinating book and then reviewing it, speaking in front of a rapt audience, was a hugely enjoyable experience. As a thank-you gift, I was given a copy of the book, which is still on my shelf.

Following the book review, I began looking for more professional experiences outside Bob's firm. Dr. Allan Korn, a personal friend and the Director of Cooperative Experiential Education at Buffalo State College, invited me to lecture to students in his class of Small Business Management in July. The students were unanimous in their positive evaluations of my lecture, and I addressed other Business Management classes again in 1982, 1984 and 1985. I was invited to lecture again in 1986 but declined, having lost interest in that type of volunteerism.

In 1981, I also planned, investigated and implemented both word and data processing for the firm. I arranged to have two word processors installed, one in the Buffalo office and one in Washington. Modems were acquired to link the two offices and enable instant communication between the two. To carry out the many clerical functions, I hired two young women, one functioning as office manager/secretary, the other as secretary in the Buffalo office, and also a secretary in Washington. Then in August I converted the firm's manual accounting and project management system to a computer-based system, developed by Harper and Shuman, based in Boston, utilized by architectural and engineering firms throughout the country.

With a staff of twelve, including Bob and I in Buffalo, and five in Washington, as well as various consultants, management of office operations had become increasingly complex in 1982, and I found myself going back to the office most Saturdays and even Sundays for a few hours just to keep caught up. Cash flow was a continual problem, with irregular payments from clients. In a meeting with our banker at the end of March, he told us that our business was going downhill and that we needed to take drastic action immediately. I had seen signs of trouble for some time, but it took the banker to convince Bob. He reacted by letting two of the Buffalo staff go and alerting the Washington office that he might need to reduce staff there as well. Our financial situation improved gradually, sufficient to mollify the bank.

On a brighter note, in May Bob and I celebrated the Friday night opening of an exhibit on Buffalo architecture at the Albright-Knox Gallery, with a lecture by Brendan Gill, New Yorker critic. The next afternoon Bob was one of the panelists in a Symposium at the Gallery, joining other local architects and the architectural critic from the Boston Globe. We hosted an open house at our home Saturday evening and more than eighty guests came. A guide to

Buffalo's architecture had been published in 1981, Bob one of the contributors. Our house was pictured in the book, described as "one of the few avowedly contemporary residential structures in the city."

Our contemporary house had its flaws: built with a flat roof, rainwater and snow melt collected on the roof, resulting in leaks inside the house. With the roofing material deteriorating, we called in a roofing company in November, 1982 to replace the roof. Unfortunately, it rained at the same time they started work. Bob had to scurry to get plastic to cover the piano and furniture in the living room. Before the roofing was completed, it rained hard one night causing a cascade of water to come pouring down. We emptied buckets as fast as they filled to keep up with the deluge. Fortunately, the rain stopped the next day and the workmen continued the job, but not until leaks in the studio several days later forced a move of most of the contents to the lower level. When it was all over, Bob conceded, "If I had to do it over again, I would design the roof with a slight pitch." The roof problem repeated itself over the years, as roofing gradually deteriorated and further roof replacements were needed.

Cash management problems continued, and affairs hit a low point in early 1983 with our banker remarking, during a lunch meeting with me, that "on paper, you're bankrupt." I took the responsibility of working out a solution. Meanwhile, as we experienced turnover among the administrative personnel, I completed an Administrative Office Manual, outlining policies and procedures for current and future staff, anticipating a time when I might no longer be with the firm.

Occasionally, we escaped from office worries. In April, Bob and I went to Boston to attend a dinner reunion of the Rotch scholars, and Bob especially enjoyed meeting scholars he knew as well as those who had received the awards since his in 1955. While in Boston, I visited Harper and Shuman and spoke with their personnel to reassure myself that installing CFMS had been the right move for the firm.

In May, I took off by myself for a trip to the West Coast to visit Marion and Darcy. After receiving his MBA degree from Northwestern University in 1978, Darcy had moved out west and lived temporarily with Marion and her second husband, Paul Brown, and his son. Since then he had worked as the Acting Director of Capital Projects and Grants Fiscal Officer for the San Francisco Municipal Railway and, most recently, as the Project Manager for AC Transit, in Oakland. Marion had since remarried, and she and her husband, Michael Ongerth, the superintendent of Operations for a section of the Southern Pacific Railway, lived in Berkeley. Marion was working as an engineer on the Railway.

Marion and Michael Ongerth at home. Berkeley, California. Summer, 1988

In November, Bob decided to work for the Jesse Jackson presidential campaign and asked me to help with the required accounting. I was not happy to do this. I resented Bob's assuming I would cooperate any time he needed my help, whether or not I was enthusiastic about the project involved. Till now, I'd always gone along with his expectations, but now I was beginning to rebel. To keep the peace, I grudgingly assented.

15

Breaking Away

In a Ma and Pa working relationship such as ours, conflicts were inevitable. Naively, I had expected that after I received my MBA degree, I would have authority on financial matters. Now I was having second thoughts about choosing to stay with Bob's practice, wondering if I'd made a mistake. Bob had always considered his judgment—in all matters—superior to mine. As early as August, 1982, he told me, "You are leaving in December because of your rigidity!" It was a remark asserting his superiority; he couldn't bear to think otherwise.

Following that remark, I began thinking of a transition to other work, ...to what, I didn't know. I considered taking a career counseling course, which would have included testing and identifying options to staying where I was. I received various advice from friends, one of whom reminded me that I'd talked about leaving Bob's firm even before I went back to school for the MBA. I formulated a transition plan, which had me leaving the firm in December, 1982, but remaining available to consult with the firm when necessary.

But I didn't leave; instead, I stayed on. Why? I found myself in the dilemma many persons face when considering a career move: the choice of dealing with the known rather than facing the unknown. And the negative remarks continued. Early in 1983, I followed advice from my friend, Dr. Korn, to apply for a teaching position at Buffalo State, based on my success in lecturing to classes there. In the meantime, I taught a credit-free course, Time Management, which I structured myself. I had half a dozen students, all of whom said they benefited from the course.

Although tensions in the office carried over to our home life, we did celebrate our 30th wedding anniversary in March, 1983, with a party. Our guests included out-of-town friend Joyce Smith, Lucas Smith's widow, who came from Minneapolis. Lucas, Bob's best friend in Minneapolis, had died in 1982, of lung cancer. But soon afterwards my morale hit a new low when, during another conflict, Bob made remarks denigrating the MBA degree. Then, in December, after I had grudgingly consented to help with accounting for the Jesse Jackson campaign, I hit rock bottom—this time when Bob once again announced, "You are resigning, as of December 31."

This time I thought to myself, "Yes, I just might do that." I actually began to move out of the office, but stayed on once again. I wasn't quite ready yet.

I endured another year of negative remarks but had the satisfaction of believing that the firm had weathered its financial crisis and that all financial matters were under control. That year, still looking for career options, I sent away for an application to the Peace Corps, but gave that up as not feasible at this point in time. In August of 1984, Bob hired a young woman, Kathy L., to take over the accounting, and I began training her, having made up my mind to leave as of December 31. In a frank discussion with Bob about my leaving, he remarked, in regard to our disagreements on financial issues, "I'm smarter than you are." He had a knack of putting me down, with no apt rejoinder. That remark really hurt, and I considered moving out of the house as well.

Badly in need of a morale-booster, in November I began a self-empowerment course. After the first session, I already felt better about myself, and I wrote in my journal, "Think a new me will emerge." Earlier that year, in February, I had stopped smoking, after many years, according to my own plan, "to get that monkey off my back." Ironically, later that same year Bob's twin brother, Bill, who was living with his wife, Alberta, in Springfield, Massachusetts; and Dick Prosser, living with his family in Buffalo, succumbed to lung cancer. Bob lost both a brother and his closest friend.

I involved myself in volunteer work for the YWCA and for the church, and these outside interests served to relieve some of the strain I felt. The red-letter day, December 31, 1984, finally arrived. I thought this would be my last day in Bob's office. Kathy, my replacement, appeared competent and ready to take over the accounting, but without the managerial functions I had assumed. In leaving the firm, I also resigned as secretary of the corporation. With Bob now the sole officer and shareholder, I would no longer bear any responsibility for whatever happened to the firm.

A new chapter of my life opened in January, 1985. Having pursued teaching positions at both Buffalo State College and Erie Community College-North Campus, and after interviews at both, I was appointed as part-time lecturer at Buffalo State and as an Adjunct Professor at Erie Community College, both beginning at the end of January. I would be teaching Introduction to Business to a class of thirty-five or more students at Buffalo State, and Marketing Management to a class of twenty-two at Erie Community College.

I was scheduled to begin classes at Buffalo State on January 23, but Buffalo was hit with a blizzard on the 19th, with twenty-five inches of snow and record low temperatures. It took days for things to get back to normal. As I was outside shoveling the front sidewalk, a pair of snow-white swans suddenly alighted on the walk near me, a startling sight! I had just enough time to rush into the house, grab my camera, and get two shots of the birds before they took flight. I was so glad I had a camera—bought when I stopped smoking—and could record this once-in-a lifetime event.

Later I took my prints to the ornithologist at the Buffalo Museum of Science, Robert Anderle, who tentatively identified the birds as European Whooper Swans, rarely seen in the United States. When I showed the pictures to my hair stylist, she was so taken with the swans that she bought an enlarged, framed print to hang on the wall in her salon.

My first class in Marketing was on February 1, and Introduction to Business on February 6. Both classes met once a week, on different days. The Marketing class began early, at 8:00 AM. With the college campus in Williamsville, a 30-40 minute drive from Buffalo, I got up about 5:00 to have time for breakfast and arrive before the students. The other class, at Buffalo State, was only a 10-minute drive away. With the semester extending until the end of May, I was plenty busy with class preparation and paperwork.

Besides being occupied with teaching, I often responded to calls from Kathy in the office, asking for help, and I usually went in and spent an hour or two with her then. As Bob had expressed misgivings about Kathy, I was not surprised when she sent him a letter at the end March notifying him she was resigning. She had apparently found the job not what she'd anticipated.

I found teaching college students more challenging than I'd anticipated. The students in the Small Business Management classes were all older professionals, attentive and interested. The students at ECC and Buffalo State were young, some bored and inattentive and, as I discovered, a few apt to cheat on exams. While there were complainers among both classes of students, there were a few who were encouraging to me, which enabled me to carry on through the semester. Dr. Korn, also continued to be supportive. He sat in on one class at Buffalo State and termed it "excellent."

My teaching ended around the end of May, rather to my relief. Reading over the evaluations from both classes, it appeared that the most favorable were from the best students, the most negative from the most problematic. Most ECC students rated my overall teaching ability between B and C, with a few A's and some D's and F's. Buffalo State student evaluations were much the same. The general complaint was that I taught classes "out of the book," and that the sessions lacked interest. Students in both classes said that the classes could have been improved by more student discussion and involvement. By the end of the semester, I had learned an important lesson: I knew the subject matter, but I did not know how to teach college students.

Despite the mixed reviews, I was invited to teach at ECC again for the fall semester. Even if I'd considered it, there was now a more pressing matter. Things were deteriorating in the office. Kathy had left in mid-May, and no one was doing the accounting. Ironically, only five months after I'd left the office, I now found myself back there, at least temporarily, tackling the financial situation, which was literally a mess. Did Kathy throw up her hands in despair? After interviewing several candidates, I selected Sharon D. as the best fit for the position, and Bob hired her, beginning June 10.

I foresaw my involvement as minimal, once Sharon was familiar with the accounting process. I certainly didn't want to find myself in the same position as when I left on December 31. To keep myself at arm's length from the firm, I registered with the Internal Revenue Service as an independent consultant, with the freedom to choose the hours I worked and to be paid an hourly fee for the work.

Going into the office occasionally to check Sharon's work, in July I found a big mistake she'd made. It was lucky I discovered it in time to correct it before real damage was done. In the process of discovering Sharon's mistake, I also found various mistakes made by Kathy and felt like strangling her. But of course, she was long gone. Meanwhile the firm's financial situation was worsening, with bankruptcy a real threat. Pressured to act, Bob reduced the staff from thirteen in January to eight by October. With the completion of the D.C. Municipal Office Building, Bob closed his Washington office in 1986.

Going into the office occasionally, as I did, inevitably, I again ran into conflicts with Bob, not only on finances but extending to issues such as obtaining professional liability insurance. He, of course, continued to assert his authority, while I realized how little he actually understood what it took to run the financial end of the office. In September, M & T Bank cancelled the firm's line of credit. The firm was again experiencing serious cash problems, with barely enough income to support staff, let alone pay consultants. As an indication of how dire the situation was, I had noted in my journal that, on October 1, the bank balance was down to $97.00.

As a relief from the depressing office situation, that summer, I escaped, once or twice a week, and engaged in my favorite sport, swimming, driving to my favorite swimming spot, Sherkston Quarry, in Canada, sometimes with a friend, sometimes by myself. There I could spend as many hours as I liked swimming, sunning, and simply relaxing.

I also joined a support group of women I'd met in church, all professionals. We met regularly, usually six to eight of us, every few weeks, each member airing her problems and, in turn, offering advice and moral support. The sessions did a lot to boost my morale and helped me weather the depressing office situation. One of the women, Gerry Evans, became one of my best friends.

As I found myself spending an increasing amount of time in the office, I was dismayed to think that, even as a consultant, I was almost back to where I'd been when I left in December. I thought again of getting a part-time job, which would take me away from the office. I did apply at Accountemps, but no positions were available at that time. Later, when there were, I had become too involved in the office. Tensions at the office invariably carried over to our home life, and, in a conversation with Bob at the end of October, I told him that, if not a separation, I needed a career for myself and a separate identity.

In the meantime, an interesting opportunity presented itself. While shopping on Elmwood Avenue, I had noticed a group of students painting the wall of a pocket park. Inquiring, I learned that the mural was intended to transform the park from a meeting place for drug addicts, as well as a respite for homeless people—both undesirables—to an attractive play area for youngsters and their parents.

To that end, a class from Buffalo State College, led by their instructor, Mary Weig, were painting a circus mural, with clowns, trapeze artists, bears, giraffes, and other circus animals. I was intrigued and began photographing the mural, meeting fiber artist Mary Weig. We made a deal: I would photograph the mural for her, put the printed sections together in a single frame, and give her the finished product. She, in turn, would create a fabric, life-size, grinning Cheshire cat, which I planned to gift to Marion. In addition, Johanna Mabrey, the owner of Preservation Hall, a vegetarian restaurant two doors from the park, bought a framed photograph of the circus bears, which she hung in the restaurant.

The class planned to return the following spring to put finishing touches on the mural; but, unhappily, over the winter, the first graffiti marks appeared, then others, defacing the circus characters. By the spring of 1986, the damage to the mural had gone beyond repair, and skateboarders and the older crowd reappeared. I was sorry to see the project ruined, but having been a part of it was a rewarding experience. That was the first of the various photographic projects I undertook in the years ahead.

In November, Bob approached me with the possibility of my doing the accounting for the Wende project as an independent consultant. It would entail setting up a separate accounting system for the joint venture of Bob's firm and that of Voinovich, Sgro Architects, based in Cleveland. The project involved renovating buildings in the Wende Correctional Facility complex and would take several years to complete. It promised to be a source of badly-needed income for the firm. After considering, I agreed to do the accounting, which must have been a relief for Bob, as he preferred to have it done in his office rather than Voinovich's.

On December 19, Sharon dropped a bombshell, announcing she was leaving after New Year's Eve. I was really disgusted, feeling that she had simply used her experience in Bob's office to get another job. The end of the year left me, once again, feeling boxed in. Out of conversations with friends, who offered helpful advice, the nagging question arose again: What is it I really want to do?

The year came to a peaceful close, as Bob and I celebrated the Christmas season with an Open House on December 30. We had a fragrant spruce tree in the living room, I put up decorations all through the house, made cookies and other goodies, and spirits flowed freely. Everyone—forty-five guests, Bob, and I—all had a fine time.

16

Trying Out New Roles

As I began going to fewer functions with Bob, partly because he was out-of-town frequently, and partly because we did have separate interests, a friend of ours inquired, "Are you and Bob still together?" I said, "Yes, we are, but I'm searching for my own identity." If other architects' wives found themselves without an identity apart from their husbands, very few wrote about it, or their stories went unpublished. I did find one story contained in the diary of Dione Neutra, married to the brilliant architect, Richard Neutra. Neutra became famous in the 1930s for developing a new concept of architecture, a style of design he hoped would be a means of bringing people into harmony with nature and themselves.

Dione, who could have had a career of her own, wrote, "During Richard's lifetime, I accompanied him everywhere. I was his secretary, his publications editor, his trouble shooter." After his death, she "blossomed," and was able to create her own rich life. "Happiness for me," she wrote, "is fulfilling my own potential." Like Dione, I began my own search for fulfillment.

A request for my help in financial matters came from an acquaintance, needing a crash course in accounting to enable her to meet the requirements for a job she was hoping to get. I began tutoring her, generally several hours a week. At the end, we were both elated when she passed the accounting exam.

Another request came from our church, and I agreed to serve, temporarily, as Interim Treasurer, and acted in this capacity for several months. Then came a request to take over the position of Treasurer for the St. Lawrence District of the Unitarian Universalist Church, the District encompassing the Buffalo, Williamsville and Rochester churches, and several churches in Ontario, Canada, including Ottawa. I assumed this position in 1986 and continued until August 1989.

When I took over the Treasurer's records, they were a mess, but I managed to improve the record-keeping and other areas, which "greatly helped the District function more smoothly," as expressed in a thank-you letter from the District Secretary on behalf of the Board. It was interesting to meet and work with the various Board members, in various locations, and the Board did pay me a nominal fee for my work, which included reporting to members at the periodic Board meetings. One of these was held over the weekend in Ottawa; and there I had the opportunity to see a few of its historic sites.

Meanwhile, in December of 1986, I answered a newspaper ad calling for applicants for the position of part-time interviewer for the National Opinion Research Center (NORC) based at the University of Chicago. The ad described the position as an "interesting and challenging" job. That certainly appealed to me! I answered the ad, was interviewed, and after training began working periodically for NORC in January, 1987, continuing through January, 1991. The initial work was the National Medical Expenditures Survey (NEMS).

NEMS was conducted throughout the country and gathered detailed information from randomly-selected individuals. The survey comprised five rounds of interviews, the interviewer returning each round to the same individual, and I completed four of the five rounds. My caseload included about thirty participants, and I managed to interview all but a few, which were turned over to a more experienced interviewer to handle.

Just as the ad promised, it certainly was an interesting and challenging job, unlike any I'd had before. Most of my cases were in Buffalo, the near suburbs, and Niagara Falls, New York. I also spent a week in the vicinity of New Haven, Connecticut, including Guilford and Brantford. This was an opportunity to see a part of the country I would not have otherwise. In Guilford, I spotted a strange structure perched on a hill on the outskirts of town. It looked like a space ship ready for takeoff. I photographed it but didn't have time to inquire about it then. Years later, I happened on an article explaining the structure, a condominium. The architect who designed it expressed his futuristic ideas in this building.

While in Connecticut, I had my longest interview, five and a half hours, with a woman who had a long history of health problems, medication and treatment. She was very patient while I filled one booklet of information after another; both of us were greatly relieved when it was over. Also, I had a harrowing near-accident one day. Driving my rented car on the thruway from one interview on a rainy day, I drove into a blinding downpour. Driving through the torrential rain probably took only a few minutes, but for me, caught up in fast-moving traffic and terrified, it seemed like an hour. Luckily, I drove safely out of the storm.

As an interviewer, I discovered how challenging that job really was. While a few of my cases were very cooperative and were there at the appointed time and place, most needed more than one contact. Initial reactions ranged from reluctance to distrust, to hostility, and a few outright refusals. There were a number of instances in which I would find the interviewee absent when I called. These needed repeat visits. Two cases involved a hard-nosed middle-aged businessman and his daughter, a college student, living in a Buffalo suburb. When I first approached him, he asked, "What's in it for me, what's in it for you?" I did my best to explain the value of his cooperation. His daughter was never at home. Finally, they both agreed to an interview, and at this point they were both completely cooperative and even cordial.

In another instance, a young woman who had never been home when I arrived at the appointed time was finally there. After we finished the interview and as I was leaving, she suddenly embraced me and said, "It was a real pleasure to work with you." That kind of gratifying experience made up for the frustration I often felt.

One of the most difficult cases was a black lady who lived in one of Buffalo's poorest neighborhoods. Her house had its windows boarded up and doors locked against intruders. After the fourth attempt, I finally found her at home and willing to open the door to me. I didn't blame her for being reluctant; she probably had good reason not to open her door to strangers—especially a white woman, who might be bringing all sorts of trouble. As we got into the interview, she relaxed, and her fifteen-year old daughter appeared, showing me her infant son.

Another elusive client, a middle-aged Italian, finally agreeing on an interview, led me up the stairs to his small apartment. He explained he had been absent when I made repeated attempts to see him because he was out deer-hunting. Several of his trophies, stuffed deer heads, were mounted on the wall. He was pleasant and the interview with him was fairly easy.

After NEMS, I participated in several other surveys. After that time, however, I found myself unwilling to do any further interviewing and informed NORC that I was not interested in future work. It was hard to obtain interviews with some people, especially older couples, not about to trust a stranger in their home, and I couldn't blame them. I began thinking myself that the interviewing process was really an invasion of privacy, and I could understand reluctance on the part of individuals. At the same time, I developed a feeling of empathy with interviewers who approached me, and after that experience, was more willing to be interviewed myself.

Besides whatever else I was engaged in, photography began to assume an increasingly important part of my life. Patricia (Pat)

Bazelon was one of the first to encourage my interest in photography. I met her in May, 1987, at a reception following an exhibit of her photographs, focusing on architectural images and including Buffalo's grain elevators. Her work was regularly published in magazines such as *Progressive Architecture*, *Architectural Record*, and *Architecture*.

After showing her a few of my photographs, she told me, "You should do more color photography." Before she left Buffalo in 1988 to become chief photographer for the Brooklyn Museum, I bought one of her photographs, a loading dock in North Buffalo. I was fascinated in the way she used the camera to reveal unexpected colors—shades of blue, gray and orange—in the weathered wood of the dock. That photograph was instructive for me, as I began to see design and color, just as Pat Bazelon did, in Buffalo's deteriorating buildings, finding them interesting subjects to photograph.

At our church, I offered my services as a "Photographer for Hire" for their auctions, and twice had buyers. The first was a mother who wanted a photograph of her three teenagers. I suggested an outdoor location, and the final photograph was of the three, a pretty young girl and her two handsome brothers, all perched on limbs of a willow tree bending over the waters of Delaware Lake. They all loved the photo. The second project was to photograph the 50th birthday party, held in the church, for Lynna Sedlak, for many years the church's office manager.

It was during the May, 1988 AIA Convention in New York City, where Bob and I attended a party, that I realized how naturally I assumed the role of a photographer. While he was off networking, I went off on my own with my camera to take candid shots of some of the partygoers. While I was busily engaged, I was taken for an official photographer and was asked by two separate groups to photograph them. The first group was an architect and his friends. The second group included the head of the El Paso Chile Company and his mother, partners in a new company, selling "authentic southwestern gourmet food," and their friends.

The black and white photographs turned out well, and both the architect and the entrepreneur liked them and paid me. Shortly after, I received a box of samples of the gourmet food. That happy episode served to validate my role as a photographer, and I had cards printed with my own logo, specializing in documentary photography.

Previously, I had had two photos of scenes in Delaware Park published in *Common Ground*, Buffalo's Pro-Choice Network's monthly newsletter. Having become an active member of Buffalo's

National Organization for Women (NOW), I volunteered to act as photographer for NOW's national convention held in Buffalo in June, 1988. My offer was accepted, and I was Buffalo's only official photographer, documenting many of the convention events, including a reenactment of the first Women's Rights Convention held in Seneca Falls, New York. I also photographed Molly Yard, then NOW's President, as well as convention speakers. After the convention, I sent my slides to NOW's headquarters for their archives and received a personal note from Molly Yard thanking me.

A long-time member of the Buffalo Museum of Science, I volunteered to photograph a special benefit, part of a year-long program focusing on Africa, held on September 30, 1988, at the Museum. During the evening, two exhibits were unveiled, "The Costumes and Textiles of Africa," from the Museum's anthropology collection, and the recreation of a Kenyan market place, displaying traditional Kenyan goods and foreign currency. Using two cameras, mine and the Museum's, I took four rolls of color and three rolls of black and white film of the evening's events, presenters and attendees. I enjoyed my role as photographer, and the Museum staff were very appreciative.

When I learned that the First International Women Playwright's Conference, sponsored by the University at Buffalo, would be held at the University's Amherst campus in October, 1988, I decided to attend the opening session. The conference was bringing several hundred women playwrights, from thirty-five countries, to Buffalo. Also attending would be Buffalo's women playwrights, including Anna Kay France, co-director, a Professor of English and Theatre at U.B. I knew Anna Kay because we were both in the women's support group I'd joined a few years earlier.

As a member of the media, representing the Buffalo Chapter of NOW, I took photos of some of the opening session events, speakers and attendees. One of my photos was later published in the December issue of *Common Ground*. I sent the photographs to Anna Kay, who returned them with thanks for my support of the conference. For me, my brief participation in the conference was an exhilarating and inspiring experience.

I photographed one more conference, in 1993. This was a two-day *Conference on the Status of Women* in Western New York, sponsored by Erie Community College (ECC) and held at its south campus. I had heard about the event from Judith Geer, co-director for the conference, and who was also in my support group. The conference speakers included professors, social and political activists, businesswomen, artists and poets, among them some of

Buffalo's outstanding citizens. I photographed the speakers and some of the attendees at the various seminars. I turned over an album of selected photographs to ECC, to be kept in the campus library. Besides a warm letter of appreciation from the co-directors, I received a modest fee in addition to reimbursement for my expenses.

That was the last conference I photographed. Previously, my focus had been on nature and landscape photography, Delaware Park a favorite subject. This led to my entering a photo contest in October, 1990, picturing Buffalo's parks, sponsored by The Friends of Olmsted Parks. Two of the color photographs I submitted were selected as among the winners of the contest.

My photo of the Delaware Park Rose Garden in Snow (taken on a February evening) was published, along with two other winning photographs, in *The Buffalo News* on October 5. The winning photos, judged by George Campos, himself a photographer and also the owner of Campos Photography, and John Pfahl, a professional landscape photographer, were displayed in the Burchfield Penney Art Center, and I was delighted to have my photographs displayed there, especially since I'd volunteered there for a time and felt a strong connection to the Center.

Lynna Sedlak, whose 50th birthday party I had photographed, co-owned a bookstore on Hertel Avenue. After the Olmsted photo contest, I started selling note cards with scenes from Delaware Park at the bookstore, and they were a popular item for several years.

By that time, I had become an avid photographer, and I found a wealth of subjects wherever I looked, my eyes open to all sorts of possibilities. One afternoon at home I stepped out on the terrace and saw a perfect photo op: an emerald green praying mantis perched on a scarlet hibiscus. I rushed inside to get my camera, came back out, took aim, and snapped several shots. It wasn't until later I discovered, much to my dismay, there was no film in the camera. I had to make this mistake several times before I, like many other photographers, finally learned the lesson: Make sure there's film in your camera before you photograph.

In the summer of 1988, I took my camera with me when I attended a reunion of my mother's extended family on St. Simon's Island, in Georgia. After the reunion I went on to the Smoky Mountains, renting a car and spending the weekend touring the bucolic countryside.

One day, while driving slowly through Cades Cove in the early morning haze, I happened to see a young girl and her backpacking boyfriend just about to turn the corner of a fenced narrow road winding through a hay stacked field. There was a tall dead tree right at the corner; opposite it stood a spreading shade tree. All the elements formed a pleasing composition and the colors were subtle but lovely: the couples' white clothes, the faintly orange road, fence and haystacks, the dead tree's gray, the green tree and shrubs lining the road, and the smoky blue haze enveloping the countryside, obscuring the mountains dimly visible in the distance. It was too perfect a picture to miss. I stopped the car immediately, got out my camera, opened the car window and managed to photograph the couple just as they turned the corner and disappeared down the road.

After leaving Cade's Cove, I drove on, stopping at various scenic sites and staying overnight in campsites along the way. At Klingman's Dome, I walked up Andrew Bald, the highest point in the Park, its summit at 5800 feet. I also hiked a short section of the Appalachian Trail, to get a feel of the trail experience. I never hear Aaron Copland's quiet piece, "Down a Country Lane," without recalling that idyllic weekend and the image I captured. I consider that photograph one of my best ever.

17

Together yet Separate

At the same time I was trying out my various roles, I adjusted to changes in Bob's office. When the bookkeeper, hired in January, 1988, left abruptly in April—the fourth since 1985—I decided that, rather than continuing the frustrating process of training and supervising bookkeepers, only to see them leave, I would simply do the work myself, in addition to acting as a Financial Consultant to the firm. I was spending considerable time in the office in that role, typically an average of one hundred hours monthly, with less time in the summer months. So now I simply added routine bookkeeping to the accounting and managerial functions I was fulfilling. It was not exactly back to "square one", since I was working as an independent consultant.

Happily, Bob and I now had fewer clashes than in the past, perhaps at least partly due to the fact that I was now engaged in various satisfying activities away from the office. Now and then, though, we would disagree on financial matters, Bob accusing me of negativism, while I considered my attitude a healthy skepticism. Bob was perennially optimistic, submitting one proposal after another, always expecting to secure a new project, while I adopted a wait-and-see attitude. Whenever Bob told me, "I see the forest; you only see the trees," I would remind him that someone needed to deal with the details, which totally bored him. Bob himself had a revelation in May, 1987, exclaiming, "For the first time, I realize we're exact opposites! That explains all the frustration I've experienced throughout the years."

In many ways, we were opposites. First of all, Bob was from Mars and I was from Venus: He seemed to thrive on conflict, while I avoided it. He grew up in the city and was most comfortable there; I grew up in the country and loved the outdoors. He was basically an extrovert, needing continual interaction with other people; I was basically an introvert, enjoying the company of others but needing more time alone. At parties, I was ready to go home after the first hour; Bob was just getting warmed up. On many occasions, I had to literally drag him away and then wait in the doorway while he said final goodbyes.

Bob had a tremendous ego, needing not only continual bolstering from friends and associates but also public recognition.

Moving in smaller circles, I was pleased to be recognized occasionally for my more modest achievements. Underlying everything was a fundamental difference: He was black, I was white. As empathetic as I tried to be, I couldn't put myself in his skin, experience the racism he encountered, and deal with it as he did.

We did share certain interests. Being married to an architect gave me an appreciation of architecture I would not otherwise have had. Our travels in Europe opened my eyes to the great European architecture but also fostered my interest in built architecture in general. Buffalo itself had many fine buildings, designed by renowned architects, including Frank Lloyd Wright, Louis Sullivan, Daniel Burnham, Gordon Bunshaft, Stanford White, and Eliel and Eero Saarinen, father and son, who designed Buffalo's Kleinhans Music Hall, known for its acoustical excellence as well as its unique design. Coincidentally, Eliel Saarinen was a critic of Bob's at M.I.T. Besides fine buildings, he designed St. Louis's beautiful Gateway Arch. While attending an AIA Convention there with Bob in 1989, I toured the Gateway area, the highlight being my ride to the top of the Arch in the elevator ingeniously designed to keep riders in an upright position while traversing the curve.

Music was an integral part of my life. I was raised on classical music, my mother a music teacher, taught me to play the piano when I was four years old and continued as my teacher through my childhood. By that time, I didn't need any encouragement to continue studying piano through my college years. While classical music wasn't listened to in Bob's household, he learned to appreciate the three B's—Bach, Beethoven and Brahms.

For several years, we held series tickets to the Buffalo Philharmonic and heard many fine concerts at Kleinhans, with some of the most celebrated artists of the time, including violinist Itzak Perlman and flutist Jean Pierre Rapal, and also rising stars such as Andre Watts. The son of a black father and white mother, Watts appeared at Kleinhans in 1980, at the start of his musical career. We were thrilled by his brilliant performance and had the rare opportunity of meeting him at the reception following that concert.

Thereafter, we made a point of hearing him whenever he appeared in Buffalo. When the Buffalo Philharmonic went to Carnegie Hall in 1986, our good friend, Harry Taub, among the musicians, we went to New York especially to hear the concert. We first heard black trumpeter Winton Marsalis when he played at

Artpark in Lewiston in 1988, and heard him again later in Buffalo at the Tralfamadore Café.

Just as Bob learned to appreciate classical music, I learned to appreciate jazz, especially the cool, John Coltrane and Miles Davis, variety. We often went to concerts featuring artists such as jazz singer Ella Fitzgerald. We were also fans of folksingers, including Joan Baez—whom we first heard in Cambridge—Roberta Flack, Pete Seeger and Arlo Guthrie.

We never missed modern dance performances—the Harlem Dance Theatre, the Alvin Ailey Dancers, the Paul Taylor Dance Theater, the Martha Graham Dance Company, and the Merce Cunningham Dancers. A modern dance fan, I tried modern dance myself, and sometimes danced around the house to the music of Copland's "Appalachian Spring." I enjoyed dancing with Bob. Whenever we attended a social affair that included dancing, we were usually the first couple on the dance floor.

Summertime for Bob meant sailing on Lake Erie; and I went sailing with him a few times every year. But while he sailed all summer long, I swam, driving to Canada across the Peace Bridge to Sherkston Quarry, next to the beach on Lake Erie. I first discovered the quarry when Darcy was still a youngster. Like me, he was a good swimmer and exulted in going off the high dive. When he stopped going with me, I went either with my friend, Carol Hibbard, or by myself. The Quarry was an ideal swimming place. Like a small lake, it was deep, with clear, spring-fed water. The sandy beach was swept clean every evening, and a concession stand and restroom facilities were conveniently nearby.

I continued going to Sherkston Quarry until the Peace Bridge traffic increased to the point where I'd sit in my car, engine idling, traffic proceeding at a crawl, while minutes ticked by and the car engine overheated. Around the same time, developers moved into Sherkston Quarry, building summer cottages on the fringe of the quarry and creating a little town with facilities to serve the increasing number of vacationers there. When the beach became so crowded that families began setting up their trailers right next to the women's washroom, I was disgusted. "That's it!" I said. I did not go back.

In the snowy winter months, while Bob sat inside and watched Sunday NBA basketball, Carol and I drove out in the country and spent exhilarating afternoons cross-country skiing along the many trails in the county parks. I had met Carol when we were both learning how to ski, and we went skiing together for many years. Besides going out in the country, I could simply shoulder my skis and walk to Delaware Park, ski around the ring road on one side of the park, cross the Expressway to the other side and ski up and down the slopes around the Albright-Knox Gallery.

While Bob involved himself primarily in architecture and issues relating to the profession, I became involved with women's issues. Continuing my initial connection with NOW, I joined the local chapter in the Pro-Choice network, participating in rallies, demonstrations and "speak outs" to counter the anti-abortion forces led by outsider Randall Terry. Terry came to Buffalo in 1988, to enlist locals in his campaign. The battling in Buffalo, which continued until 1992, included demonstrations outside the clinics offering abortion services. Terry and his supporters had expected Buffalo to be "another Wichita," where he and his supporters had been welcomed. Instead, he was defeated by the strong support shown by Buffalo for a woman's right to choose.

In April of 1989, I joined other Buffalonians, leaving at 10:49 PM for an overnight bus ride to Washington, D.C. There we joined others in a massive demonstration demanding preservation of the 1972 Supreme Court decision granting women the right to legal abortion. More than 15,000 buses carried demonstrators from all over the country. Delegations from twelve foreign countries joined in a crowd estimated at 300,000—of which 40% were men—the largest demonstration ever held there. Speakers at the rally near the Washington Monument included politicians Jesse Jackson and Bella Abzug, folksinger Judy Collins, and actress Jane Fonda.

During the rally, I made my way through the crowd and climbed up a tower used by the media, got out my camera, and took a picture—a sea of people stretching as far as the eye could see. I took more pictures as we marched down Constitution Avenue to the Capitol. Along the way, both pro-choice and pro-life supporters lined the sidewalks, shouting slogans and cheering the marchers. I had never been in a crowd like this and found it exhilarating but also frightening, being swept along by the mass movement. Altogether, the demonstration was an unforgettable experience. I enlarged the photo I took of the crowd during the rally to poster size and mounted it. It hangs on my office wall, a priceless souvenir.

I had another unforgettable experience, of a much different kind, in August, 1989, when I left for Africa. Always looking for interesting new opportunities, I had begun subscribing to the journal which detailed all the trips available through Earthwatch. A non-profit organization, partially funded by voluntary contributions, Earthwatch sponsored many research expeditions around the globe.

I was intrigued by all the possibilities open in various areas of interest embracing all the sciences.

One expedition was especially inviting, titled "The Semliki Expedition: Searching for our Earliest Ancestors", it was described by a volunteer as "the most beautiful dig in Africa." It was a three-week trip to Zaire led by paleontologist Noel Boaz, who had been working in the Semliki River region and found elephant fossils and stone tools. These discoveries pointed to the possibility of finding human fossils in that region of the same age as the famous 3.5 million year-old Lucy. I applied in January, 1989, and was elated when in February I received notice from Earthwatch of my acceptance as part of a team working that summer from August 15-30.

In the months ahead, I read books from a list suggested by Dr. Boaz, the team's principal investigator, to give team members a background for discoveries in Africa, where the oldest fossils, dating 3-4 million years old, had been found. The list included D.C. Johanson's *Lucy: The Beginning of Humankind*, about his discovery of the female ape-woman; J. Desmond Clark's *The Prehistory of Africa*; Phillipson's *African Archaeology*; and Henry Stanley's *In Darkest Africa*, the account of his quest to discover the true source of the Nile. The reading not only prepared me for the expedition but served as a most interesting short course in paleontology, the study of fossils.

When I told people about the trip, which might include spending some time in Rwanda, someone suggested I talk to Alison Des Forges, who had lived and worked with her husband in Rwanda for some years and was considered an authority on that country. My conversation with Alison was very helpful: She dispelled a good bit of my apprehension about traveling in that part of Africa and loaned me a book on Rwanda. She also advised me to learn a bit of French before I left, so I obtained a book of conversational French and also a book of traveler's French, taking the latter with me to Africa.

Further travel preparations included booking airline passage from Buffalo through London; Nairobi, Kenya; and to Kigali, Rwanda; securing a passport and visas to Kenya, Rwanda and Zaire, getting all the required inoculations; and buying camping equipment and clothing suitable for travel and work in Africa. Having been cautioned by Earthwatch to take only as much luggage as we could carry ourselves, I managed to cram everything into a backpack and duffel bag. Finally, with the blessing and good wishes of family and friends, I began my African adventure.

18

Getting to Goma

To reach our final destination, I would be joining the other expedition team members in Goma, Zaire to take a chartered flight to the project site. Getting to Goma was complicated. Flying on August 11 from Buffalo to London and on to Kenya, I arrived in Nairobi late that night. Checking into a hotel, I got a few hours of sleep and then left that morning for the airport. My flight to Kigali was via Cameroon Air Lines, and the ticket counter didn't open till 9:30; I waited in line to get my boarding pass. Then someone told me I would have to pay a $20 airport tax, so I got in the Tax Control line. Waiting there took even longer, as the tax official ran out of stamps and left to get more, returning after about 20 minutes.

Finally it was my turn. But then the official told me that the tax had to be paid in U.S. dollars, not Kenyan currency, which was all I had. Leaving that line, I rushed over to another part of the airport and got in the Exchange line. I'd been standing there for about ten minutes when it suddenly dawned on me that I'd left my duffel bag—with all my camping gear—at the Tax Control counter. My heart sank, as I pictured myself getting to camp with no camping equipment! Hurrying back over to the Tax Control counter, I saw—to my great relief—my blue duffel, exactly where I'd left it. Telling myself how very lucky I was, and never, ever again to lose sight of my backpack or duffel bag, I snatched it up, sped back to the Exchange counter and got in line again. Finally I got the $20 U.S.

By the time I paid the tax and got the stamp affixed to my airline ticket, it was about ten minutes to flight time. Just then, Frank Spignola, Buck Braswell and John Hembree came up and introduced themselves to me as fellow Earthwatchers, also bound for Goma. We scrambled to the boarding gate and ran for the Cameroon plane, which was standing on the tarmac ready to take off. Just made it!

Frank, from Union City, California, and I had talked over the telephone. A veteran Earthwatch volunteer, he had given me some travelling tips and also told me what to expect on an Earthwatch expedition. The best piece of advice turned out to be that their tents were not dependable. I had bought a tent the week before I left and took great care to seal all the seams, an act that later proved well worth the effort. Buck Braswell, a retired army pilot from Miami, was a friend of Frank's and had travelled all over the world. This was John Hembree's first Earthwatch expedition. John, an insurance salesman from Lexington, Kentucky, collected Indian arrowheads.

John Hembree, Paluka, and Sylvia, preparing to motor down the Semliki River Zaire, Africa. September, 1989

Arriving at the Kigali airport about 11:30 a.m., we were greeted by two more Earthwatch volunteers, Nancy Law, from San Antonio, and Tom Staley, a microbiologist from Beaver, West Virginia. Debating how to get from Kigali to Goma, about 100 miles away, we decided to hire two drivers and taxis. It was an expensive way to go: We each paid about $40. However, it was Sunday, and we didn't know whether any other transportation was available. So, John, Tom and I got in one car and Nancy, Frank and Buck rode in the other. We passed quickly through Kigali, the capital of Rwanda, a small city of about 60,000, and then were out in the countryside.

At that time, Rwanda, with a population of 6,320,000, occupied 10,169 square miles, densely inhabited, compared to neighboring Zaire, with 905,567 square miles and 34,520,000 inhabitants. Truly "the country of a thousand hills," it appeared that just about every available bit of land was being cultivated, with crops planted in the valleys and also up the terraced hillsides. We'd never seen anything like it; and as our driver sped along, we got out cameras, hoping to get some good photos. We met streams of men, women and children walking along the roadway, the women dressed in brilliantly colored turbans, skirts and blouses, the men and boys in T-shirts and pants. Huge banana trees towered everywhere.

Arriving in the border town of Gisenyi, we passed through Rwandan customs, our drivers paying the official a small bribe to ensure there would be no problems. Repeating the procedure a few hundred feet away at the Zaire border, we entered Goma. Then a little town of 15,000, it was a jumping-off place for tourists. Here, at the Amiza Travel Agency, one could book a tour to see the mountain gorillas, the volcanoes, or other local attractions. We had expected to find rooms in one of Goma's several hotels, but we didn't know that a presidential delegation convening here over the weekend had booked all the rooms.

After an hour of driving around, our last stop, and last hope, was the Hotel Karibu, about four miles out of town, on Lake Kivu. But here, too, all the rooms were full. Tired, hungry and desperate as we were, Buck, who spoke some French, talked to the manager and managed to negotiate a deal: We could pitch our tents on the hotel grounds that night (free) and then have rooms the next day. It was after 6:00 p.m. and dark when we got out our camping gear and other belongings and said "Au Revoir" to the drivers, who must have been relieved to be rid of us.

Fortuitously, I had practiced setting up my tent at home, so even in the dark, it went up easily. Nancy and I shared my tent; Frank had his one-person tent, and Buck and John shared their big tent with Tom. We all met in the hotel bar for drinks and then had a delicious, though expensive, dinner in the restaurant. Soon after dinner, Nancy and I settled in our tent and soon were fast asleep. It rained during the night, but we were snug as bugs in a rug.

The next morning we took down our tents and moved indoors, each of us enjoying the luxury of a private "room with a view" of the expansive hotel grounds and beautiful Lake Kivu. Seen in the daylight, the Hotel Karibu looked every bit the resort hotel it was—complete with swimming pool, beautifully landscaped grounds, and white stuccoed cottages. Adding to the charm of the place, crested cranes and other fowl hunted for insects on the lawn, completely unafraid of people; and songbirds filled the air with their music.

That morning we met Rome Spognardi, a young archaeology student from Illinois, and Dennis Londergan, a rehab counselor from Las Vegas, each of whom had arrived at the hotel the evening before. They told us about their disconcerting experience in the Kinshasha airport: Recognized as tourists, they were besieged by peddlers and beggars, but were eventually rescued by the Zairean police patrolling the airport.

That morning Tom and I decided to see Goma. Upon inquiring at the hotel desk, I was told that we could get a ride with the hotel van and return with it in another hour or so, or get back on our own. One of the guidebooks I had read described Goma as "a spearhead in the touristic development of the province of Kivu....on the north shore of Lake Kivu, it nestles in a huge amphitheater formed by the impressive chain of the volcanic heights of the Virungas, two of whose craters are still active."

Our first stop was at a post office, where we bought stamps and mailed postcards. We then walked along the main street, noting the shops and restaurant we thought we might try when we returned from the expedition. We could see two of the eight volcanoes that stretch from west to east around Goma. We stopped at the Hotel Masques for a sandwich and the local Primus beer and got into a conversation with a Dutch trader. He was surprised to learn we were going to Ishango, "in the bush," as he put it. We did a bit more exploring and then took a taxi back to the Karibu.

That evening we met for dinner but didn't linger as we needed to be up before dawn the next morning to meet our chartered plane at the Goma airport at 7:00 AM. As it turned out, the plane was delayed. In the meantime, Marie Curtis, a real estate agent from California, and her son Matt, a young archaeological student at Berkeley, California, and Bob Turk, a surgeon from North Carolina, who had lived in Kinshasha in the 1970s and worked in the hospital there, had arrived.

The twelfth member of the team had decided to opt out, going on another expedition instead. But Mike Ruddy, a journalist from the Reuters News Service, accompanied us. He would be staying in camp with us several days and writing an article about the expedition.

The plane finally came. Our baggage was loaded along with food and other supplies for camp, and we clambered aboard. Cameras were busy as we photographed the scene below: volcanoes, then savannah, followed by Lake Rutenzige and Ishango. Suddenly the plane set down on an airstrip in the middle of the vast African savannah. Descending from the plane, I was profoundly moved. I could hardly believe that I was in a part of the world where the human race began.

19

The Most Beautiful Dig in Africa

Dr. Boaz was there to welcome us to the Semliki Research Expedition, as was also Dr. Paris Pavlakis, another paleontologist, from Athens, Greece, who would supervise the excavation. Waiting to take the plane back to Goma were members of the second team, who gave us glowing accounts of their experience in camp. We piled our luggage in the camp truck and Land Rover and climbed aboard for the bumpy ten-minute ride to camp. Those of us in the truck shared space with chickens, potatoes, vegetables and other provisions that had been on the plane with us. Now, in the Virunga National Park, we gaped at the hundreds of antelope and other animals near the road and ranging as far as we could see.

Arriving in camp, I was totally unprepared for the beauty of our surroundings. Certainly, the black and white photos in the Earthwatch briefing hadn't begun to convey a sense of the colorful landscape. High on a bluff overlooking the Semliki River, we had a magnificent view of the river, the river valley, and the mountain ranges looming to the west and north. In the park, we were in the midst of abundant wildlife and exotic plants. For a city dweller like me, this was paradise.

We spent the first afternoon in camp setting up tents, taking a walking tour to the excavation site, down to the beach by the river and around the camp grounds, and then settled in. At lunch, we introduced ourselves and volunteered to be on one of the various committees—water, lantern, latrine, and dessert—that would keep camp life running smoothly. Rome, Matt and I signed up for the Water Committee. Our job was to make sure an adequate supply of boiled water for drinking (from the Semliki River) was always at hand. Dr. Boaz laid down the two and only camp rules: 1) don't complain, and 2) don't do anything stupid.

That first night we had our rain initiation, as a thunderstorm broke around midnight, with the rain continuing until early morning. Those of us who had water-tight tents weathered the storm; others with leaky tents had to dry out everything the next day. Neither Nancy nor Tom had brought their own tents but each had set up an Earthwatch tent. They both found, to their dismay, that the tents leaked. Tom abandoned his in the middle of the night and took refuge in the work tent, amid sand for screening, skulls and bones, books and other equipment. Nancy endured the night, having moved off to the side of the pool of water that collected in the middle of her tent. The next time it rained, Tom slept in the Land Rover. But when Mike Roddy left—he had a dry Earthwatch tent—Tom moved in.

Rain or shine, a typical workday began about 5:30 a.m., as we rose at dawn. The moon might still be shining palely in the sky before the sun emerged over the horizon. Hidden in the bushes and trees in and around the camp, birds of many species filled the fresh morning air with their beautiful songs. By 6:00, we would be gathered at the breakfast table for a stick-to-your-ribs meal of cereal, fresh fruit, scrambled eggs, toast, peanut butter and jam, and coffee or tea. We listened to the BBC morning news broadcast on Dr. Boaz's radio to find out what was going on in the rest of the world.

By 6:30, we would be ready, with water canteens, sunscreen and other supplies, to start the ten-minute walk from camp through the grassy savannah, past thorn bushes, termite hills, and acacia trees to the excavation site. There we gathered pans, picks, brushes and other tools and set to work within our assigned squares, measured off and delineated with string. Our task was to excavate through the surface layer several inches down to the sand, where we would find most of the fossils.

Those of us who were novices soon learned from "Paris," Dr. Pavlakis, to distinguish between lumps of ironstone and real fossils. As we worked to unearth the fossils, Paris, assisted by one of the team, would survey to determine each fossil's exact location, which was numbered and logged. Standing under the shade of a picturesque "candelabra tree," a euphorbia, was Paluka, the park guard, who lived in camp with us, rifle at the ready in case of danger.

Around noon, when the sun was high in the sky and the temperature had soared from the cool of the morning to the eighties or lower nineties, we were glad to stop work, get out of the hot sun, and head back to camp. We might enjoy a quick swim before lunch. The mid-day meal always included soup, fresh fruit—pineapple, bananas, passion fruit, all grown locally—and, most days, delicious fresh fish caught in the river and prepared to perfection. After lunch there was time for reading, bird-watching, or napping.

At 2:00 PM we returned to the site and resumed excavating, surveying, or wet screening. Being near the river, we heard hippos, gathered in herds in the river grunting to each other as they surfaced to breathe. At night, the hippos left the river to come up on shore, up "hippo paths," to graze all night. Besides the hippo sounds, we listened to the wild cries of a pair of fish eagles, whose territory was along the opposite river bank, as they soared high above the river searching for prey.

According to a 1986 edition of the *Traveler's Guide to Central and Southern Africa*, the central part of Virunga Park contained the largest concentration of hippopotamus in the world, estimated at about 26,000, and many of the 1,086 species of birds in Zaire were also found in the park. Besides hippos, animals we saw in or near camp included antelope, water buck, buffalo, warthogs, hyenas, mongoose, and lions.

With wild animals all around us, we also found plentiful evidence of those that had been here in another time. The site we were excavating, one of a number of Lusso beds in this area, was dated at 2.3 million years old, so all fossils found here were of that age. Crocodile teeth, turtle shells and fish bones unearthed pointed to the possibility, Paris said, that the site may at one time have been a stream bed. Other, mammalian, fossils suggested the presence of manlike apes.

The first day of the dig, Rome found a bovid (a cow-like animal) tooth, intact, buried in the sand. On another day, Dennis unearthed a huge elephant molar, perhaps from the same elephant of which parts had been found previously. A few days later, I myself found three pieces which, when Paris glued them together, formed the partial jawbone and molars of a bovid. What a thrill! Paris said these were some of the most significant finds of the 1989 survey year.

While the usual routine was to go to the dig site, there were a few days when rain made it too wet. The second day in camp was one of those days. We then worked in camp at another task. Seated at the table under the sun-rain canopy, we took small containers of sand, previously collected at the site, and sifted through these with picks and tweezers, identifying and separating tiny bits of bones and teeth from grains of sand. Paris collected these for micro-faunal analysis, adding to the inventory of fauna at the site, named Senga 13B. While we sieved, we listened to Frank's taped collection of jazz and blues dating back to the 1940s, told jokes, and talked. Taking a break from micro-faunal analysis, we also helped clean skulls and bones of a collection recently brought to camp, which Dr. Boaz planned to use for teaching purposes.

Our workday ended at 5:00 p.m. Except on rainy days, we headed to the river for a dip or swim, keeping a respectful distance between ourselves and the ever-present hippos. Dr. Boaz had told us about a traveler in this area who had ignored an important rule:

Don't get in a hippo's way. Enraged, the hippo charged, with fatal consequences. One evening Nancy and I watched three hippos on the opposite bank. Two adults, one apparently the mother, gently nudged a baby to its feet and into the water, where all three submerged.

In the time remaining before dinner, we might listen to a seminar by Dr. Boaz or Paris. In one of those sessions, we listed as Paris told us about the discoveries made in the Semliki area. The first discovery of fossils was made at the Ishango I research site in 1936, followed by other discoveries in later years. Dr. Boaz himself began research in the Semliki-Ishango area in 1983, identifying and excavating numerous sites. Although no Pliocene age (that of the famous "Lucy" skeleton) fossils had been found thus far in the Western Rift Valley of Zaire—where we were—Dr. Boaz continued to believe they were here, waiting to be discovered. With that possibility in mind, he had brought a bottle of rare champagne to camp, to celebrate if such a find were made.

Within our campground was another excavation site, Senga 5, dug the previous summer, which had yielded numerous 2.3 million-year-old fossils. The first morning in camp, after the rain, some of us walked over to the site on the way to the beach, to see whether we could see tracks of the lions we had heard in camp the night before.

As we walked the muddy "hippo path" up the hill to Senga 5, we saw what appeared to be lion tracks. Standing on the crest of Senga 5, I looked down and saw what appeared to be an unusual rock, and picked it up. Curious, I showed it to Dr. Boaz. Surprised, he told me that it was the molar of a 2.3 million-year old pig, as large as the present day rhinoceros. Evidently rain and wind had eroded the site since the previous summer and exposed the molar. Needless to say, I was tremendously excited to have found something so significant early on...a good omen for the rest of the expedition.

If no seminars were being given, we were free to explore within the camp's boundaries. Birdwatchers Bob and Tom had many birds to identify. There were fish eagles, ibis, sandbill storks, speckled mousebirds, Egyptian geese, weaver birds, whose nests we saw in the trees at the river's edge, and countless more. We gave our own descriptive names to the ones we couldn't identify: the "organ bird" whose song was very melodic, and the "scowl bird" which sounded the way a scowl looks.

I had brought along a tape recorder, planning to record the sounds of Africa, whatever they might be. The best time to listen to birds was in the very early morning when, from their cover of trees or bushes, they engaged in a veritable concert. Their songs grew less frequent and more subdued as the day grew hotter, then picked up again before evening. One of the most distinctive sounds was the wild cry of the fish eagles as they circled above the river. I also captured the pig-like grunts of the hippos as they "talked" to each other in the river. After dark, crickets and other insects shrilled; then frogs croaked in chorus somewhere upstream. While I had hoped to hear a lion's growl or hyena's bark during the night, I was disappointed—I was too sound a sleeper.

As we were located just ten miles south of the equator, dusk fell about 6:00. By 6:30, it was pitch dark, lanterns were lit, and dinner began. This meal was a time for relaxing and relating the experiences of the day. It was also a time to hear Dr. Boaz and Paris talk about their work and their many interesting experiences in the field of paleontology. Promptly at 6:30, dinner was brought from the "kitchen" to the dining table. Amade, the oldest of the cooks, supervised Katanje, Kimbo, and Joseph. One of the cooks also fished for the daily catch from the river.

The dinner itself, usually accompanied by beer and tea (wine on Saturdays), was either rice or pasta with a meat or chicken sauce, or a stew of fish or beef, accompanied by salad and bread, and—the highlight of the day—dessert. Creatively using whatever ingredients were on hand, the Dessert Committee, headed by Nancy, produced delicious treats, the best of which was undoubtedly the cake with chocolate sauce. The only flop was the pineapple-banana medley: Someone had mistaken the salt shaker for sugar.

Having risen early, we went to bed early, most of us retiring soon after dinner to our tents to read, listen to music, and then fall asleep. My tape recorder was also a tape player, and each night I listened to Astor Piazzolla's Concerto for the Bandoneon and three tangos for bandoneon and orchestra. The music had a haunting quality which seemed just the right music to listen to in Africa.

Several trips out of camp varied the usual routine: a walking safari, a ride to the market, site surveys, and Ishango. One Sunday morning after breakfast, several of us went on a long walk out of camp, accompanied by Paluka. As we walked over the grassy terrain, we kept on the alert for all forms of wildlife—especially snakes. Marie had seen what she believed was a python one afternoon near the path that led from camp to the excavation site. We thought maybe she had exaggerated, but about a mile out of camp, we suddenly saw one, about 30 feet away. We had apparently surprised it as it was dragging an antelope to the cover of a bush before devouring it. The python dropped its quarry, crawled under the bush, and stayed under cover until we passed by. Nearby, vultures perched in a treetop.

One afternoon Dr. Boaz, Tom, John, Bob, Paluka and I took the pontoon Zodiac down river to survey several sites. Looking for fossils that may have become exposed on the surface, we found several near Katango 10. John spotted something that turned out to be the inside of an antelope horn. "Interesting find," Dr. Boaz remarked. Motoring back in the middle of the river, we avoided the hippos on either side, but one hippo, disturbed by our presence, lunged at us. Paluka had his rifle ready to fire, but we were soon out of reach.

Another day we piled in the truck and rode the bumpy road to Ishango, one of the park's headquarters. The park maintained an office there, and park staff and their families lived nearby. The panoramic view from Ishango, at the top of a sheer cliff, was spellbinding: We could see that portion of Lake Rutenzige (formerly Lake Idi Amin—and before that, Lake Edward) that spills into the Semliki River, the River itself, the River Valley, and the Ruwenzoris, the famed Mountains of the Moon in neighboring Uganda.

From Ishango, we took a long walk downhill through brush and jungle growth, to the river's edge, and then surveyed several sites, looking for Pliocene fossils. But although we searched, we didn't find any. I was delighted, however, to find a piece of quartz that had been shaped into a scraping tool. Since it wasn't significant for our expedition, I kept it as a souvenir. On the way back to camp, we got our photo opportunity: a pair of lions, lying peaceably in the grass about fifty feet from the road.

Dr. Boaz had told us, "Don't do anything foolish", and I believe all of us heeded his message. So we were shocked one night when, unaccountably, a small but very poisonous snake crawled into the cooks' tent and bit Joseph in the right wrist. Dr. Boaz immediately administered anti-snake serum, and then he and Bob rushed him in the Land Rover to the nearest hospital, in Beni, about fifty miles away. Fortunately for Joseph, the attack was not fatal, but he spent the rest of the time in the hospital and did not return to camp. The snake, killed after its attack, could not be identified. Dr. Boaz put it in a jar of preserving alcohol for later classification.

Aside from this episode, life in camp was usually non-threatening. It was with mixed feelings that we reached the end of our stay in camp, but we all agreed that two weeks in camp was just about right. We were all beginning to long for soft beds, hot baths, and ice cold drinks. I especially longed for a frosty bottle of Coca-

Cola and a big dish of chocolate ice cream. But we had all gained a better understanding of paleontological research, enjoyed new friendships, and had the satisfaction of knowing that each of us had contributed to the success of the expedition.

20

Back to Goma

Although we were originally scheduled to be in camp until August 30, this was cut short. Dr. Boaz decided that the best way to transport all of us and the camp equipment would be to pack everything in the truck and Land Rover and go overland over the mountains to Beni, and then south back to Goma. We left camp on the morning of August 27. When Dr. Boaz said that all the camping equipment, tents, fossils, books and research equipment; kitchen and food stores; the three cooks; eleven volunteers; and Paris and himself; all the baggage, petrol and water, and one live goat could all be contained on the truck and in the Land Rover, no one believed him.

However, just as soon as we finished breakfast, we all started this impossible task. We had to believe Dr. Boaz, as this was our only transportation out of the park and back to Goma.   And then, as we helped Dr. Boaz pack, we watched the most awkward objects meld into an organized whole, orchestrated by Dr. Boaz, with food and baggage packed in last, to be readily accessible. Tarps went over everything, and ropes were lashed down and around the sides to secure the load. Finally, the goat, bleating in protest, was hoisted to the top.

Early on, Nancy had assumed a position in the space behind the cab in the truck. Joining her were Matt, Rome, John, Kimbo and Katanje. Buck sat in the cab, with Paris at the wheel. The rest of us, Frank, Tom, Dennis, Bob, Marie, Amade and I, rode in the Land Rover with Dr. Boaz. Pulling out of camp, we headed north to the mountains. Dr. Boaz's plan was to drive north as far as Beni, make a stop at Matsuro, cross the Semliki River, then head south to Goma, camping overnight near Butembo and a second night near Rwindi.

We left the savannah grassland for the mountains and tropical rain forest. As we drove along, the landscape became lush and green, dense with trees, shrubs and all forms of plant life. About noon, we stopped at Matsuro, the headquarters of the Virunga Park Commissioner. While Dr. Boaz settled some business with the Commissioner, we walked about the park grounds, admiring the luxuriant foliage and beautiful flowers including hibiscus, poinsiettas, and many others I couldn't identify.

Leaving Matsuro, we drove on to Beni, arriving there about 3:30 PM. The Land Rover was ahead of the camp truck; and we parked and sat down at an outdoor café for a bite to eat. Just then, the threatening storm clouds that had followed us all the way from camp finally broke and a torrential rain ensued. Marie and Dennis, who had gone down the street to try to find a tobacco store for cigarettes, came back, drenched. After the rain stopped, we sat and ordered sandwiches and Primus beer, wondering where the others were.

Soon the truck appeared and pulled up to a stop near us. All except Buck and Paris, who had ridden in the truck's cab, were soaking wet, cold and miserable. Not only all the riders but some of the luggage on the truck had been soaked. Nancy discovered later that her suitcase contents were wet and her camera and film ruined.

At that point, dissatisfaction about the project itself, which had apparently been mounting among Buck, Frank and John, came to a head. They announced they were leaving the group and would stay in Beni, where they hoped to get a direct flight back to Goma. With that, they left the group and went off to find a hotel. The rest of us finished lunch and set off again, this time everyone squeezing inside the truck and Land Rover. From Beni, we headed forth on the "highway" that runs all the way from Cairo to Capetown, little more than a narrow, barely two-lane, gravel road. Halfway to Butembo, we stopped at a roadside market for fresh pineapple, for sale by women vendors, who, shy at first, giggled and "hammed it up" for photographers.

Because of the wet weather, Dr. Boaz—with our unanimously hearty approval—abandoned the plan of camping out that night and decided to try a hotel in Butembo. It was getting dark when, just about a mile away, disaster struck! The Land Rover had a flat. Springing out, Dr. Boaz stripped off his raincoat, laid it on the muddy ground underneath the chassis, lay flat on his back on top of the raincoat, and went to work with the jack. But despite repeated attempts by him and then by Tom and Matt as well, it wouldn't work. What to do? Just then the camp truck drove up.

The solution: All hands lifted up the Land Rover; the flat tire was removed and replaced with the spare. That done, we soon climbed up the slippery road to the hilltop, where we found the Hotel Kikyo. Fortunately, there were rooms available; and Nancy and I shared one. Being in a hotel again, with running water, electricity and soft beds seemed positively luxurious. That night we feasted on a delicious meal, supervised by Paris, of goat hors d'oeuvres, goat stew with rice, fresh pineapple, and red wine.

Rising before dawn the next morning, I got up and had a look around. While the hotel had been partially constructed by the Belgians, one part of the complex remained unfinished. Blackened, it looked burned out. In contrast, a bush of snow-white trumpet lilies bloomed next to it. Fog veiled the valley between the hotel and the village on the opposite hill. The sight was both mysterious and beautiful. After breakfast, just before we left, native vendors appeared with ebony wood carvings for sale; and some in our group bought a few things.

After stopping in Butembo to have the flat tire fixed, we were on our way again, passing through spectacular scenery as we crossed the equator. We passed through quite a few dairy farms between here and Goma. Dr. Boaz told us this part of Zaire was called its Switzerland. We sampled the local cheese for lunch and agreed it was very good. We also saw numerous coffee plantations. Interspersed with the dairy farms and the numerous coffee plantations were mountain villages, one so densely populated that its thatched huts perched all the way up to the mountaintop.

Scrapping the camping plan completely, Dr. Boaz decided to push on to Rwindi and stay in a hotel there that night. At dinner that night in the hotel, the last together as a group, Dr. Boaz opened the bottle of rare champagne he'd been saving as he announced we'd celebrate a very productive season. That set the tone for the evening and everyone got very happy.

Up early and underway the next morning, we stopped in Rutshuru and had a breakfast of chappatis and tea in a Muslim restaurant. Back on the wet and slippery narrow road, Dr. Boaz and Paris drove cautiously: A slip into the ditch would have been disastrous. There was one bad moment when we encountered a truck as large as ours coming from the opposite direction. We stopped. Dr. Boaz got out of the Land Rover and acted as traffic director while Paris and the other truck slowly edged past each other. Before descending from the mountains, we saw a family of baboons, a spotted hyena and a hartebeest in the brush near the road. Then, as we neared Goma we saw several of the eight massive volcanoes that range from east to west in the area and stopped to photograph one of them. We reached Goma a bit before noon.

We were all relieved to be back in Goma, and Dr. Boaz helped us find rooms, Marie and I at the Catholic Mission. That afternoon I went with Marie, Matt, Bob and Rome to the Amiza Travel Agency, where they arranged a mountain gorilla tour for the following day. I would very much have liked to join them, but at the park fee of $100 and $50 taxi cost, I couldn't afford it—my cash supply was dwindling due to unexpected expenses.   They left for the tour very early the next morning and returned that afternoon positively ecstatic: They'd seen the gorillas—a silverback and his family—and spent some time in their midst, almost within touching distance.   Moved by her experience, Marie said she'd felt a strong sense of kinship with the gorillas.

21

Rwanda

We would all be leaving to return home or our next destination in the next few days. Tom was the first to leave, and I accompanied him, walking across the border from Goma to Gisenyi. With a map of Gisenyi, we walked along Lake Kivu and to the bus plaza. There, buses and taxis were loading passengers bound for various destinations. After I spotted a white man in the crowd and asked him for help, he directed us to a taxi-van headed for Kigali. Luckily, the fare was right ($6) and there was room for Tom and his baggage. We hugged, with a "Goodbye and Good Luck," and Tom was on his way.

My new friend walked with me part of the way back to Goma, as he was going to the post office down by the lake to mail letters. A Belgian, he told me he and his wife had been living in Rwanda for the past four years, he assisting the Rwandans in a new enterprise—cultivating mushrooms—and she teaching in a private girls' school in Gisenyi. He told me I could probably find inexpensive lodging either at the Presbyterian Mission or the Jesuit Mission. Continuing on alone, I felt very happy: I'd helped Tom on his way and I'd found Gisenyi much nicer than Goma.

The next morning I packed, said my goodbyes and headed for Gisenyi. Bob decided to walk with me, just as I'd done with Tom, and I was grateful for his company. During our walk, we made an expedient exchange: He gave me $45 U.S. for the equivalent of my Zaire francs. At the border, the official took a dim view of our mode of travel: "You should have taken a taxi," he said. We didn't tell him we knew he would have demanded a bribe from the driver.

We found the Presbyterian Mission up the hill near the bus plaza. The Mission buildings included an office, motel-like rooms, a central meeting-dining area, washing facilities, and two charming gazebos, in African mud-hut style, set in very attractively landscaped grounds. From the Mission, I had an excellent view of Lake Kivu in one direction and the mountains in another. The manager, who spoke a little English, was friendly and booked a bunk in a room for me for one night for only $5. Bob and I wished each other "Good Luck," and he left for Goma. Now I was on my own once again.

For the rest of the day, I explored Gisenyi, from the hilltop where I was, down to the lakefront and back again. Alison Des Forges had told me how charming Gisenyi was, and it proved to be true. Part of its charm came from its location next to Lake Kivu. Belgians had built resort hotels and other commercial buildings near the waterfront, and a few expats still lived in beautiful homes facing the lake. There was a public beach, and I waded out into the water. It was clear and inviting, and I was sorry I hadn't brought my swimsuit. A further walk down the lakefront revealed wide boulevards, lined with palm trees and other tropical plants—a Caribbean look. Luxury hotels and shops were located in this part of Gisenyi.

Back on the hilltop, many people were at the central market, encompassing several city blocks next to the bus plaza. I walked into the market and marveled at the great variety of food and goods of all description: tiny silver fish, live chickens and goats, fresh pineapple, bananas and passion fruit, rice and manioc, cosmetics and trinkets, household goods, and petrol for those who had vehicles. Men sat at long lines of sewing machines, tailoring and mending clothes. Trying to be inconspicuous, I sat down and watched the show. However, after a few minutes of curious stares directed at me, I moved on.

Out in the streets and in the open, I walked along the main street and observed some of the busy life of the village: people selling trinkets and food at roadside stands, men removing shoes before going into a mosque for noonday prayer, a class of adults exiting from a Catholic Mission school. Getting hungry, I was tempted to buy some sugar cane for a taste, but settled for a handful of peanuts instead.

Dinner that evening was a delightful surprise. I had signed up to have the meal cooked by the Mission for $5; it was both simple and delicious and attractively served in one of the gazebos. There I was delighted to have a dinner companion. Christopher, a young medical student from Brussels, told me he was staying at the Mission while receiving medical training at the Gisenyi Hospital.

At the end of our meal, we were joined by another couple here on holiday, from Sydney, Australia. They were doing missionary work in Zambia, they said, and had come through Kigali to Gisenyi to arrange a mountain gorilla tour. When I told them I planned to be in Kigali the next day, they pulled out a list of places to stay, ranging from the most expensive hotel, about $65, to one of the least expensive—the Catholic Mission, at about $5.

The next day I got up early, excited at the prospect of leaving Gisenyi and going on to Kigali. There was nothing open for breakfast on the hill, so I set off for the waterfront, hoping to find a restaurant open in one of the hotels. The Palm Beach Restaurant was, in fact, open for breakfast. I dined like a proper tourist, at a tourist price. Taking one last look at beautiful Lake Kivu, I went back to the Mission, packed, and trudged with backpack and duffel bag to the bus plaza.

Just as I'd expected, there were buses and taxi-vans loading passengers. I picked a taxi-van bound for Kigali, paid the $6 fare, and settled in a window seat. Eventually, the van filled with fifteen passengers, two men sitting beside me. To our mutual delight, we found we could communicate, to a limited degree. The young man next to me, Calvin Munyarukato, worked in Gisenyi; he knew a little English, having studied it in school. The other man was Leonard Rashidi, a college professor, who lived and taught in Kigali. Monsieur Rashidi was very friendly and curious, wanting to know all about me and my family. As we said "Au Revoir", we exchanged addresses and promised to write.

As the van entered Kigali, I spotted my destination—the area near the Catholic church. Getting off the van, I shouldered my backpack and duffel bag and started walking. With a little help from a young girl, who I rewarded with a tip, I found the Mission. There the person in charge agreed to $5 for a bunk for the night and handed me the key.

After settling in, I spent the rest of the day exploring Kigali, beginning with its elegant section up on the hill, including the famous Hotel des Milles Colonia. Dianne Fossey used to stay there before heading to the mountains to be with her gorillas. My walk wound down through the downtown section, where I mailed postcards and bought a map of Kigali, to the lower hillside, where the common folk congregated. Late in the afternoon, starved, I started looking for a place to eat an early dinner.

The Restaurant Café Flora, with sidewalk tables, looked inviting. My selection among the menu of petit friture poisons was a happy choice. It arrived, a beautifully-served platter of tiny, crisp-fried fish arranged in a ring around cole slaw and tomato slices. With a glass of Primus beer, it tasted better than anything I'd had in a long time. The pleasant waitress was happy to receive my generous tip, my thanks for such a nice meal. Going back to the Mission, I was full and content.

That evening it rained steadily. As I had no place to go, I couldn't have asked for more than being warm and cozy, with a good book to read. Naipal's novel, *A Bend in the River*, is about an Indian merchant who settles in an African country but becomes a victim of upheavals as the country adjusts to the new African nationalism. I'd read it on the flight to Kigali. Now, as I read it a second time, and having had a first-hand glimpse of Africa, the message of the book became clearer.

The next morning I woke up hungry again and was lucky to find the Restaurant Café Flora open. There I had a delicious and satisfying meal. Thus fortified, I returned to the Mission, packed, and left for the airport. There, it was a long wait, as my flight didn't leave until 10:30 that night. In the meantime, I learned I would need to cash my last traveler's check to pay airport fees, and there was no place to cash it. Fortunately, a sympathetic airport official came to my rescue, as he opened his office and—after lengthy negotiations and filling out forms—cashed my check for me.

Finally, our flight left for Nairobi. There we learned that our flight to London had been delayed until the next morning. Some of the passengers left to get a few hours' sleep in a hotel; others—including me—dozed in our chairs. The announcement of another delay prompted loud cries of outrage from the complainers. The rest of us lost no time in following the British Airways agent up to the fourth floor and the Simba Restaurant for a free breakfast. Eventually, our flight left and I was on my way to London, and then, back to Buffalo. What a wonderful trip this had been!

22

Bob in Academia

Bob had for some time been considering teaching as a sideline to his practice. In March, 1989, he was invited to give a series of lectures at the University of Kansas in Lawrence as a visiting professor. He was there about a week, and I came for a visit while he was there. Having enjoyed that experience, he was open to other teaching opportunities. In January, 1990, John Eberhard, who had been head of the Department of Architecture at U.B. and was now a professor and head of the Department of Architecture at Carnegie Mellon, suggested, "Bob, come to Pittsburgh and have a look around." Responding to the invitation, we drove to Pittsburgh and stayed overnight with John and his wife, Lois.

Soon afterward, I accompanied Bob to Tampa, Florida, where he gave a well-received lecture on "Urban Access to the Waterfront" at the Tampa Museum. Afterward, we met the museum head and the mayor. Bob also gave a lecture to students on "The Practice of Architecture." Following that lecture, we rented a car and drove to St. Petersburg and beautiful Long Boat Key, and walked along Bradenton Beach stretching along the Gulf.

In April, we went to Tallahassee, Florida for a look at the School of Architecture, where Bob was also considering teaching. After he presented a lecture there, we drove around Tallahassee and its outskirts, wondering whether we could be comfortable in that southern environment. Had Tallahassee been in southern Florida, near the Everglades and the Florida Keys, I would have seen a positive aspect of living there. Since it wasn't, it held no appeal for me; and Bob had his doubts, so he didn't pursue it.

About the time we went to Tallahassee, Bob learned of a potential new project, the renovation of a public school in Brooklyn for the New York City School, and asked me whether he should pursue it. Conservative as always, I said "No, it's too large a project." Bob went right ahead with it and, in fact, was selected as the architect. Sometimes it appeared that Bob asked my opinion just so he could counter it.

Good news came with a letter from John Eberhard on June 18, 1990, inviting Bob to join the department as a tenure-track Associate Professor, beginning September 1, and Bob signed on. The next month, Bob and I both went to Pittsburgh, and while there looked at apartments. While Bob was busy, I explored Pittsburgh. By the time classes began in September, we had leased an apartment in the Shadyside neighborhood, within walking distance of the University, and moved some of our furniture from Buffalo to the apartment. During the next trip to Pittsburgh, I saw Bob's office and met his secretary.

The Carnegie Mellon appointment came at a critical time: Bob's IRA savings were depleted, and I had had to withdraw savings out of my own account. While I was billing the firm for my services, I held off paying myself to conserve the firm's funds. The staff now was down to one architect in the New York project office, and an architect, intern architect, and administrative assistant in the Buffalo office. Beginning that September, and continuing through his engagement at Carnegie Mellon, Bob's schedule generally had him spending four days in Pittsburgh and one day either in the Buffalo office or in New York, administering projects there—both P.S. #233 and the new Ambulatory Facility for Harlem Hospital. After finding air travel to Pittsburgh inconvenient, he drove back and forth.

I frequently went to Pittsburgh, either driving there with Bob or going via bus by myself. We met several faculty members at a party given by Lois and John Eberhard, and after that we occasionally hosted gatherings of our own in the apartment. While Bob was occupied at the University, I spent much of my time there walking out from the apartment in the Shadyside area and beyond, always with my camera at the ready. In March, 1991, Bob was offered a 5-year Associate Professorship; naturally, he was elated. A month later I met him in Pittsburgh, and together we drove down to see Frank Lloyd Wright's incomparable *Fallingwater*.

David Lewis was one of the professors we met at Carnegie Mellon and with whom we became friends. He invited us to dinner one evening at his house in a suburb of Pittsburgh. David prepared a delicious dinner, and we had a delightful evening. Finally we said "Goodbye," and returned to our car, only to discover that Bob had locked it with the keys inside. David was surprised when we appeared at the door, and Bob explained our dilemma. But, being the gracious host he was, he offered us a double bed in the guest room, and we spent the night there. On another occasion, following another delightful evening with David and his lady friend, we said "Good night," and Bob started driving. Bob, however, had had too many glasses of wine, and we found ourselves miles out of the way, finally ending at the Allegheny county airport. We did get back eventually, in the wee hours of the morning, but I was fuming all the way.

At the AIA Board meeting held in Washington in May, Bob was elected Secretary for the College of Fellows. He was pleased and so was I, especially since his costs in travelling to Board meetings and convention expenses would be paid. Following the Board meeting, we drove to Hampton, Virginia and visited Hampton University, where Bob had spent two years of his undergraduate studies. Then we went on to Gloucester, Virginia for a mini-reunion with Bob's aunt and his cousins.

We both went again to Washington in December for the College of Fellows affairs and met the new Chancellor, as Bob's San Francisco friend and former Chancellor, Bob Marquis, retired. While there, we went to the Smithsonian Museum to see "Degenerative Art," an exhibit of works by artists banned by Hitler.

Bob had been experiencing shoulder pain for some time and decided to have corrective surgery done in a Pittsburgh hospital in March, 1992. I spent that week in Pittsburgh, taking Bob to the hospital, visiting him, and then picking him up a day after the surgery. Although the hospital deemed him ready to be released, Bob was reluctant to leave. He had been self-administering morphine to alleviate the excruciating pain he said he felt following the surgery. He was released despite his objections and given prescriptions for pain-killers. Unfortunately, they were not entirely effective, and he spent a miserable week recovering. It was a miserable week for me as well, since I could do little to help but had to witness and bear the brunt of his discomfort.

To make matters worse, Bob learned in a telephone call to his office that the administrative assistant had lost a $58,000 check on the way to the bank. Bob was furious. "The bank is just across the street from the Ellicott Square Building; how could she lose it?" Fortunately, he was able to stop payment on the check, and the client issued a new one soon afterwards.

When I returned to Buffalo the following Monday, carrying Bob's dismissal letter to the administrative assistant, she didn't seem too surprised—she'd probably been expecting it. She left soon after and I assumed her duties. Actually, there wasn't that much work in the Buffalo office, so I had time for other projects. I hired temporary personnel when I was out-of-town.

Bob and I took a trip to New England in May, first visiting friends in New Hampshire and Worcester, Massachusetts and then attending the annual AIA conference in Boston. While there, we revisited Alpine Street, finding it much changed since we lived there.

One of the AIA events was the College of Fellows reception, during which Bob and I were delighted to be in the receiving line. After the convention, we drove to Lincoln for a brief visit with Bob's favorite M.I.T. professor, Lawrence Anderson, and his wife. Sadly, Anderson was then almost blind. That was the last time Bob saw him, as he died not long afterwards.

We went on to Cape Cod and South Orleans to see Jim Robinson, who had been a client of Bob's when he lived in Buffalo, and met his artist friend, Barbara. Going on to Providence, Rhode Island, we met Don Conlon, one of Bob's joint venture partners, at one of their projects, the renovated railroad station. Bob and Don discussed a pending lawsuit brought by the attorneys for a young boy who had slipped and fallen downstairs in the station. The lawsuit was later dismissed, to everyone's great relief.

In Lyme, Connecticut, we stopped to see Elizabeth Ross, on Bob's staff years ago. Finally, on the way back to Buffalo, we saw Howard Koch and his wife, former clients. Howard was famous (or infamous) for having produced the Orson Welles' radio show with a realistic depiction of an invasion from Mars—scaring many people out of their wits.

We took another trip in July, this time to see my relatives. My mother was one of fourteen children of a Lutheran minister, Paul Bunge, and his wife. The Bunges traced their roots back to the Hugenots, who had fled religious persecution in France years ago and settled in Germany. Subsequently, some of the Bunges came to America, along with other Germans. The Bunges held a family reunion every three years, and I had gone to several of these over the years, beginning as a child. This year the reunion was held in Estes Park, Colorado; and Bob and I decided we'd both attend, staying at the park's facilities reserved for the Bunge clan.

My mother had been close-mouthed about my marrying an African-American, and I had kept that fact a secret from most of my Bunge relatives—many of them conservative Lutherans. We weren't sure what the reaction to Bob would be, but generally everyone was friendly, and we joined in the activities. A photograph taken by a professional photographer of the assembled group, gathered on the lawn with the Rocky Mountains looming behind, showed all one hundred and twenty or more of us—babies, kids, teenagers, parents and grandparents—with Bob the only dark face in the crowd.

After the reunion, we drove up to Longs Peak, at 14,256 feet the highest point in the Rockies, for a spectacular view. We stopped at the Alpine Visitor's Center and took the 250-ft. ascent walk. Leaving Colorado, we drove to Scottsbluff, Nebraska, for a visit with

Janet, Richard Prosser's widow, who lived out in the country with her father near Scottsbluff. Before seeing Janet, we stopped at the Scottsbluff National Monument. I persuaded Bob to walk with me on the winding, vertiginous trail up, around, and back down the monument, rather than driving to the top, as most tourists did. We stayed overnight with Janet and her father, then drove back to Denver and flew home to Buffalo.

Considering some of the stressful situations we'd endured during the year, I decided to buy Bob a humorous gift for Christmas. Shopping at the Nature Company, I found the perfect present: an inflatable life-size, Emperor penguin. When Bob opened his present and blew up the penguin, which bobbed at his feet, he burst out laughing, a sound I hadn't heard in a long time. The penguin was great fun to have around, like a pet, and I even used him in some comical photographs. I took him to Delaware Park, setting him up on a pair of skies, on a hill overlooking Hoyt Lake, poised to take off down the slope. In another scenario, I set him on the terrace, ready to dine on a platter of fresh fish garnished with parsley and lemon. Finally, I posed him standing in the snow in the back yard, watching television (I'd brought our set outside). The resulting photos were hilarious. Sadly, the penguin slowly deflated. Bob and I missed him. The Nature Company didn't sell any more penguins, and, in fact, went out of business a few years later—a pity, I thought.

23

The Byron Dig and Other Pursuits

While Bob was occupied with teaching and the New York City projects, I was busy with my own activities outside of office work. When I returned from that "most beautiful dig" in Africa, I looked for digs closer to home, and heard about the Buffalo Science Museum's Byron Dig. This dig, at a site near Byron, about an hour's drive from Buffalo, had been conducted every summer since 1983, when ice age bones including mastodons were first unearthed in a farmer's field. The Byron Dig was considered one of the richest ice age sites in North America.

In April, 1990, I heard Dr. Richard Laub, Curator of Geology at the Museum, speak about the dig, to be held three weeks in July and early August, attracting as many as 150 volunteers, and I decided to sign up for it. That summer I spent five days out at the dig site, camping out in the open and working with about twenty other volunteers, trowelling through various layers of earth in the excavation pits, or sieving to find small bones. Besides directing the dig, Dr. Laub worked alongside the volunteers, as did Bill Parsons, the Museum's scientific illustrator. In addition to working at the Museum, Parsons did illustrations for *Time*, *Discovery*, and *Natural History* magazines. His sketch of a meat-eating dinosaur recently unearthed was featured in a 1996 article in *Time Magazine*.

High school teachers and students were among the volunteers, mostly from Western New York, with a few from other places. While working, I had some fascinating conversations, one with Gearhardt, a long-time veteran of the dig, who had also been to many others, including some in Israel. Ute, from East Berlin and now teaching science in Rochester, told me she'd also been on a Semliki dig, in 1984. Small world!

One day, Grant, a barefoot taxidermist living in Toronto, visited the dig with his girl-friend. When I asked her whether he wears shoes in the winter time, she said, "Grant always goes barefoot, except on very rare occasions." Grant said he had mounted just about everything under the sun and that his clients included zoos, museums, bars and restaurants, and that he got a lot of his material from road kills. It was fascinating to hear him about his work and the unusual people he met in that line of work; Grant himself was a real character.

At the dig, we worked long days, up early for breakfast, with work beginning at 7:30, lunch at 1:00 with an hour's break afterwards, then work again till 7:00, with 15-minute breaks in mid-morning and mid-afternoon. We had three hearty meals and snacks of delicious, nourishing food prepared by the cooks, who lived in nearby Byron. In good weather, the night skies were crystal clear, and as we sat around the evening campfire, we could see all the major constellations, something I missed, living in the city. I went back to the dig for a few days every summer for fourteen more years, working in all kinds of weather. On rainy days we stayed good-natured as we worked in wet and muddy conditions, sometimes retreating to our cars to wait out a severe thunderstorm.

The best "find" I made during those years was a mastodon rib, in August, 1993. Dr. Laub pronounced it a significant discovery, and I was a celebrity for a day. All bones and other found items, including fluted points, were taken to the Science Museum, where they were cleaned and stored, with the major finds put on display. At the dig, I had my camera ready to take photos of the volunteers and the most interesting finds, keeping them in a scrapbook with an account of my experiences each year. I went back to the dig every year till 2005. One of the volunteers I met during the digs, Brenda Runk, became a good friend. As I told Dr. Laub in a letter telling him I wouldn't be returning for another dig season, it was one of the most rewarding volunteer experiences I'd ever had.

Meanwhile, I'd become increasingly involved in photography, ranging from campaign to wedding photography, creating note cards for the Book Revue, to occasionally responding to requests from others for photos and reprints. After winning a prize in the Olmsted Parks exhibit, I focused for a time on photographing scenes in Delaware Park and used these for note cards at the Book Revue. By January, 1992, I'd sold more than a hundred. I also made up a dozen little books with scenes picturing the park in various seasons, sold several copies to friends and a half-dozen through the Burchfield Penney gift shop. On seeing the note cards and books, Bob commented, "Maybe you should have gone into graphics." Well, perhaps I should have.

Encouraged by Ruth Heintz, an accomplished photographer and herself a member, I joined the Science Museum Camera Club in December, 1990. The Club met twice a month: a program night featuring a guest speaker, usually accompanied by slides, and one print and slide competition night. Becoming active in the Club, I submitted the best of my photographs in the competitions. I was elated in November, 1991, to receive the highest possible score from juror Jim Cavanaugh, a professional photographer, for one of these photographs.

I took another photograph, which I considered one of my best, as I walked in Delaware Park on a brilliantly sunny February afternoon in 1992. Seeing footsteps left in the icy crust on top of several inches of snow, I hurried home to get my camera and came back to photograph them. That photograph was one in a series of Delaware Park photographs I donated to the Olmsted Parks Conservancy, and they used "Footsteps in the Snow" for the cover of their 2002 seasonal greeting card. Several years later, that same photograph was used as the cover photo for the Winter 2006 issue for a new magazine, *Buffalo Rising*, a shopping and activity guide. That issue highlighted skiing and other winter sports accessible in Buffalo and outlying areas.

Noted photographer-mountain climber Galen Rowell came to the Science Museum in February, 1992. Rowell had photographed the people, scenery and wildlife of all seven continents and was noted for his remarkable ability "to find details in a landscape that others might not notice but which bring out the underlying elemental strength of a place," according to author and film producer Rick Ridgeway. I attended a workshop he presented on "Mountain Light," with helpful pointers in photographing landscapes. The next day I went back to the Museum to see more slides, on "The Spirit of Adventure and Environmentalism." I was very impressed with Rowell and his photography and was shocked when only a few months later, in August, he and his wife were both killed in a plane crash. Bob gave me his book, *Mountain Light*, and I turned to it repeatedly as both a guide and inspiration.

At Campos, a photography center in Buffalo, I learned how to develop prints from both negatives and slides. Attending the annual weekend convention of camera clubs from Buffalo, Western New York and Southern Ontario, I participated in workshops and lectures, gaining useful information. At the first of these conventions, I was delighted that one of my photographs, "Reflections," submitted for the slide competition received a high score. I remained active in the Camera Club until 2005 and during that time served on various committees and as President one year.

24

Bob Changes Course

The year 1993 began on a positive note, as we hosted an open house on January 2, for about fifty guests. In March, Bob and I flew to San Antonio Texas for the AIA Executive Board meeting. We enjoyed being in this charming city, with its various attractions including the Riverwalk, lined with inviting shops and restaurants. Patronizing one of these one evening, we dined on authentic Mexican cuisine. Needless to say, I took many photographs.

Bob and Sylvia, in San Antonio, Texas, for the College of Fellows Board Meeting.
April, 1993

Our Canadian friends, Ken and Anne Terriss, from Vancouver; and Doug and Donna Jean Gilmor, from Winnipeg; came in June for a weekend mini-reunion, and we all stayed at the historic Post and Pillar Inn, in Niagara-on-the Lake, Ontario, a charming little town, with attractive shops and restaurants catering to the tourists who came to see plays produced in the theatre there during the Shaw Festival season.

Soon afterwards, Bob and I went to the annual AIA convention in Chicago. Coincidentally, I saw Michael Stransky, now an AIA Board member; and I was delighted when he remembered me as having photographed him and his friends in New York during the AIA convention there several years ago.

On July 8th, the World University Games opened here, with venues both in Buffalo and at U.B.'s North Campus. Several of the events took place at the HPER Complex Bob designed. Naturally, Bob was pleased to have "his building" receive wide recognition, and we attended one of the events there.

Until September, I had no inkling of the change in course that Bob would take. I had always considered Bob a "Type A" person, with boundless energy and the ability to successfully confront most challenges he faced. I was aware that he had been under a great deal of stress, what with his teaching commitment at Carnegie Mellon while at the same time coordinating staff in projects both in New York and Buffalo. Perhaps he himself was not fully aware of how much strain he could tolerate. A week after he resumed teaching, he told me, "I'm feeling very low." He saw a psychiatrist, recognizing that he'd been doing too much and would have to cut back.

Meanwhile, I continued my usual activities, including spending Wednesday afternoons at the Science Museum, working on the New Guinea project, seeing friends, and, as Print Chairman for the Camera Club, becoming still more involved in photography. Also, I seriously considered applying to U.B. for graduate studies in Anthropology.

In September, Bob decided to take a leave of absence from Carnegie beginning January, 1994, till the end of August. So, in early November we drove to Pittsburgh and, during the weekend there, sold some of the apartment furniture, taking other items back to Buffalo.

In December, Bob and I went to Washington for the College of Fellows Dinner. While in Washington, we visited the new Holocaust Museum, and I was moved to tears upon seeing the heart-rending exhibits. The year ended, as it began, on a positive note. Before Bob closed the office for the Christmas holidays, we had a little party in the office, with architect Chuck Lynch, intern Timothy Mertzlufft, the new Administrative Assistant, Karen Thomas, Bob and I, toasting the season with champagne. Bob and I went to one

Christmas party, and on New Year's Eve we went out to dinner with Suzanne and Harry Taub.

25

Moving On

Early in January the next year, following through on my plan, I submitted an application to U.B. for graduate study in Anthropology, using both Kevin Smith and Richard Laub as references. They were both very encouraging and wrote letters of recommendation. While I was working in the Anthropology Department one afternoon, Kevin introduced me to visitors as one who was inspired as a volunteer to go on for formal study. He apparently was pleased with my decision.

In April, I received a letter from the University informing me that I was not admitted to the program, since "...competition among students was very strong, while our budget continues to decline, and we must reluctantly deny admission to many." Still interested in graduate study, I then applied for the Master of Science in the Social Sciences program, and was accepted for admission, beginning in the fall 1994 semester.

In early May, Bob and I headed off to the West Coast for an extended trip, seeing friends and family along the way and then attending the annual AIA convention in Los Angeles. We went first to Vancouver, staying with Anne and Ken Terriss. Doug and Donna Jean Gillmor were also in Vancouver. Anne and Ken took us to see Granville Island, with interesting shops, fresh fish markets, restaurants, and other attractions, all very picturesque. One day we all went to the Whistler ski resort—about one hundred miles from Vancouver with beautiful vistas all along the way. We spent a couple hours at Whistler, winding through the streets lined with shops and cafes, and ate lunch there.

After our visit, Anne drove us to Seattle and dropped us off at the airport. From Seattle, we flew to San Francisco and rented a car, driving into the city. There we met architect friend Bob Marquis, who gave us a tour of his office and introduced us to his staff. Leaving the office, we walked past a fountain designed by David Halpern to an Italian restaurant, where Bob's wife, Ellen, met us for a sumptuous dinner. Afterwards, we drove to the Berkeley Marina, where Bob usually stayed when in San Francisco.

Leaving the Marina the next morning, we drove to Sacramento, staying at a motel there. Darcy was still living in nearby Davis, although he was no longer working at the University of

California in Sacramento, where he'd been campus Traffic Manager. He picked us up at our motel for a drive around the University campus and then to Davis, a pleasant, bicycle-friendly university town, and took us out for dinner at a Thai restaurant. Conversation during dinner was pleasant. Darcy seemed relaxed: He told us he was no longer frantically seeking new work, getting one rejection after another. He said, "I might even leave the field of transportation."

Leaving Sacramento, we stopped to see a friend in Carmichael and then went on to Palo Alto for a brief visit with George and Nell. From there we went to Big Sur, driving along the coastal highway, "seventy-four miles of hills and curves." It was my turn to drive, and cruising cautiously along, I was relieved to be in control of the car and on the inside, not forced to look out the passenger window, our car only a few feet away from the edge of the cliff dropping to the ocean below.

After that heart-stopping drive, we arrived safely at Jill and Richard Russo's home. Jill had divorced sculptor Jack Solomon, left Buffalo for Big Sur, and married Richard Russo. She had hired an architect to design the house—a stunning contemporary wood and glass structure, placed less than a hundred feet from the cliff overlooking the ocean. Jill proudly showed us her "knitting room," a whole wall filled with rows of yarn from which she knit handsome sweaters, caps, gloves and other things. That Christmas, she sent me a knitted "vase," with a red neck and multi-colored bowl. Near the knitting room was "Sylvia's Wall" of photographs I'd sent her over the years.

Jill made a special chicken dish for dinner, with a salad of vegetables from their garden and a lemon pie made with fruit from their lemon tree. After dinner we sat in the living room and watched the sun set over the ocean. After breakfast the next morning we left, Bob driving this time, and stopped in San Simeon for a walk along the beach and fishing pier. Going on, we saw the Hearst Castle in the distance. At the Los Angeles airport we dropped off the car and took a shuttle to the Hilton Hotel in Los Angeles, where we settled in and dined in an Italian restaurant with an elegant décor straight out of a Fellini movie.

The next day we headed to the Convention Center for the AIA's opening ceremonies. At the entrance we met Frank Gehry, who greeted Bob warmly. Gehry was one of the convention speakers, and he showed slides of his architecture. After lunch, we went on a Frank Gehry tour, seeing several of his buildings and including a visit to his studio, where we viewed models of the new

Symphony Hall. That evening we attended the New York State reception and went to a NOMA affair. A number of black architects showed slides of their work; and Bob also showed slides of some of his buildings, including the renovated War Memorial Stadium in Buffalo.

The next morning Bob had breakfast with the College of Fellows Executive Committee, and later we met for the Past Chancellors' Luncheon, leaving halfway through to go on a tour of LA, including Santa Monica, the Hollywood section, passing near Rodeo Drive with its elegant mansions and exclusive shops and restaurants. Later, at the New Fellows' Investiture, Bob congratulated several new Fellows including Randy Vosbeck.

The last day at the Convention, I went with Bob to hear Sir Norman Thomas, that year's Gold Medalist, an Englishman of unusual creativity, who showed slides of his work. Bob considered him a modern-day "Bucky Fuller." A special characteristic of his buildings was that they "glowed" with light while incorporating energy-saving features, the buildings producing their own heat and electricity through solar energy.

While Bob attended the COF Business Luncheon, I joined wives for the "Venice Art Walk." This turned out to be more of a bus than walking tour, but we did stop at several galleries to see the artists at work. We also stopped at Frank Gehry's Rebecca Restaurant, which featured his fish icon together with a glass octopus and two glass crocodiles hanging from the ceiling, one wall covered with velvet paintings.

That evening was the final event, a formal dinner. I dressed in my one formal outfit, a pretty gown I had sewn of silk I bought in Thailand years ago and a pink shawl. Before the dinner, Bob joined Chancellor Tom Teasdale and his wife and other Board members and their wives in the receiving line. During dinner, we were honored to sit on the dais with dignitaries including Dr. Jonas Salk, the keynote speaker. I found his speech obscure and completely missed his point. After dinner, however, an orchestra played dance music, and Bob and I joined the dancing couples—great fun. As the evening ended, we passed up going to a party afterwards; I was only too happy to get to bed.

In early June, I spent my last afternoon volunteering in the Anthropology Department and was pleased when Kevin and his assistant, Mignon, presented me with a thank-you note, a book, Clifford Geertz's *Interpretation of Cultures*, and a chocolate bar, "for quick energy." I bought a computer and printer and learned to use them that summer while housebound for several weeks after corrective foot surgery. Then I went through Geertz's book, chapter by chapter—dense reading—summarizing each one as an intellectual exercise and preparation for the courses I'd be taking. In September, I began classes at U.B. It was stimulating to be in school again, with mostly younger classmates, and I looked forward to the challenge of completing the program.

In December, we were off to Washington for the AIA events. The high point for us was Bob's inauguration as Chancellor of the College of Fellows. I was ready with my camera to photograph outgoing Chancellor Tom Teasdale hanging the Chancellor's medal around Bob's neck, and then Bob as he gave a brief speech, expressing his hopes for the year. It was a great honor for Bob—the highest position he could hold in the AIA—and I was happy for him. Guests at our table included Randy Vosbeck; Kathy Prigmore, who worked in the Washington office; architect Terry O'Neal, who had also worked with Bob, and his wife; and friends Jim Harkless and Eve Epstein. Also seated at our table were Raj Bar, a former Chancellor, and Michael Stransky.

Bob with Randy Vosbeck and Kathryn Prigmore at the College of Fellows Dinner. December, 1994.

The next day we went for a long walk in Georgetown and had lunch at a French restaurant. Back in Washington we saw the exhibit, "Imagining Families," including photos by our photographer friend Fern Logan, at the Industries Museum, and an exhibit of Robert Frank's photographs, "Moving Out," at the National Gallery. Then it was back to Buffalo. In December, I received my grade report for the two courses I'd completed and was thrilled to see I'd received A's in both.

26

A Pivotal Year

When I heard the news of the Rwandan genocide in 1994, I was shocked and saddened, thinking about the two men I had met in Kigali and wondering whether either or both had been killed. Compelled, I wrote a paper for the course in "History and Culture" entitled "Rwanda and other African Studies." In the paper, I outlined the history of that country, including the long enmity between the Hutus and the Tutsis, and detailed the events since 1991 leading to the genocide. I argued that the Hutu-controlled media had inflamed the Hutus' deep hatred of the Tutsis, inciting them to turn savagely on their Tutsi countrymen and even those Hutus who had married Tutsis or befriended them.

Further, I argued that American media in the past had failed to communicate meaningful cultural information to the public regarding African countries but, rather, focused on the sensational— coups, corruption, chaotic economies, quaint tribal rites and the like. Because of its recent negative experience in Somalia, the U.S. government decided to take a neutral stance in Rwanda. Activist Alison Des Forges had been there both before and after the genocide. She reported that General Romeo Daillaire, a former commander of U.N. forces in Zaire, had stated that the U.S. could have stopped the killing in the first week. For most of the American public, Rwanda became just another tragic story.

Leonard Rashidi and I had corresponded fairly regularly for some time, but I last heard from him in 1991, and now feared he had been among the victims. Then I was surprised when in February, 1995 I received a letter from Calvin Emanuel telling me that he had lost his father, grandfather and two sisters, but that he'd escaped, fleeing to Zaire. There he had found work and was pursuing his studies at the University in management. But his contract with an organization called Care International was ending soon, and he would then be without funds to continue his education.

As there was no one else he could turn to, Calvin pleaded, "Sylvia, you are my mother, you are my last hope, and I hope that you will listen." He probably figured that I was well-to-do, as many tourists were. While happy to know that he was alive, I was sorry to answer his letter, explaining that our own situation was such that we couldn't provide the financial support he needed. I never heard from him again, but I hoped that somehow he'd be able to achieve his goal.

At the beginning of 1995, I signed up for more courses at U.B. In February, Bob flew to San Francisco to investigate possible projects and while there saw Darcy. Bob said the visit had not gone well, as Darcy had expressed a lot of bitterness. "I think Darcy hates me," he said. But in a call to me in March, Darcy said he didn't hate Bob but resented him for what he did not to do as a father. Marion had made that same accusation years before, at the point where she estranged herself from Bob. I myself hadn't heard from her since 1993, when she wrote a terse letter to me saying she was undergoing intensive therapy in a process that involved "careful examination" of her childhood.

While I continued steadily on my course of study at U.B., the office financial situation was critical once again. Bob dismissed the administrative assistant replacing Karen Thomas, who had resigned in January. After a meeting with our accountant, I was reassured, but Bob called his attorneys and told them he was considering bankruptcy. Bob was feeling increasingly depressed, indecisive and pessimistic. He said to me, "I don't know how I can get through the next few months, teaching, the College of Fellows meeting here in Buffalo in April, and the annual AIA convention in May."

Bob decided to resign as Chancellor, and his resignation was accepted by the College of Fellows. He did, however, go to Pittsburgh and teach two more classes. Later that month, at the end of the semester, Bob was elated when his students gave him a standing ovation—a heartwarming "goodbye." Also, he had a good talk with some of the Carnegie Mellon faculty and left on a positive note. Attending the AIA Convention in Atlanta, he was happy to be recognized for his efforts while Chancellor.

In one of my spring courses at U.B., I learned how to prepare a proposal for my Master's thesis, and I decided to write a paper on the conflict between Canisius College and the neighboring community, the Hamlin Park area, where Bob and I lived. My proposal was accepted, and I began interviewing people in the community and at the College.

Besides what they saw as encroachment by the College, a continual source of irritation to the Hamlin Park residents was the presence of transient students living in rented rooms in houses owned by absentee landlords, the original owners having left Hamlin Park for the suburbs. Elderly residents were especially annoyed by the students' many weekend parties, involving drinking and loud music.

At the end of the spring semester in May, students traditionally celebrated with "Quad Day," when they took over the entire block of Loring Avenue, near us, partying in the street and holding night-long keg parties on porches along Loring as well as on other blocks in the neighborhood. Some years, other residents resorted to calling the police to shut down the parties. Our next-door neighbor complained to me and said he was thinking of selling his house and moving.

It was an opportune time to be taking classes. While Bob was still involved with the New York City projects, office work was light enough for me to manage spending only a few hours there daily in addition to keeping up with coursework and attending class. The one aspect of office work I utterly despised was helping prepare proposals for acquiring new contracts. I knew that Bob depended on continually getting new work as projects were completed, but I questioned his approach: He cast a wide net, preparing and sending out one proposal after another, while rarely securing one in this manner. It was depressing to me to see so much time and energy wasted, but he was the boss and that was his strategy, and I couldn't change it.

In mid-May, Bob and I went together to Indianapolis to see my nephew, Jim, and his wife, Monica, and to celebrate her graduation with a degree in Interior Design from Purdue University. While in Indianapolis, we took a side trip to Columbus, known for its architecture. Although a small city, with a population of less than 40,000, it has a high number of notable public buildings and sculptures, designed by architects and artists including Eero Saarinen, I.M. Pei, Robert Venturi, Cesar Pelli, and Richard Meier. Six of its buildings built between 1942 and 1965 are National Historic Landmarks, and sixty other buildings sustain its reputation as a showcase of modern architecture. We visited at least a dozen of these, and I enjoyed the experience just as much as Bob, even getting a shot of myself reflected on the glass wall of one of the buildings.

Returning to U.B. in the fall, I took two more courses. For one, I wrote a paper, "Anthropologists in New Guinea," describing how the first anthropologists had gone there to study the culture, considering the people exotic subjects and fostering negative images. While contemporary anthropologists built upon previous studies, they also recognized misinterpretations by the early anthropologists. Female anthropologists, in particular, had contributed to revising the view of women's roles in New Guinea societies. I suggested that New Guinea's struggle to find a place in the modern world offered a new role for Western anthropologists, while thinking I would have liked to be among them. Doing the research for this paper heightened my interest in New Guinea and strengthened my resolve to travel there someday.

One weekend in October, I went with Bob to the annual New York State AIA's annual convention, this year held in a historic hotel in Cooperstown, New York. It was exactly the right time to be there, the fall foliage at its most splendid peak. During the weekend, Bob and I walked downtown to visit the Cooperstown Baseball Hall of Fame, finding the display interesting, but resisting the temptation to buy any souvenirs.

At the convention banquet, we sat at a table with Barbara Rodriguez, the state AIA's president, other AIA members and friends. Jack Miller, a friend of Barbara's, was seated next to me, and I struck up a conversation. It turned out we had a number of common interests, among them music and art. I was surprised when he said he'd seen the movie, Koyaanisquatsi, "Life Out of Balance," with the musical score by Phillip Glass. Until then, Suzanne Taub was the only other person I knew besides myself who had seen the movie. As Jack also loved to travel, he was engrossed when I described some of the exotic trips Bob and I had taken. I did see him again at future AIA events, and we kept in touch.

On March 28, 1996, Bob and I celebrated our 43rd wedding anniversary. Bob didn't like my card to him, which said, "We made it through another, sometimes trying, year." Bob said, "It was a great year!" ...Well, maybe it was for him.

27

A Close Call

By this time, we should have begun expecting the unexpected, but another crisis in August, 1996, caught us off guard. Till then, the year went smoothly. Ever since beginning the graduate program, I had been thoroughly enjoying each of my courses. The various required papers for each of the courses involved a lot of interesting research and writing. I was always pleased when I received top grades, and especially when two of my professors requested a copy of the paper I'd written for the courses I took with them.

Besides a paper, another requirement for one of the courses was to give a presentation to the class. When it was my turn, I put a lot of effort in preparation and was rewarded by the professor's evaluation: "excellent—clear, lucid, easy to follow." For another course, I wrote a paper on the increasing number of homeless people in America. For the cover, I used a photograph I'd taken recently in Washington, D.C. of a homeless man huddled under a blanket, a sign on the cart with his belongings next to him asking for help. The comment on that paper was, "This is a wonderful paper; I enjoyed reading it." He gave me an A-plus.

In May, we attended the 1996 AIA convention, held in Minneapolis. Bob went to the College of Fellows business meeting, and we both went to some of the affairs. It was also an opportunity to connect with our Minneapolis friends, and we gave a party in our hotel suite the first night we were there. One afternoon we met architect Jim Stageberg and his new wife, writer Susan Toth. I had read an amusing article she wrote, "Living with an Architect," in which she described how, otherwise compatible, they seemed to have completely opposite tastes in home furnishings, and Jim's opinion overruled hers. How familiar that sounded! She and Jim did, however, collaborate in writing, *A House of One's Own*, an architect's guide to designing the home of one's dreams.

Back in Buffalo, Bob was honored to have his architectural projects on display in an exhibit at the Burchfield Penney Art Center, which opened May 18. We invited out-of-town friends, and after the opening we all went out for dinner with curator Gerald Mead, acting Director Peter Fleishman and his wife, Don Metz and his wife, and photographer friend David Gordon, who took pictures at the opening. While the affair was well attended, Bob noticed the absence of most of Buffalo's other architects as well as black professionals. Following the opening, Bob gave a "gallery talk" at the Center.

Bob and Sylvia at Bob's Burchfield Penney Exhibit. May, 1996

Steve Giacci was a young architect who had worked with Bob occasionally, and he and Bob became friends. Steve introduced us to his fiancée, Cindy, and when they decided to get married that summer, invited us to their wedding in the Catskills on August 24th—the same day as Bob's birthday. We drove to the Catskills, arriving the evening before and stayed at the Pine Hill Inn, some twenty miles from the hotel where the wedding would take place. We had a nice dinner in the Inn that evening, and the next morning we left for the wedding.

We met Steve and Cindy, beaming with happiness, at their hotel. They were married outside the hotel in a scenic setting, and I took pictures. The ceremony took place a little before noon and was followed by a long afternoon of eating and drinking in the hotel. Steve's parents were especially nice, even arranging to have Bob's birthday celebrated by having the hotel kitchen prepare a little birthday cake bearing two candles. Although I had had enough celebrating by mid-afternoon, Bob was not ready until around 5:00, when we left. His driving back to the hotel seemed erratic to me—I presumed he'd had too much to drink—and we got into an argument on the way back. It was a relief to get back to the Inn. I took a long walk and Bob went to sleep.

We drove back to Buffalo the next morning, both of us glad to be back home. The next day, Bob went off in the afternoon to the Small Boat Harbor, intending to go for a sail; but he was alarmed when he almost fell in the water while trying to board his boat. He came home shaking: "I think I've lost control of my right side." Hurrying to the nearest emergency room, Bob saw a neurosurgeon there, who said he thought he might have had a stroke. Back home, Bob called his doctor friend, Frank Evans, and then his psychiatrist, who advised him to call his regular doctor.

When Bob saw his regular doctor, he prescribed a CAT scan at the nearest facility, Sisters Hospital. The CAT scan revealed that he'd experienced a head injury, causing bleeding inside the skull. The blood clot formed was pushing his brain to one side, affecting his right side. The neurosurgeon who examined him considered his condition critical and scheduled surgery for the next morning. He asked Bob, "What hit you on the head?" Bob couldn't recall anything specific; he thought it could have been a swinging boom on the boat, or perhaps that he'd bumped his head on the overhang alongside our house.

We were back at Sisters Hospital the next morning, arriving at 6:30 to meet the neurosurgeon. He told us there was a 2% chance something could go wrong but there was no alternative. As I sat at Bob's bedside, waiting, we said the things couples usually say to each other when facing a serious operation with an uncertain outcome: "I love you," "Love you, too," and hope for the best. I stayed with Bob until they wheeled him away for surgery and returned home. To my great relief, the neurosurgeon called at 10:00 a.m. telling me that the surgery had been successful.

I stopped by to see Bob later that afternoon. He was conscious but intubated. I came by again that evening and fed him dinner, he was hungry—a good sign. Bob was released two days later, with instructions to "take it easy," with no driving or sailing for the next few weeks. It was fortunate that Bob was diagnosed and had surgery immediately; a day or more might have been too late to prevent serious brain damage.

As hard as it was for Bob to do that, he managed to stay away from the office until the following week. While he was home, I used the opportunity to air my various grievances. I was also concerned about his forgetting things; for example, he'd forgotten where he put my birthday present I'd given him in the Catskills. (He did find it sometime later.)

When he did come in the office, architect Chuck Lynch was shocked to see the scar on Bob's shaved head. I think Bob was rather proud of it. I'd taken a picture of Bob showing the scar, and Bob passed it around to illustrate the harrowing episode he'd survived. In the midst of my own sort of gloom, one day I happened on a good omen, lifting my spirits instantly. I had parked Bob's Camry in the parking garage near the Ellicott Square Building, and when I left the garage, I noticed a monarch butterfly on the cement floor. Wondering how it got there, and how it escaped being crushed, I picked it up and saw that, although lifeless, it was intact. Treasuring the butterfly as a symbol of hope for the future, I brought it home and put it in a wooden box, where it has stayed beautiful through the years.

Bob saw the neurosurgeon on October 3, who told him that the recent CAT scan "looked good," also, that he doubted that any kind of rehab would help Bob's memory lapses. I was at the point where I didn't know whether to laugh or cry over Bob's forgetfulness. At least he was back to being more on his own again, and back to his independent self, including violating the "no driving" order. This began one afternoon when I declined to drive him to the Small Boat Harbor so he could have a look at his boat; defiantly, he drove off himself. When he came home, I asked him, "Did you actually drive there?" "Yes, but I was shaky," he admitted. After that episode, Bob decided to ignore the doctor's orders entirely and went back to driving full-time. While concerned, I was also glad to be relieved from that responsibility.

As we'd done in previous years, Bob and I went to Washington in early December for the inauguration of the new Chancellor. The year ended on a high note, as we had a nice Christmas, Bob back to normal, great news from Darcy—he'd had a good year consulting as an independent contractor—and I finished two more courses, only one more term to go.

28

What Matters to Me

As a long-time member, actively involved in the Buffalo Unitarian-Universalist Church, I was invited to speak one Sunday on "What Matters to Me." In my address, I said that my experience in Africa had strengthened my conviction that we are all members of only one race—the human race—and need to treat each other with respect and kindness. "What matters to me," I said, "besides my family, is that we should all reach across the barriers that divide whites and people of color and work cooperatively, in our neighborhoods and in our communities, to make them better living places for everyone." My speech was well-received, and Bob, who made a rare appearance in church to hear me speak, said he was impressed.

My conviction led me to write my Master's thesis on the conflict between Canisius College and the predominantly black neighborhood surrounding the college. I had hoped, with my study, to provide both the organization representing the community and representatives of the college a scholarly perspective on the problems encountered in their relationship, with the expectation that each party would gain a better understanding of the other's position, leading to positive change.

I began writing my thesis in January, 1997. After an initial draft was severely criticized by my two thesis advisors, I wrote another draft, and this one was approved. Relieved to have passed this hurdle, I ordered my cap and gown for the graduation ceremony. I had fifteen copies of my thesis printed for distribution, to the Independent Studies Department at U.B., the community organization, and the college staff I'd interviewed. I also sent a copy to Canisius College President Cooke and to then Mayor Anthony Masiello. I did receive an acknowledgment from Cooke, who said he had found the report "enlightening."

The graduation ceremony was held on May 16, 1997, in U.B.'s Center for the Arts. Friends Suzanne Taub and Carol Hibbard were there to see me walk up to the stage to receive a handshake from my favorite professor, Phillips Stevens, and then my diploma, Suzanne snapping a picture of me on stage. Bob came late and missed the degree awarding. But we all attended the reception afterwards, I basking in a warm glow of accomplishment. That evening Bob and I celebrated with dinner at E.B. Greens, one of Buffalo's best restaurants. Later that year, in August, we had a backyard summer party. The weather was perfect, and about forty guests came, among them one of my sociology professors, who brought two of his friends. Bob said, "It's your party"; ...and so it was.

Bob and Sylvia, after receiving her Master of Science Degree.
SUNY at Buffalo. May, 1997

Bob also had his share of awards that year. In February, he was honored with a plaque reading "Citizen of Distinction," in a ceremony held in Buffalo's City Hall council chambers. A number of our friends and I attended the ceremony and listened to Bob's responding speech. Afterwards, he said, "I'm sorry I didn't acknowledge you in my address." Since he rarely acknowledged me, the omission didn't surprise me, but his admission that he should have did.

Several months later Bob received a medal as an honored University of Minnesota alumnus. We flew to Minneapolis for the ceremony, on June 14, and met Tom Fisher, Dean of the College of Art and Landscape Architecture, at a reception in the new art museum designed by Frank Gehry. After the commencement exercises, during which Bob received the medal, and the following reception, we held our own party, on the 50th floor of the IDS Tower in downtown Minneapolis. About thirty guests attended, among them friends of ours. However, Bob was disappointed that only two of his Minnesota classmates and several of the faculty showed up.

With more free time now and still interested in volunteering at the Science Museum, in September, 1997, I committed myself to working one afternoon a week in Registrar Betty Robins' office. Besides acting as Registrar, Robins maintained the Museum's collection of slides donated by photographers. Her current project was the organization and weeding out of thousands of slides, with the discarded slides to be passed on to schools or organizations which would find them useful. I found viewing the slides, the majority of them taken during trips to various African countries, engrossing. At the same time, I used my judgment to select the best among many similar photographs; e.g., a half-dozen out of the fifty or more similar photographs of elephants.

I had also told Anthropology Curator Kevin Smith I'd be interested in once again working in that department. During a brainstorming session with him in October, to discuss possible opportunities, he suggested I might photograph the New Guinea collection. While intrigued, I was doubtful that I, with no experience, would be able to accomplish this, but I decided to at least explore the possibility, consulting with experienced photographers David Gordon and Patty Wallace, both of whom offered constructive advice. I incorporated their suggestions with my own research into a report for Kevin Smith. Meeting with him in early October, he was encouraging, and said he would use my report to bolster his request for the necessary lighting equipment. He said he should know by December 31 whether or not the project was a go.

With the project in mind, I decided to buy a more advanced camera, a Nikon 80 SLR, which had the capability of doing the kind of photography the project required. However, not too long afterwards, despite the Museum's approval of the New Guinea project, it stalled. Mignon Johnson's recent retirement had left Kevin without an assistant, and he was fully occupied with mounting a major installation—the Whem Ankh exhibit depicting Egyptian life in the era of the Pharaohs. That done, Kevin was off to Iceland to continue research on a project he was doing there. Eventually, I came to the conclusion that the New Guinea project had been shelved.

That fall, we received the sad news that Bob's brother, George, had died after failing to recover from a stroke. Bob flew out to stay with George's widow, Nell, in Palo Alto, until the memorial service. Darcy drove from Davis to meet Bob in San Francisco, and they attended the service together. George's ashes were scattered in the Pacific Ocean, a fitting burial for a former submarine commander.

The 1998 AIA Convention was held in San Francisco in May, and Bob and I flew out, staying at a hotel near Union Square. One gorgeous day I walked out from the hotel and all the way to the Golden Gate Bridge, across, and back to the hotel, not realizing until later that I'd sustained a sunburn that turned my face beet-red. We had breakfast one morning with Herb Korner, who had worked with Bob in Buffalo briefly some years ago, and his wife, together with Jack Solomon, our sculptor friend, who had moved to San Francisco. Jack had adopted a new persona, calling himself Jake and engaged in a new enterprise.

I saw an exhibit of Keith Haring's work at the Museum of Modern Art. Not sure whether I liked it or not, I did find it intriguing. I went with Bob to the various parties before the banquet and then sat at a table with other Fellows we knew and their wives. Leaving the city, we went to Palo Alto for a visit with Nell Coles and then to the hotel at the Berkeley Marina. There we met Darcy and his cousin, George's son, for dinner. The next day Darcy took me for a ride to Mount Tamalpais State Park, across the Golden Gate Bridge.

I first experienced Mount Tam, as it's known locally, in 1984, when Darcy picked me up and drove to the top, where we had a spectacular view from its 2,574-ft. peak and a hike along one of the ridge-top trails. When I visited Darcy and Marion again in 1986, Marion took me back to Mount Tam; and she and I took photos of each other, sitting on a rock at the windy summit, the rolling hills below and San Francisco and the Pacific Ocean in the background. Facing into the wind, the look on my face reflected my elation at being there. Whenever I'm in San Francisco, I look for Mount Tam, clearly visible from the city. Seeing it reminds me of those happy times.

In June, I spent a week with Helen, retired from teaching, in Ellis, Kansas. I had been going to Kansas annually to see her, usually in early summer. For several years, we had been touring Kansas. Although Helen lived in Kansas, she had seen very little of the countryside. During our trips we visited many historic and scenic sites, testifying to the great diversity to be found in this state. This year the highlight of our trip was visiting the Tallgrass Natural Preserve which encompasses nearly 11,000 acres of rolling hills, native grasses and wildflowers, one of the few remaining areas of the United States to retain its tall grass prairie ecosystem.

The Preserve is located in Chase County, a sparsely populated tract in the Flint Hills of Central Kansas. This county was the subject of the book, *PrairieErth* by writer William Least Heat-Moon, in which he lovingly details the history of its 774 square miles and 3,000 souls. After returning to Helen's home, we decided that this would be last of the touring: It had become too tiring for her. But I continued to visit her every year.

In April, Bob had been selected by the Hamlin Park community organization to assist them in obtaining historical landmark status. This involved surveying all the houses in the Hamlin Park neighborhood and recording the results. On September 10, the completed application, including a history of Hamlin Park and the detailed survey, was presented to the Preservation Board; and in a hearing on December 8 in City Hall, it was approved. The organization's members were jubilant; and Bob and I were gratified, both of us having worked on the application.

I had also taken on another role within the organization, having been asked to chair its Audit Committee, which would oversee the Treasurer's records. In that role, I became familiar with the inner workings of the organization and its sometimes stormy inner conflicts. I continued in that role for a few years before excusing myself.

My brother Werner's youngest son, Steve, his wife, Heidi, and their eleven-year old son, Kieran, moved from Connecticut to Toronto in 1998 and lived near the University of Toronto. Steve had a teaching position there and was also engaged in DNA research, while Heidi practiced as an attorney. It was the first time they'd lived near us, and we enjoyed getting to know them better. One weekend in August we drove to Toronto and had dinner with them. There, we also celebrated Doug Gillmor's birthday at a party given by his niece, who lived in Toronto.

In October, Werner flew to Toronto for a visit with Steve, Heidi and Kieran. They all drove down to Buffalo for a Sunday dinner with us, leaving Werner to spend a few days in Buffalo. On Monday I took Werner downtown to show him the office, then on a walking tour to City Hall and up to the Observation Deck. Later I drove out to Athol Springs, where Werner and I sat on the beach and contemplated Lake Erie, Buffalo faintly visible in the distance. Over the years, walking along the beach, I'd found interesting rocks and driftwood that I brought home. It was one of my favorite spots.

Another day Bob took Werner out to the Amherst campus to show him the HPER Complex; then I took him to Delaware Park, the Albright-Knox Gallery, and the Burchfield Penney Art Center. One evening he and I met Suzanne Taub for a delicious French dinner at the Coda Restaurant, opposite Kleinhans Music Hall, and then heard a concert of works including the premier of a new quartet by Lukas Foss, who gave a pre-concert talk. While Suzanne and I, fans of Foss, were enthusiastic about his new work, Werner, turned off by atonal music, said he was glad when it ended. The next day I showed Werner pictures of Marion's quilts. She'd become an accomplished quilter, showing her quilts in a number of galleries, including those in the Bay area. She also had been invited, along with other quilters, to show her work in a gallery in Japan. That same afternoon we also dropped by to see our friends, Lydia Wright and Frank Evans. Both medics, Frank and Werner exchanged medical horror stories. The next morning I drove Werner to the Toronto airport for his flight back to Eugene.

That Thanksgiving we drove to Toronto to share a feast with Heidi, Steve and Kieran. Heidi's twin sister, Faedra, had come with her husband and three daughters from Indianapolis, and three of Kieran's classmates also came for dinner. A month later, Steve and Heidi drove down to Buffalo to spend Christmas Eve and Christmas morning with us.

For several Thanksgivings in a row, we drove to Toronto. Their dinners became international affairs, as both Steve and Heidi invited people they worked with, many of them foreigners temporarily working in Toronto, and interesting to talk to. Steve and Heidi's spending Christmas or Christmas Eve with us became a tradition, as they came without fail, inclement weather or not. With Darcy out on the West Coast and Marion estranged from us, Bob and I cherished our relationship with Steve, Heidi and Kieran.

Heidi and Steve Meyn celebrating Christmas with the Coles. December, 2009.

29

Prelude to a Big Trip

I'd been thinking about travelling to New Guinea ever since working on the Science Museum's extensive collection of New Guinea artifacts. Actually, my interest in that country, "the last unknown," had begun years ago when I was a child: When I was about nine or ten, my minister father invited a Lutheran missionary, recently returned from New Guinea, to speak to his congregation about his experience there. With his talk, the missionary showed artifacts he'd brought back—bows and arrows, spears, and other objects. I was absolutely enthralled, and the idea of some day traveling there remained with me.

Recently I'd been reading travel packages offering trips to Papua New Guinea and kept looking for one that especially appealed to me. Among these was a two-week tour sponsored by the Nature Conservancy. Focusing on wildlife, the tour was scheduled to take participants to the Highland Forests, renowned for their exquisite birds-of-paradise, to the Sepik River region and to a marine wildlife preserve on the island of New Britain. In addition to seeing rare species of wildlife, we would visit culture groups and witness the Goroka annual sing-sing, spectacular dance performances celebrating the country's Independence Day, September 18.

The tour seemed exactly right for me, and I put down a deposit. I called my painter friend, Catherine Parker, to tell her about my plans, and she invited me over to see the artifacts she'd brought back from a recent trip to Papua New Guinea to visit her daughter and son-in-law, who were working in the capital, Port Moresby. Catherine showed me her treasures—beautiful carvings and decorative items such as necklaces—and also paintings she'd done while she was there. "You'll find it a fascinating experience," she said.

The tour was scheduled for September 11-26. In the meantime, I kept to a regular routine of working part-time in the office and volunteering at the Science Museum. I also went to see my college friend, Marianne Pearson and her husband, Tom, in Knoxville, Tennessee in early April, and later that month to visit Helen; then, in May a visit with Darcy, now living in Davis, a bicycle-friendly, university town. Darcy had moved to Davis while working at the University of California and stayed on after he left that position. While I was there, Darcy and I drove to Sacramento to see the Pacific Rim Festival, featuring costumed dancers from different countries. We stopped at one display to talk to the vendor about the New Guinea items she had for sale. "I go to New Guinea regularly to buy things for my shop," she told us. When I told her of my impending trip, she assured me I'd find it an incomparable experience, and advised, "Just don't look like a tourist."

In July, Bob and I threw a big party to celebrate his upcoming 70th birthday, inviting out-of-town friends, including Ken and Anne Terriss, Doug and Donna Jean Gillmor, photographer Fern Logan, and my nephew, Jim Allen, and arranging lodging for them nearby. On the 28th, the day before the party, the poplar tree stump we'd kept as a piece of towering sculpture but which had decayed, suddenly collapsed in the back yard. Fortunately, it fell—all twenty feet of it—parallel to the yard, just behind the large tent which had been erected (in case of rain) the day before. It was a conversation piece that evening. One of the young guests scrambled up to sit on the stump and stayed there, obviously enjoying her seat above the crowd. I took a picture of her there.

Seated on the balcony, Buffalo's venerated musician Al Tinney played jazz on his keyboard and accompanied singer Peggy Farrell, entertaining us for an hour or more. Guests came and went all throughout the evening, beginning at 5:00 and ending around 8:00. They sat at tables set up in the yard and ate the catered food, "delicious," I was told—I hadn't had a chance to taste any myself. The efficient caterers had everything packed up by the time the last guest left, at which point the rain—which had been threatening all evening—poured down. I said to Bob, "How lucky could we get?" Later, looking over the guest list, we counted one hundred fourteen, probably the biggest party we'd ever given. I think Bob and I enjoyed it as much as the guests, who all told us they'd had a great time.

The next day we took Fern, Jim, Ken and Anne, Doug and Donna Jean to the Albright-Knox Gallery to see the famed Monet exhibit, then had an elegant lunch in the gallery restaurant. That afternoon Bob took Fern, Ken and Doug sailing while I took Jim to the airport for his flight back to Indianapolis. A few hours later we all went to Harry's Harborside for dinner on the patio, where we had a fine view of the Niagara River and the sunset.

Before I left for New Guinea, I got all the shots required—typhoid, tetanus and a script for malaria pills to begin taking the week before leaving. In August, I received my passport and a packet of information on Papua New Guinea, including an itinerary and the names of the sixteen participants. As an amateur anthropologist, I was intensely curious about the people I would encounter. Also, the tour promised to provide me, an avid photographer, many rare "photo ops," to record unique places and people. Finally, as a nature lover, I looked forward to seeing some of the few pristine areas still remaining in the world. Altogether, this trip promised to be one of the most extraordinary experiences of my life.

30

Papua New Guinea – The Highlands

I left Buffalo on September 11, 1999, arriving in Los Angeles around noon, LA time. That afternoon, friends Fern and Louie Angelikus picked me up at the airport and took me to see the new Getty Museum. Perfectly sited on the crest of one of LA's highest hills, the architecture is striking—with numerous pavilions leading to separate galleries on several different levels—much more interesting, I thought, than the art collection itself. We enjoyed a light lunch in an outdoor café and then left just as the Museum was closing. Fern and Louie returned me to the airport, and I checked into the Quantas flight, scheduled to leave at 10:30 p.m.

After I checked in, I met Mary Enstrom-Warner, the Nature Conservancy escort for our group, and Penny and Barry Glunts, a couple from Woburn, Massachusetts. Others in our group arrived, and we took off about 11:34 p.m. We arrived in Sydney about 6:30 the next morning, a stop before we'd fly to Port Moresby, New Guinea's capitol and largest city. In Sydney, young Mary explained her role: "Primarily, I'll be handling travel details, but I'll also help you have a great time." Then we all introduced ourselves: Besides Mary and the Gluntses, my companions were Wilma Acheson, from Foster City, California; Leona and Daniel Green, from Sarasota; San Dee Kreger from Los Angeles; James Marcetich from Silver Springs; Pamela and Stephen Marsh from Colorado Springs; Elaine Nonneman from Seattle; Drs. Vera and Anthony (Tony) Oregon from Pueblo, Colorado; and Carol and Malcolm Stevenson from Englewood, Florida. San Dee, in her 30s, was the youngest in our group; Leona and Daniel Green, 90, the oldest.

Leaving Sydney, we arrived in Port Moresby around 2:30 p.m., went through customs, and then went by van to the Islander Hotel, where we spent the night. Elaine—who I judged to be in her forties—and I were paired as roommates for the duration of the trip, and we shared a room on the eighth floor with a nice view and even a balcony. The weather was muggy, and I enjoyed a refreshing swim in the hotel pool. Then I met Jenny and Mark, Catherine Parker's daughter and son-in-law, who came to the hotel with their two young children, and listened as Mark described his activities as director of the Peace Corps in Papua New Guinea. They were leaving that week, with Mark assuming a new position as administrator of a charitable foundation in St. Paul, Minnesota.

The next morning we ate breakfast in the hotel and then went to the airport for our flight to Mt. Hagen. Flying high over Papua New Guinea, I got a good look at the island's rugged landscape. Lying in the middle of the long chain of islands which forms part of a great arc of fold mountains stretching from the Asian mainland through Indonesia and into the South Pacific, the mainland of Papua New Guinea forms the eastern half of the second largest island in the world. In our flight to Mt. Hagen, we passed over the Central Highlands, part of the massive mountain spine of the island. More than a dozen of the peaks in the Central Highlands rise to over 10,000 feet. The highest, Mt. Wilhelm at 14,793 feet, is often covered by a layer of snow. Deep gorges plunge between the mountains, and rushing streams lead to rivers and waterfalls.

After a brief stop at the Goroka airport, we flew on to Mt. Hagen. There we encountered a problem—passengers and luggage exceeded the weight limit for the plane. Our mood was glum as Mary and the airport officials failed to come up with a solution, and we faced the prospect of spending hours, if not days, in a place not prepared for tourists. Fortunately, the pilots hit upon an idea which worked: The flight attendant scheduled to travel with us was "bumped," thus achieving a tolerable load.

While we waited, I struck up a conversation with a man from Tari, bumped from the flight himself because our group took priority. "The government is making a mistake in training young people for jobs but not teaching them how to sustain the land," he told me. As many young men leave for the city, those who don't find work turn to crime, as was the case in Port Moresby.

As we flew on to Tari, I was fascinated with the view below— rugged hills and deep valleys, with only a few signs of habitation. Landing at the Tari airport, we were met by Eric, our local guide, who took us by van to the Ambua Lodge. He explained that the many people gathered at the airport were awaiting the arrival of Highlands government officials, who would be speaking there as part of the country's Independence Day celebrations. Driving through the countryside and telling us about local customs, Eric confided that his father was "very rich" and had nine wives. "But," he said, "I am a Catholic and will have only one wife; we've been married twenty-five years."

As we drove through the village of Tari, we got our first look at the famed Huli wigmen, wearing large wigs made from human hair and adorned with bird-of-paradise feathers, yellow daisies and cuscus fur. Some men also wore a band of snakeskin on their foreheads and a cassowary quill through their nasal septa. Everyone in our group reached for cameras to take photos of those extraordinary-looking men—handsome fellows with fine physiques among them. The wigmen were among crowds of people along the road and at an outdoor market. Other men, women and children were gathered on top of a hillside, some of the men playing darts, where they waited for the government officials.

After a long ride, going higher and higher up into the Southern Highlands, we finally arrived at the Ambua Lodge, spectacularly sited at an elevation of about 6,000 feet. The lodge, known worldwide as a favorite destination for bird watchers and orchid lovers, included a meeting center and dining area, and twenty or more individual lodges clustered on beautifully landscaped and meticulously maintained grounds. The lodges were round, thatch-roofed huts, copying native dwellings but comfortably furnished in western style, with windows opening to a superb view of the countryside.

After settling in, all except two in our group went walking along the "Scenic River Trail" through the moss forest near the lodge, led by our guide, Joseph. Cautiously, we crossed streams on hanging vine bridges and passed near two waterfalls. Joseph told us, "These waterfalls supply hydro-electric power to the area." After we returned, I took my camera and walked around the beautiful grounds, taking a few photographs. That night we ate dinner together and then watched a video documentary on the Mendi people, who lived in the Southern Highlands and were one of the few groups that still maintained traditions.

The next morning I got up at 6:00 AM to join others in a bird-watching trip. We went in the van with Joseph, travelling higher up in the mountains. At one point, Joseph stopped the van abruptly, as he sighted a bird. Quickly getting out of the van we stood on the road and got out our binoculars. Soon we were treated to the sight of a King of Saxony bird-of-paradise perched high in a distant tree. Then we saw another close by. Excited and eager to see more, we followed Joseph deep into the forest. For the next hour or so, we had the pleasure of seeing more varieties of birds-of-paradise and also other species. One bird was so close we could see its beautiful, iridescent blue-green plumage and observe it eating fruit and seeds. These were only a few of the species we anticipated seeing, based on the tour literature sent by the Nature Conservancy.

Back at the lodge, we ate breakfast and then went on our next trip, visiting the Huli people. Peter, our van driver and guide, took us to see a Huli village and witness a sing-sing there by the Huli wigmen. I had not anticipated actually coming face to face with individuals, to say nothing of photographing them. But the tourist business is a way for people to make a living, so they are accommodating.

On our way to the village, we met one of the Huli wigmen walking along the road, in full regalia and carrying a bow and arrows. Since it was a great photo opportunity, Peter obligingly stopped the van, and we all got out our cameras and started photographing. The arrows the man was carrying were for sale at 10 kinas (about $5 U.S.) each, and I hastened to buy one as a souvenir.

Sylvia with Huli wigmen, in Papua New Guinea. September, 1999

When we arrived at the Huli village, we were treated to a "welcome sing-sing" performed for us by a troupe of dancers, a dozen adult men and one young boy, the son of the village "head man." The dancers, their faces and bodies painted a brilliant red and yellow and their wigs bedecked with bird-of-paradise feathers and other ornaments, performed several stamping dances, accompanied by two men playing small drums and one a Jews harp. Following the example of others in our group, I posed for a photograph with two obliging fellows.

Snapping photo after photo, I was dismayed when my Nikon went dead, and I searched in vain in my bag for the extra batteries I thought I'd packed. Fortunately, I'd brought along my Olympus "point and shoot" camera, loaded with film, so was able to continue photographing.

After the sing-sing, our guide took us to another village. There we were shown the lifestyles of the villagers—the men and boys occupying the "men's house," and the women, girls and little boys relegated to the "women's house." Our guide, having overcome any resistance on the part of the men beforehand, we had a look inside their dwelling and the women's house as well. A brief look inside the women's hut left me dismayed as I surveyed the dirt floor with a fireplace in the center for cooking, and the bare wood walls. In one of the spaces—perhaps used as a bedroom, since a few garments were hanging there—someone had put up several newspaper clippings—for decoration? The visual evidence of the gap between our two cultures was wrenching. Before we left, we witnessed the conclusion of a pig roasting done by the women, mainly as a demonstration for us. Taken from the roasting pit and uncovered from its wrapping of cabbage leaves, the pig's choicest parts were given to the men. Since the pig was roasted with hide, entrails and all, we politely declined a taste and ate our bag lunches.

Finally, we went to a third village, for a weaving demonstration by some of the women. As we watched, we noticed they were wearing billums—colorful woven bags—and ropes around their necks. Peter explained: "Huli women have a hard life and sometimes use the ropes to hang themselves." One of the four women was also covered in gray clay and wearing several necklaces of Job's tears seeds, a sign of mourning for a dead husband. She was required to wear the necklaces and clay for a year, after which she could marry again.

Peter told us that the Huli clans used to fight—he himself did—but that they'd given up warfare. As we asked about a skull and bones displayed in the grassy area where we were gathered, he explained that these were from the former head man. He said his grandson was now the head man. We thanked the villagers and said goodbye, some of us leaving a small donation in the collection box set up at the exit gate. That ended the day's tour, and we headed back to the lodge.

That evening, Leona and Dan invited us for cocktails in their lodge. During the party, Mary told us she was concerned about exceeding the weight limit for our charter flight from Goroka, our next destination, to the Sepik River region. "Please leave behind any excess baggage you might have," she admonished. With the party, Dan and Leona got rid of a few bottles of liquor; others left other things behind—magazines, paperbacks, and the like. Vera and Tony reluctantly jettisoned the supply of drinking water they'd brought from the States. I couldn't help feeling smug as I knew I'd be way under the weight limit, having brought along a minimum wardrobe and belongings.

At dinner, Mary read us an excerpt written by a Nature Conservancy staffer in regard to deforestation in Papua New Guinea and the Conservancy's attempts to control it. Tony opined that it was already too late, and I couldn't help thinking that the Ambua Lodge itself was a prime example of deforestation, done to advance tourism.

After dinner I watched a video documentary, *First Contact*, about the encounter between white explorers and the Highlands people in the 1920s. Michael Leahy was one of the explorers who were amazed to find a stone age culture of nearly one million people who had had no previous contact with the outside world and thought the white men were ghosts of their ancestors. He took thousands of photographs and shot many reels of film footage of the encounters between the two cultures. He remained steadfast in his belief that he and the other white prospectors had helped the people by taking over their land for gold mining and introducing them to western civilization.

The next morning we left the lodge and went to the airport. While we waited for our plane to Goroka, a man from Tari came up to me and began a conversation. When I told him I was headed for Goroka with a group travelling around the country for two weeks, he said, "You should have come when you were young!" Laughing, I told him I was very fit and would have no difficulty with the trip. As a memento of our meeting, I gave him a Buffalo postcard, signed with my name.

It was a short flight to Goroka, and I was curious to see what it would be like. I'd read anthropologist Kenneth Read's account of his experience living among the Highlanders back in the 1950s. He'd returned recently and was pleased to find that some of the people he had known then were still living there, and they welcomed him back. Goroka had been transformed from a village to a population of 20,000 and the capital of the Highlands, a pleasant little city, with shopping and transportation facilities.

The airport appeared to be in the center of Goroka, and we were at the Bird of Paradise Hotel within minutes after our local guide arrived with his van to pick us up. Elaine and I settled in our room and then went to lunch in the hotel dining room, sampling the generous buffet set out for hotel guests.

After lunch we all took a van ride up in the highlands to Mt. Gahavisuka, a national park nestled in a rainforest at an elevation of more than 7,000 feet. It was a long ride, up a bumpy road, but we were looking forward to an hour's hike through the forest among orchids and rhododendrons up to the summit. We also hoped to see a few Birds of Paradise in the forest canopy. Unfortunately, the weather was threatening, and our guide decided to limit our tour to a brief visit to the "orchid house" in the park. We were disappointed as well, when we found only a few orchids blooming, and those not particularly fragrant. We did have a fine view, and one of the photographs I took outside the orchid house—exotic flowers in the foreground and distant mountains swathed in the descending clouds—is among my favorite PNG shots.

Back at our hotel, Elaine and I both took a walk to the town center, and I made a mental note of places that might sell the lithium batteries I needed for my camera. Both she and I bought bottled water in the Bintango Supermarket. Most of the folks shopping there were men and women in traditional dress, but I also spotted a few young men in western dress, using cellphones. As we walked along the town square, we looked at the wares people spread out on the grass—billums, carvings, little whistles and other things—but resisted buying anything.

Dinner that evening was a sumptuous buffet with a great variety of dishes including beef, chicken, seafood, fresh vegetables and fruit; and I filled my plate with shrimp, oysters, crab and an unfamiliar fish. We would have a variety of delicious food such as that all during the trip.

The Goroka Sing-Sing, which we'd been eagerly anticipating, was held the next day. That morning, I left early with others in our group to go to the Goroka High School grounds, where various groups were rehearsing for the mini sing-sing scheduled to begin later this morning. The regular sing-sing, with thousands of participants from all over the country, and lasting two or three days, had been cancelled by government officials because they feared clashes between rival clans. As we walked around the grounds, we photographed some of the performers, good-looking young fellows and girls, decked out in spectacular costumes. A woman with whom we spoke told us she was the principal of a girls' school and that, in addition to basic subjects, the students were learning to use computers, taught by a Peace Corps volunteer.

I had my picture taken with an exceptionally handsome young fellow, in traditional dress, wearing an elaborate necklace of cuscus fur, seeds and shells and crowned with a towering headdress of cassowary feathers. I barely reached his shoulders. His mother, with a sour expression—and his brother and younger sister, all smiles—waited nearby.

After a look all around, I came back to the performance area, where admission was by ticket only—the officials apparently intending to keep out any mischief-makers—and settled myself in a grassy area near the stage, in a prime position to photograph performers. A little after 10:00 a.m., an official took the microphone and announced the beginning of the sing-sing, with about twenty groups performing. The first were a group of young men and boys from Asaro, a village northwest of Goroka. They came dancing in, their bodies painted half white and half black, wearing headdresses of cassowary feathers and switching monkey-like "tails," amusing the audience.

Certainly the most curious performers were those portraying the "mud men" of Asaro, their bodies covered in grey clay and wearing grotesque clay masks. Legend has it that a long time ago the Asaros lost a battle with their rivals and decided to portray themselves as fearfully as possible in the next bout. When these ghostly apparitions—covered with grey mud and huge mud masks—emerged from their hiding place among trees, their opponents scattered in terror. Nowadays, the capers the "mud men" perform are greeted with laughter from the audience.

I stayed to watch about half the performances, then left, observing some of the groups lined up, waiting to perform. The beautifully costumed dancers, some bearing magnificent paper "masks" twelve feet tall, in striking colors and patterns, were perfect subjects for photographs. Going downtown after lunch to search for a store that sold lithium batteries, I found one that did. The batteries were selling for much more than I would have paid in the States, but I wasn't going to quibble, just happy to be able to resume using my Nikon.

That afternoon we left for a trip in the van up the winding, hair-pinned mountain road to Daulo Pass, elevation 6,750 feet. We stopped halfway up and then at the summit to enjoy the panoramic view encompassing Mt. Wilhelm, at 14,790 feet the highest mountain in Papua New Guinea. At the pass, we visited a village with our guide and greeted the villagers, who stared at us. As we walked along, I noticed a few modern locks on the huts' wooden doors, and was delighted to see beautiful Jacaranda trees, with fragrant lavender flowers, blooming outside several of the huts. As we were leaving, I stopped to grasp the outstretched hand of an old woman sitting on the ground with a tray of fruit and tree tomatoes, and she beamed at this sign of friendship.

On the way back, we passed a large coffee plantation near our next stop, the village where one of our guides lived. As we got out of the van and walked up to the village, with a population of about 1,000, we met people coming and going, who all appeared happy to see us. It was a long walk, up a steep hill, and some in our group waited while the guide and a few of us continued to the top and visited briefly with the villagers. On the way back, I persuaded Mary to pose with a group of smiling children gathered to see us go.

Riding back to Goroka, our guide informed us of the respective roles of men and women in his culture: Briefly, the women assume a submissive role, with the criteria used by men in selecting a mate being whether she has a strong body and can perform the hard work women are expected to do. The way women carry a billum identifies a women as single, married, or widowed. As an example, a woman carrying a burden of wood with the billum band strapped around her forehead clearly signifies she is married. Hanging the billum backwards off her neck identifies her as a widow, while a billum draped over the head, hanging across the body signifies she is a virgin. If a woman is not carrying a billum, it signals she is a prostitute.

Before dinner that evening, we went to see a performance by the Raul Paul Theatre, housed in an attractive building, a rare example of modern architecture in that part of PNG. The theater in the round was based on the rebirth of Papua New Guinea and featured excellent dancing and singing by a cast of men and women. After the play, we returned to the hotel to pack and prepare for leaving the next day.

31

The Sepik River Region

At the Goroka airport the next morning, we checked in and boarded our chartered plane. I had a window seat and thus had a fine view of the mountains over which we flew. Our MAF (Missionary Aviation Fellowship) aircraft, according to information printed on the reverse side of the map of our flight in the seat pocket, "can carry 19 passengers in and out of the shortest, steepest, and most remote airstrips in PNG." When we neared Timbunke, I was thrilled to see the Sepik River—one of the world's great rivers-- meandering through the countryside. According to *The Lonely Planet Guidebook*, "...to travel on its broad waters is to experience the heart and soul of this amazing country."

Stepping out of the plane after it landed, we immediately felt the temperature change—from the cool mountain air to the heat and humidity of the Sepik River region. At Timbunke, just a little mission station, we were taken by speedboat to the Melanesian Discoverer, the vessel which would take us on our river trip. After a briefing by the tour director, we were assigned to our cabins. Elaine and I found our cabin quite comfortable, with bunk beds, bathroom and ample storage space, even a TV. The porthole windows afforded a good view of the river and the countryside we passed. As we unpacked, I said to Elaine, "It's good to be 'at home' for several days."

Meanwhile, the Discoverer motored up the river, reaching our first destination, the village of Kaminimbit, in mid-afternoon. The whole village, it seemed—men, women and children—was waiting for us. Their wares—carvings, jewelry, flutes and other objects—were laid out on cloths spread along the river banks. I shot half a roll of film, of the people, the men's house, the women's house and a special performance featuring two men playing the sacred flutes. These flutes, almost as long as the men were tall, were kept in the men's house and used during initiation rites. Traditionally, women were forbidden to see or hear the sacred flutes; obviously, that rule didn't apply to women tourists.

After the performance, we watched some of the village women demonstrate weaving and baking a sago pancake. We were offered samples of the pancake, and I tried a bite. The taste was not unpleasant; rather, it was tasteless. Sago is a starch processed from the sago palm, common in the swampy areas of Papua New Guinea and a staple in the diet of the people who live there.

Then we took another look at the many interesting objects for sale, and I decided to start collecting souvenirs, all very inexpensive, for gifts or to keep. I chose a curious necklace with a small grinning "face" fashioned from the jaw of a cuscus (similar to an opossum), tiny shells, seeds, and fiber. I also selected a small wood carving of a half-bird, half-human figure ending in a sort of hook made from a pig's tusk.

After our visit to the village, we returned to the Discoverer. As the afternoon had been very hot and muggy, I was glad to come back to our air-conditioned cabin and take a refreshing shower. Mary treated us all to a pre-dinner drink: "It's your reward for jettisoning excess baggage," she said. Before dinner, we listened to an informative briefing by Nancy, an anthropologist and guide for another group also on the ship and taking the same Sepik River trip. She told us a bit about the Iatmul people, since the villagers we had visited that afternoon were part of that culture.

According to Nancy, the Iatmuls stressed revering family and passed knowledge about ancestors down through the generations. This to them was of the utmost importance, as contrasted with the focus by the Highland people on accumulating wealth. Also, she said, they were generally more assertive than other coastal people. As Nancy had been living among the Iatmul people for some years, she was obviously a good source of information. Later, before going to sleep in my comfortable bed, I read about the geography of Papua New Guinea in a book borrowed from the ship's library.

After an early breakfast the next morning, we got into speedboats, half our group in one speedboat and half in another, and motored down the Sepik, then down a tributary to the Chambri Lake, a vast and beautiful expanse of shallow water. At times our passage was impeded because of salvinia molesta, an invasive floating water fern which covered much of the lake. The fern had been a problem for several decades, as it had grown to form a barrier to canoes and fish traps. Since the people living on the lake subsisted entirely by fishing, the effects of the fern had been catastrophic. Although efforts to eradicate or even contain it had thus far been unsuccessful, lately, scientists thought they had identified an insect that might inhibit its growth.

Along the way, we saw many water birds including the Great Egret, the Little Egret and the Lesser Egret, Cormorants, the Brahmini Kite, pigeons, a White Cockatoo, and more. I wished I'd brought my binoculars for a better view; but as I was sitting next to James, our local guide, he let me use his now and then.

The people of the Chambri region, part of the larger Iatmul culture, had been subjects of study by a number of anthropologists, including Margaret Mead and Reo Fortune, who worked there in the 1930s, and Deborah Gewertz, who lived among the Chambri in the 1970s. Having read their impressions, I was looking forward to a first-hand experience, as we would be visiting three villages in the region—Kirimbit, Wombun, and Aibom—that afternoon.

We stopped at each village and at each had a brief tour led by James. In the villages, we observed one of the most interesting features of the Iatmul culture, the haus tambaran, a unique architectural style. The haus typically has a front façade that is highly ornamented with carved figures and brightly painted. Spirit figures and other sacred objects are contained inside the haus, a gathering place for men only; women are forbidden to enter. Once again, we found that female tourists were allowed to overstep that rule.

In Kirimbit, we were invited inside the haus tambaran to see and hear men playing the large drums, carved from tree trunks. We were also treated to a sing-sing performed by a group of men. At Wombun, we visited another haus tambaran, enjoyed another sing-sing, and then looked at the many beautiful articles for sale. Adding to my collection, I bought a carved fork with a handle in the shape of a man's head, a miniature drum in the form of a crocodile, a beautifully carved little crocodile, painted red, and a billum in which to carry these things. I especially admired the red crocodile and persuaded Garbriel, the maker, to pose for a photograph with his young son, holding the crocodile.

We stopped briefly in Aibom, the village James was from. Aibom was noted for its fine pottery, and I had planned to buy a piece here. However, looking over the collection I decided any of these would either be too heavy or too fragile to carry back to the States, so gave up that idea. After our visit to Aibom, we motored back to the Discoverer for lunch.

Later, we set out again for a trip by speedboat to Tambanum. I was quite curious to see the village, as Margaret Mead had lived here during her research. Tambanum was much like the others we had seen that morning, but I was pleased to note an interesting difference: The haus tambaran here had a female figurehead, which seemed to suggest that women here were held in higher regard than in other villages. Here, at Tambanum, I planned to engage in a unique experience—having my face painted by a village artist.

James had told us the previous day that he would call on volunteers for the face painting. I volunteered immediately, followed by Elaine and then San Dee. In the village, we were led to the shelter of a hut and lay flat on mats covering a table as the artists carefully painted intricate designs on our faces. During the half hour or so it took to finish the painting, I lay still, feeling the soft brush applying the paint to my forehead, around my eyes, cheeks, around my mouth and chin, and wondered what the result would be.

As soon as the artist told me he was finished, I sat up and looked in my hand mirror. I felt absolutely transformed! I thought the painted design beautiful and was very pleased with my new persona. Elaine and San Dee were delighted with theirs, too, and we posed for pictures. We agreed we'd keep our faces painted until after dinner that evening to celebrate this rare experience. After the face painting, our visit to Tambanum was over, and we returned to the ship. The face paint washed off easily, but the memory of that experience would last a lifetime.

After breakfast the next morning we got into the speedboats and went down river, which branched off on the Kerom River, to our destination, Chimundo, a village of about one hundred. There, villagers were waiting for us with a great many wooden "story boards" spread out on the upper floor of the village haus tambaran. The boards were all sizes: a few small enough to fit into a large suitcase; some were three, four and five feet long and half as wide. They bore elaborately carved "stories" depicting village life. Several of our group bought boards. I looked at them and admired them all but decided not to buy any. I was limiting myself to acquisitions that would fit in my duffel bag; however, I photographed several.

As I was looking at the story boards, a young girl, speaking quite good English, came over to me, told me her name was Georgiana, and engaged me in conversation for the next half hour. Georgiana told me she was sixteen years old, had eight younger brothers and sisters, and that her mother had died in childbirth a year ago. Her father was the prayer leader in the Catholic church and she was in grade 5 in the village school, taught by a woman from the village and a man from Wewak, on the northern coast. She pointed out two women in the group that performed a sing-sing for us later, who she said were her grandmothers. She explained that the fiber for the beautiful grass skirts the women wore came from the bush. "But," she said, "I don't ever wear grass skirts, only Western clothes." When I asked about marriage, she said that, although most girls in her village get married at age nineteen or twenty, she doesn't want to get married.

Having this conversation was an unexpectedly welcome experience, and I asked Barry—a fellow in our group—to take a picture of us together. As I thought about it later, I should have asked Georgiana to give me her address so I could send her a copy of the photograph and perhaps begin a correspondence. It was sad to think that the potential for bright young people like her might never be realized, considering that only a very few achieved a level of education higher than high school, or even finished elementary school.

When it was time to leave, the various storyboards collected by people in our group were loaded onto the boat. We waved "goodbye," then sped back to our ship. After lunch we motored to two different markets at Angoram. Two pretty seed and shell necklaces caught my eye, and also a very nice wood carving. As I was in the process of paying for these, I struck up a conversation with a man from the village who told me he was a policeman, had three children, and learned English in school.

The next morning I joined others for an early morning bird-watching trip with James. We were rewarded with seeing many birds, among them the Dollar Bird, White Cockatoo, Whistling Kite, Cormorant, Rufus Kingfisher, Brass Cuckoo, Sea Eagle, Yellow Mynah, Red and Green Parrots, and the Rufus-Breasted Kookaburra. Although we didn't see the Lesser Bird-of-Paradise, we heard its call.

Later that morning we took the speedboats to Bien, a large village on the Sepik. Here we were entertained by a group of young girls, in traditional dress, led into the performing arena by a young boy. In full regalia, he stood solemnly at attention at the head of the troupe as they sang and danced. We sat on the sidelines, along with friends and family, an appreciative audience. After the sing-sing, we visited the Catholic church and two elementary schools, where several grades were being taught. It was very hot and humid that morning, and we didn't linger long but were back on the ship by 11:00 a.m.

The buffet lunch that day included several platters of prawns and some unfamiliar food. I helped myself to several prawns and a few of the other, crisp, crunchy and rich-tasting, rather like pork. I learned later that these were sago grubs, deep-fried, and was amused to think that I'd unknowingly relished a sample of native food I would ordinarily find revolting.

After lunch we motored up the Murik Lakes to Wendam, a village larger than Bien. There we looked at yet another display of crafts and saw yet another sing-sing. By this time, the excitement of sing-sings and displays had worn off, and we were all feeling over-exposed. Nevertheless, we were amused by a little play put on by a half-dozen of the village men, the basic plot that of the good guys vs. the bad guys. Accompanying the action, two men beat a large slit gong drum, eight feet long, hollowed out from a tree trunk with long narrow slits along the top and decoratively carved along the sides. Two other men played guitars. We applauded heartily to show our appreciation.

After the play, I looked for subjects to photograph and found several, among them a tame cockatoo perched on his owner's shoulder; two pretty little sisters, in crisp white dresses, standing with their father; and another pretty little girl. She was all dressed up in a fine costume—a miniature red and yellow grass skirt, a flower lei cascading down to her waist, a pig's tusk pendant around her neck, and a flaming red hibiscus as big as her face fastened in her hair. She sat in her mother's lap while I photographed them.

Later, back on the Discoverer, we spent our last evening on board. Those in our group who had acquired articles claimed them, and those with large items such as storyboards arranged to have them shipped to the States. I was pleased to find that all my souvenirs fit in my duffel bag, just as I'd planned. At this point in our trip, everyone in our group was tired of visiting villages and eager to move on to the next phase—a stop in Madang and then on to Kimbe Bay.

As we slept that night, the Discoverer left the placid Sepik River and entered the choppy Bismark Sea. It took me a while to get used to the pitching and rolling, but I did finally get to sleep. The next morning we left the Discoverer and went by speedboat to the village of Banara. On the banks of the river, with thatch-roofed huts set on stilts some ten feet above the ground and luxuriant tropical plants, it was attractive in the same way that South Sea Islands are usually pictured. In fact, a German film crew was hurrying about, shooting scenes for a film. After a short wait, we boarded a bus that took us to Madang, a ride of two hours or so.

We ate lunch at a hotel in Madang—a pleasant city, much more amenable to tourists than Port Moresby. After lunch, we went for a tour of the Cultural Center. There we saw a fine exhibit of artifacts, and I bought a blue cotton lap-lap, a souvenir of a cultural festival held at the Center in 1998. It seemed perfect to wear as a wrap over my swim suit in Kimbe Bay, where I planned to swim and snorkel.

   After returning to the hotel, we gathered our belongings and went to the airport. There we boarded our plane for the short flight to Port Moresby. Back at the Islander Hotel in Port Moresby, we all repacked to leave things we would not need at Kimbe Bay in a bag kept until our return. Elaine and I went to bed and slept until 3:30 the next morning, when our wake-up call came.

32

Kimbe Bay

After leaving the hotel and arriving at the airport, I saved the orange and orange juice included in the box breakfast given us while we waited for the flight. I had gotten up that morning with a sore throat—a warning sign of a cold coming on—but had taken two Anacin's, hoping to head it off. As we flew over Papua New Guinea and then the island of New Britain, we saw how rugged that island was. According to Shannon Seeto, our guide in Kimbe Bay, one of the island's many volcanic mountains remains active.

Shannon, Project Coordinator for the Conservancy's Marine Project in Kimbe Bay, met us as we landed at the Hoskins Airport. The 45-minute van ride from the airport to the Walindi Resort, where we'd be staying, took us past villages and miles of palm oil and coconut plantations, which have converted nearly all the native lowland forest on this, the western part of the island.

We arrived at the Walindi Plantation Resort and found it, as expected, near the waters of Kimbe Bay. We were a little disappointed, however, to find out that the sandy beach we'd envisioned, perfect for swimming and sunning, was instead, a volcanic shore. One had to walk out on the rocky beach and then wade out into the water until it was deep enough for swimming. At any rate, the resort grounds were attractive, with lush tropical foliage all around; and Elaine and I found our "lodge" quite comfortable.

After settling in, I spent the rest of the morning walking about and photographing. Then I discovered that the beach was remarkably rich in all kinds of seashells. I collected about a dozen, variously shaped and colored, most of which I'd never seen before, including a beautiful little tiger cowrie, and put them in a pile. I also found two halves, perfectly intact, of another beautiful, cream-colored shell. This last find was especially exciting, and I stepped back to get in a better position for photographing this shell, now with its halves put back together.

Focusing on the shell, I forgot about the rocks. But as I backed up to get just the right shot, I stumbled and fell. Feeling myself falling, I wanted above all to protect my expensive Nikon. So, as I held the camera in my right arm, I fell on my left side and got a nasty scrape on that arm. When I got up, the camera was intact, but my arm, now bloody and with some debris in the wounds, was an alarming sight. I hurried back to my room, thankful that Elaine wasn't there. I wasn't ready to admit to my clumsiness.

Donning my swim suit, I headed back to the beach, thinking that the best thing I could do was to immerse myself in the sea and let the salt water cleanse the wounds. I stayed near the shore but in water deep enough to swim. After my swim, I showered and cleaned the scrapes as well as I could. Unfortunately, I'd forgotten to pack my first-aid kit when preparing to go to Kimbe Bay. Since I didn't have antiseptic and bandages, I decided I would simply "tough it out." I put on a long-sleeved shirt to hide my injuries and ate the orange and drank the orange juice I'd saved from breakfast, skipping lunch at the resort dining room.

After a nap, I joined the others at the Mahonia Na Dari Conservation and Research Center, established by the Nature Conservancy in 1996, to hear Shannon and Margaret, his volunteer assistant, explain the project. Mahonia Na Dari meant "Guardians of the Sea," and the principal mission of the center was to educate people in ways to support conservation of the pristine reefs and marine life of Kimbe Bay. The center held classes for people of all ages, from elementary school age to adults.

In recent years, fisherman had been using poison and dynamite to bring in larger harvests of fish. Now they learned how harmful this practice was, not only reducing the numbers of fish but also damaging the reefs. Shannon said that the Center's program had been making a difference, as educated communities were changing harmful ways to methods that preserved the marine wildlife, ultimately proving beneficial to themselves.

Later that afternoon, Elaine and I joined several others for a short trip up the mountain for bird watching. But a light drizzle turned heavier; and it grew too dark to see more than a bird or two. I felt feverish, but I couldn't tell whether this was a fever from my cold, now full-blown, or from too much sun that morning. By dinner time I was starved, and filled my plate with lobster, vegetables and eggplant casserole, topping off the meal with a generous slice of lemon meringue pie. Back in the lodge, Elaine got a glimpse of my scrapes and was shocked. "What happened to your arm?" she asked. I told her about my fall, and I gratefully accepted the ointment she gave me to put on my arm.

The next morning I woke up to a sunrise which—I could see through our window—was awesome, and I dressed hurriedly. Outside, I rushed to the beach to photograph the scene encompassing the bay, the distant mountains, and the sky in shades of pink and lavender—beautiful beyond description. Photographing it, I felt particularly fortunate to be here at Kimbe Bay, witnessing this exceptional sunrise.

After breakfast, everyone but Wilma and I prepared for snorkeling in the Bay, some distance away from Walindi. Wilma didn't care to snorkel, and I—with a sore throat and injured arm—was in no condition to. I planned to enjoy a quiet day, relaxing and reading a book Jim lent me: *Undiscovered Country*, a novel set in the Papua New Guinea Highlands. After everyone left, I did some more photographing, napped, and read. I also went back to the beach where I'd seen the beautiful shells. They were there, just as I'd left them; and I gathered them all in a bag to take back to Buffalo. The snorkelers returned in early afternoon, having had excellent weather conditions and seen many species of fish.

Later that afternoon we left in the van and trucks to go to the "hot river," an hour's drive through the countryside. As we reached our destination, we left the road and drove a short distance through dense jungle. There we stopped, got out, and walked a few yards to the river. At that point, it was drizzling, and I suspect we were all thinking that maybe this wasn't the right kind of weather for this experience. Nevertheless, we all stripped down to swim suits and entered the river. To our surprise, the river was very warm, if not exactly hot, apparently the result of volcanic activity.

Fed by a rushing stream cascading from the mountain, the river was no more than twenty feet wide and several feet deep—in some spots just over our heads. Immersed, we cavorted in the water, oblivious to the drizzle; and bathing in the river had a wonderfully soothing effect on all of us. We stayed in for about a half hour, then got out, dried off, and headed back to Walindi.

Before dinner that evening, we gathered to hear Wep Kanawi, the Conservancy's PNG Program Director, describe the program. Then Mary surprised the group by presenting a PNG T-shirt to San Dee. While we were on the Sepik River, San Dee had remarked, "I don't know why you all bother to go out in all that heat and humidity to look for rare birds. You could stay cool inside and just look at pictures in a bird book." Apparently Mary had been amused by the remark, an expression of non-enthusiasm for a group activity. Needless to say, we all—San Dee, too—laughed at Mary's joke.

After breakfast the next morning we left for the airport. While we waited for our flight, I noticed blood on the sleeve of my white shirt: Apparently a bump had reopened one of the sores and caused it to bleed. This drew the attention of several in our group, and Tony, of the doctor couple, looking at my bleeding sore, noticed loose skin hanging off it. "That will have to come off," he said, and offered to do the job right then and there. I shook my head - No! But I did accept the ointment and a large bandage, along with expressions of sympathy from the group. Later, flying over New Britain, I saw beautiful Kimbe Bay below and had a momentary feeling of regret at having missed an opportunity to snorkel in those pristine waters.

We arrived in Port Moresby and at our hotel about noon; there we checked in, picked up our "excess baggage" from storage and settled in our room. That afternoon we left for a bus tour of Port Moresby. According to the 1998 *Lonely Planet Guide*,"...the city has a population of 260,000 of which about 7% are expatriates. Representatives of every cultural and/or tribal group in the country make up the rest of the population. The mix is reflected in the city's housing—there are a small number of palatial residences dotting the hillsides, mainly occupied by wealthy expatriates, and ever-growing squatter settlements around the outskirts."

In recent years, young men had been coming to the city from the countryside looking for work. According to the guidebook, although the country's population was over four million, only 225,000 (about 5%) were employed. Since opportunities were so few, unemployed men turned to crime, preying on tourists and other easy targets; and Port Moresby had gained an unsavory reputation because of its high crime rate. That was unfortunate because it also had many positive features, some of which we saw on our bus tour.

Our tour took us through the city's downtown, and I noticed quite a few modern office buildings and hotels. We stopped to see the Catholic Cathedral on Musgrave Street, its contemporary façade designed in the style of a Sepik haus tambaran. Then we were taken to what was perhaps the highest point in Port Moresby—the site of a Japanese bunker, a relic of World War II. Here we had a panoramic view of the sprawling city and its superb harbor. In another part of Port Moresby, we passed by the Parliament Building, an impressive structure, also built in the style of a haus tambaran, and the University of Papua New Guinea. We glimpsed both women and men students strolling through its attractive campus.

Our next stop was at the National Botanic Gardens which, according to the guidebook, was one of Port Moresby's gems. I certainly found it a lovely place. Besides flowers and plants of many varieties, we saw rare birds such as the Bird of Paradise, cockatoos, parrots, and even cassowaries—caged, of course. I was thrilled to finally get to see this strange bird, fantastic-looking, with a blue head topped with a crest, red wattles and neck, a sharp beak capable of tearing prey to shreds, and covered with coarse, black feathers. There were two frames left in the last roll of film in my camera, and I used these on the cassowary.

The final stop was at an arts and crafts warehouse, where we found many items selling for reasonable prices, about the same we were paying in the Sepik villages. I finally found a souvenir for Bob—a penis guard, once a customary part of men's attire—which I meant as a joke. I also bought an illustrated booklet about Port Moresby, including some of the places we saw on the tour, and another about PNG's artifacts and crafts. That was the end of my buying.

That night we all gathered in Vera and Tony's room for a party to celebrate our last night together. We helped ourselves to wine and snacks, and Penny set up her camera for a group photograph, including herself—good thinking on her part. After the party, dinner that night was anti-climatic, and I didn't wait for dessert. Back in my room, I finished *Undiscovered Country* and went to bed.

Today—Saturday, September 26—was departure day, and we left for the airport soon after breakfast. The trip back to the States was uneventful, and we arrived in Los Angeles the next afternoon. I was relieved to clear customs without having to have my checked bag inspected: I was afraid they'd want to disinfect all the wood artifacts. As I waited for the flight back to Buffalo and reflected upon the trip, I felt that my expectations had been realized. Sojourning in the Highland Mountains, the Sepik River region, and Kimbe Bay, each distinctly beautiful; meeting friendly and fascinating people in their villages; witnessing their colorful ceremonies and admiring their unique art; getting a glimpse of the exotic birds and wildlife—all this made for an extraordinary experience.

Our adventure took place in a very brief period of time, but I was sure that each of us on the tour would never forget it. Undoubtedly, the high point of the trip for me was my face painting in Tambunum. When the artist's design transformed my features, I felt myself transformed, as though I'd crossed a great divide, assuming an identity—even as an outsider—common with the Iatmul. It was a profound moment and one I would cherish for the rest of my life.

33

After New Guinea

When I arrived at the Buffalo airport, Bob had a surprise for me, a welcoming party with friends Suzanne and Harry Taub, Lydia Wright, and Chuck Jameson and Marcia Burke. After hugs all around, we went to the Landmark Café in the airport for breakfast where—still virtually up in the air—I gave them a glowing account of my trip.

I thoroughly enjoyed reliving my New Guinea experience by sharing it with friends and others in travel talks and slide shows at home, for the Women's Society at the church, at the Niagara Falls Library for the Niagara Falls Camera Club, and as a travel talk at the Buffalo Museum of Science. Bob, who was in the audience at the Museum, complimented me with "That was almost perfect." I transcribed my notes, selected a dozen photographs, and combined them in a little book, with a cover picture of me with my face painted. I had several copies printed and gave them away.

Soon I settled back into the familiar routine of working in the office part-time, and I also took on a more active role in the Science Museum Camera Club. In 2000-2001, I handled publicity for the club, which included having a column in the Museum's monthly newsletter. At the club's annual banquet in May, 2000 I was gratified when Tony Avelanosa, one of the club's best photographers, told me that my encouragement led him to be actively involved in the organization. Not long after the banquet, I drove to Rochester to see Sebastian Salgado's "Migration," exhibit at the Eastman House. I was very moved by this exhibit, which included photos of refugees fleeing from Rwanda after the 1994 genocide.

In February, Bob took an unscheduled vacation. That year the Buffalo Bills went to the Super Bowl, in Hawaii; and as the architect for the project which replaced the lower bowl seating in the Bills' Orchard Park stadium, the Bills' owner provided him with an all-expense trip for two to Hawaii and tickets to the game. Bob invited me to go, but I, not a football fan and having been in Hawaii once before, wasn't interested, so he invited a friend, Wilbur Trammell, to accompany him. They had a great time.

July 1, 2000 marked a milestone for Kieran, Steve and Heidi's son, as he celebrated his Bar Mitzvah. Bob and I drove to

New Haven, Connecticut and were part of the congregation witnessing the ceremony, held in the chapel of Yale's Divinity School. Steve's brother, Richard, had come from Oregon, as did Werner, who played the music for the service. Heidi and her twin sister, Faedra, officiated; and Bob and I were pleased to be part of the ceremony, as we each read a brief passage. We attended the reception afterwards and then the celebratory dinner at the County Club. I was happy to sit next to Werner and have the opportunity to talk with him. The next day we left New Haven, stopping in Boston and also in Springfield, where we saw Bill's widow, Alberta, on our way back to Buffalo.

In September, Bob and I flew to Vancouver for a weekend mini-reunion with Ken and Anne Terriss and Doug and Donna Jean Gillmor. While there we all went to see the Simon Frazier University with its impressive buildings designed by architect Arthur Erikson, evoking enthusiastic responses from Ken, Doug and Bob. Bob and I also took a day trip to Vancouver Island via ferry, a huge, six-deck ship holding about one thousand passengers. In Victoria, we saw the Parliament buildings and other historic places.

Back in Buffalo, Bob and I faced the ever-present cash flow problem. When a possible new project in Dallas failed to materialize, Bob said to me, "Maybe I should move home and just work as a consultant." That was the first time he'd voiced his doubts about continuing his practice. But since the firm was engaged in an ongoing project—the design and construction of a new library on Buffalo's east side— any doubts he had about the future were set aside for the time being.

As a member of the Sierra Club, I received their bi-monthly magazine, which included trips they sponsored. One of these immediately aroused my interest: a service trip removing invasive plants at selected sites in Point Reyes National Seashore. It sounded perfect—an opportunity to see a rare part of California while making a positive contribution to the environment. I sent in my application and was accepted.

34

Point Reyes

In May, 2001, I flew to San Francisco. Darcy picked me up at the airport and we drove to Pleasant Hill, some forty miles east of San Francisco, where he now had an apartment. The day after I arrived, Darcy drove us to Mount Diablo, also known as Devil Mountain, a focal point throughout the Bay area. At the top, approximately 4,000 feet, we could see for miles around. Darcy said, "On a clear day, you can see San Francisco, 37 miles away, and even points further south." I was impressed. From then on, each time I flew to San Francisco, I looked out the window for a sight of Mount Diablo.

Darcy Coles at summit of Mt. Diablo, California. May, 2001

The next day we drove from Pleasant Hill through Berkeley, Oakland and San Francisco, north onto the Point Reyes Peninsula, a narrow strip of land that juts out into the Pacific Ocean. After a long drive up and down and through winding hills, some swathed in fog making driving perilous, we finally reached the historic boathouse where I would be staying. There we met several of the other seventeen members of the group and the leader, her assistant, and the cook. As Darcy left, he said, "See if you can find another way back to San Francisco." I couldn't blame him; I certainly wouldn't want to make that trip again.

Named by a Spanish explorer, Point Reyes has been called "The Enchanted Shore." I spent only a week in this beautiful place, very little time, but long enough to have felt that enchantment. As several of us hiked on the Tomales Point Trail one afternoon, we found ourselves wending our way through a waist-high garden of delicately colored lupines and other wild flowers, blooming in beautiful profusion. The fog that swept inland from the Pacific Ocean on a daily basis provided moisture to the plants and softened the landscape.

Further along the trail, we glimpsed a herd of grazing tule elk in the distance, moving like shadows in the fog. In late afternoon, we reached the end of the trail, terminating abruptly on the cliff facing north to the Pacific Ocean. We had a brief view of Bird Rock, where birds flocked to perch, before it was enveloped in fog. We were careful to stay away from the steep cliff edges, which were likely to crumble and slide down into the ocean if one ventured too close. I photographed the other five hikers, huddled together right on the edge.

With ocean, I expected sandy beach, but I wasn't prepared for towering sand dunes, some as high as fifty feet, near Abbot Lagoon. The beautiful ice plant, common in California and its most invasive species, was introduced here years ago. The plants thrived and multiplied in places like these, so our task was to remove as many as we could at various sites. Another invasive plant, Scotch Broom, had established itself in the Mt. Vision area, and we spent one morning chopping and digging out many of these stubborn bushes. With invasive plants eradicated or controlled, native plants had a better chance to survive and re-establish themselves.

One of the surprises Point Reyes held for visitors was the variety in landscape and climate. We hiked one day on trails leading to Mt. Wittenberg, at 1,407 feet the highest point on Point Reyes, encountering many different species of evergreen as well as deciduous trees. In some places, the growth was as dense and the foliage as luxurious as you would find in a tropical forest. I was surprised to see pink, red, and even white blooming foxgloves along the trail.

Because it was a national park, wild animals outnumbered the few human inhabitants, another aspect of the place making it unique: Where else would you happen to spot a rare white deer, grazing in a distant field? We did, one afternoon while hiking on the Estero Trail. ...Or have a bobcat dart in front of your car, as happened to us one afternoon while we were driving back to the boathouse. Harbor seals cluster on rocky beaches; and migrating gray whales pass by the Point on their way south.

The Point formed a menacing hook for ships, and for more than a century, a lighthouse at its tip warned mariners of the danger. We were housed on the other side of the tip in the historic boathouse, formerly a Coast Guard station, on Drake's Bay. We slept in bunks in the boathouse, women on one side and men on the other, sharing bathroom facilities; ate meals in the dining room; and gathered in the recreation room upstairs after dinner.

One day we had the rare experience of seeing the sea at an annual low level. We walked along the beach that morning and saw countless starfish, anemones, and other sea creatures trapped in the tide pools left on the beach by receding waters. I marveled at the starfish. I had never seen them in such colors—red, purple, orange—and in such profusion. Among them was a large jellyfish, a creature I'd never seen before. Walking along the beach, I spotted a piece of iridescent abalone shell with a small hole worn through it. I picked it up and saw that, with a chain through the hole, it would make a stunning necklace. Every time I wear it, I think of Pt. Reyes.

Another day we walked along the Earthquake Trail, near the Bear Valley Visitor Center, to see the effects of the 1906 San Francisco earthquake. During that earthquake, the peninsula leaped twenty feet northwestward. An old fence had been preserved along the trail, on the San Andreas Fault, showing a wide gap between two sections of the fence. Point Reyes, as a whole, had been inching slowly northward for millions of years. At Tomales Bay, the split between it and the mainland was most apparent. Sandwiched between a great continent and a great ocean, it remains an enchanted shore.

The euphoria I felt from the Point Reyes experience gave way to shock not long after returning home. On June 9, I woke up abruptly at 2:05 AM when I heard a loud crash downstairs. "Bob," I said, "wake up! There's someone in the house." Together we got up and hurried downstairs. Apparently, someone had thrown a rock through the dining room window, reached inside, unlatched the sliding door and entered. Whoever it was had left. We called 911 and looked to see what, if anything, had been stolen. Nothing had. When the police came, they took a report and left, telling us, "Be careful."

We went back to bed, but a half hour later the doorbell rang. Bob got out of bed and went downstairs to answer the front door. I stood in the upper hallway to see what was going on. Standing outside was a man who told Bob he was a neighbor, had heard there was some trouble here, and had come over to see if we were okay. Bob, half asleep and off-guard, let him in—a big mistake, I thought. The "neighbor" suggested that he go through the house with Bob to check all the rooms, and Bob agreed. I stayed in bed, not wanting to confront the stranger myself. They finished in about ten minutes. After the man left, I got up and went downstairs and told Bob about my misgivings. It was only then that Bob noticed that the billfold he'd left on the kitchen counter that night was missing; and he confirmed my suspicion that the "neighbor" was a thief.

While we were standing in the dining room, I happened to look out and saw the thief. "Bob," I warned, "he's coming around the back." Moments later, the thief, a big, burly fellow, burst through the sliding door, knocked Bob down, brushed me aside, and rushed to the room where I'd left my camera bag with my Nikon, my purse, and a book bag with two library books, all ready for the trip to visit Helen I'd intended to take later that day. As we stood helplessly by, he grabbed everything and ran out the door. We called the police again. They came, and we gave them as much information as we could.

Later that morning, Bob urged me to carry on with my intended trip, and I did. I flew to Kansas City using the electronic round-trip ticket I had. Once there, my aunt lent me the money to buy a round-trip bus ticket to Hays. So my visit with Helen went almost as planned. Oddly enough, in Buffalo, the day after the burglary, Bob found the bag with the library books and my billfold, empty, on the doorstep. Insurance paid for a new Nikon; but the burglary had a lasting effect on Bob, making him paranoid, constantly fearful of future threats, both at home and in the neighborhood.

35

I Discover Relatives in Germany

Neither the office computers nor my computer had access to the Internet, so I was very interested when, in April, 2000, I read about an appliance called the I-Opener. This could, with a screen and keyboard, and via telephone, easily connect to the world-wide web. I paid $99.95 for one, connected it to the Internet, and immediately began sending messages to friends and relatives. It was wonderful! My e-mails included letters received from my friends Trudy and Andy Anderson.

They had been working abroad in the Peace Corps and were now spending a year in a "trip around the world" before settling down in the States. When they returned from their travels, I gave them a little book in which I had transcribed all the trip letters they sent during their travels. The cover was a photo Trudy had sent me showing them exultant, at the summit of Huayna Picchu, the mountain behind Machu Picchu. They had made the perilous 2,000 foot climb, on 18" wide and foot high steps on the side of the cliff— no place for anyone with acrophobia.

Heidi, a linguist as well as an attorney, encouraged me to explore my father's German genealogy. I knew a lot about my mother's Huguenot background, but my father, Claus Meyn, never talked about his family. He'd left Germany in 1908, at the age of 22, met and fell in love with my mother while at Wartburg Seminary in Iowa, studying to be a minister, and they married soon after.

I knew that he had returned to Germany several times, as he thought he might inherit land there. I was born during one of my father's trips, in December, 1929. He had been replaced as minister at his last congregation and, to save money, my mother, sister and brother were staying with one of her cousins in Pasadena, California. My father tried to persuade my mother to leave the States and live with him in Germany, but fortunately for us all, she refused. As it turned out, the land went to another relative, at which point my father cut off all contact with his relatives.

One of the first discoveries I made on the Internet was that the village where he was born and raised, Cadenberge, had a web site. Encouraged, I sent out e-mails to various officials in Cadenberge inquiring about my father. In the meantime, I went to the Latter Day Saints Family Center near Buffalo and spent hours searching records there. I could hardly contain my excitement the day I scrolled through microfilm records and found my father's name on the passenger list of a ship leaving from Hamburg bound for America.

In response to my e-mails, a reply came from a gentleman living in Cadenberge. He sent me a brochure, in German, describing historic Cadenberge's 850th celebration in May, 1998. Knowing a bit of German, I got the gist of it. Hoping to elicit more responses, I put an inquiry out on the Hanover Research list and was elated when a German by the name of Albin von Spreckelsen answered. He said he had found some information on my father's ancestors in Cadenberge's church books. He said, further, that he was a researcher and could, for a fee, trace the Meyns back through the beginning of the church books. I agreed to the modest fee and he began the research in early September, 2001.

On September 11, the unthinkable occurred: Terrorist planes crashed into the World Trade Center Towers, destroying both buildings and killing countless persons trapped inside, as well as would-be rescuers. Coincidentally, von Spreckelsen's son had been working in an office in the Towers, but luckily happened to be at home in Chelsea with his wife when the attack occurred.

When von Spreckelsen concluded his research and sent the report to me, I not only had a history of my father's relatives going back to 1709 but also the exciting revelation that I had a cousin, Elfriede Jagst, the only living daughter of my father's sister, still living in Cadenberge. I wrote to her immediately, in English, and soon received a letter from her, in German, expressing her surprise to hear from me. Apparently, she'd given my letter to a relative to translate. Thus began correspondence between us; and I also received e-mails from Elfriede's niece, Ingrid Schumacher, living in Hamburg. Ingrid put me in touch with her cousin, Carlos Rodriguez, a student living in Bilboa, Spain, and Ingrid, Carlos and I exchanged e-mails. As a young woman, Ingrid's sister, Monika, had left Germany for Spain to work, married a Spaniard, and had two children, one of whom was Carlos. Bilbao became famous because of the Guggenheim Museum there, designed by Frank Gehry.

On October 31, I wrote to Elfriede: "It is very exciting to learn that I have relatives from my father's side. It makes me consider a trip to Germany, to get aquainted with them, as well as to see Cadenberge." Elfriede and I continued writing each other and exchanged Christmas cards. I envisioned a trip to Germany in the near future, perhaps in 2003.

.

36

Looking For the Real Me

Living with Bob took continual adjustment. Lately he had taken to scrubbing pots and pans, after I'd already cleaned them following a meal, and frequently mopping the kitchen and dining room floors, more often than I thought necessary. When I commented on what I saw as a new phobia, he said, "I'm doing this to keep us both healthy." I retorted with "I've been healthy all my life, and it has nothing to do with clean floors and twice-scrubbed pots and pans." Another habit was especially irritating: He had a habit of turning on both the radio and the TV at the same time. When I told him this bothered me, he said that he "has to fill silence with noise." I wondered what he meant.

Shortly before Valentine's Day, 2002, he walked in the house at 6:15 p.m. on a Sunday evening announcing, "Your lord and master is home." He probably thought it was funny, but I didn't and avoided speaking to him for the rest of the evening. At one point he said, "Are you mad?" Yes, I was. Perhaps to make up for that, on Valentine's Day he gifted me with a nice black dress, in addition to a valentine. We did always manage to give each other valentines every year, regardless of however annoyed we may have been with each other.

Bob, of course, always considered himself the arbiter of good taste. Inspired after a visit to the Albright-Knox Gallery, where I'd seen a sculpture of a bicycle wheel, created by a well-known artist, I bought a pair of bicycle wheels on sale—only $5.00—at a bicycle shop on Elmwood Avenue. I set them up in the gravel in the back yard and admired my new sculpture. But when Bob came home later that day, he was furious. "Take that piece of junk down, or I'll do it for you!" Crushed by his reaction, but not wanting to create a mountain out of a molehill, I moved the wheels to a less conspicuous place, hanging them on one of the walls on the terrace, basically out of his sight. There they've stayed.

That spring, Bob was pleased when the director of the Buffalo Historical Society invited him to show some of his architecture at the Museum. He agreed, and on May 19, 2002, an exhibit of some of Bob's completed designs, including models, renderings and photographs, opened. After the opening, we had a reception at our house, and forty-seven people came, including

Steve and Heidi, who'd driven down from Toronto. We had a tent set up in case of inclement weather, with our friend, Lou Brehm, playing jazz on his keyboard in the tent. As it turned out, it was chilly and most people stayed inside.

At the end of May, I flew out to the West Coast, first spending a few days with Darcy and then going on to see Werner, now living in a retirement hotel in Eugene. While I was there, I sat in on a weekly practice session, listening to Werner and his friend, Candyce, play their pianos together in her living room, working through the entire "Concerto in F" by Gershwin. Werner, then eighty-five, and Candyce, a beautiful, married, fiftyish mother of grown sons, had met when Werner moved to Eugene; and they had been playing together ever since, occasionally performing in public. Werner, an accomplished pianist, had been playing most of his life. With his Baldwin grand temporarily at Candyce's, he practiced daily on a small piano in his hotel apartment. I loved hearing him play.

Werner and Candyce, duo pianists, at her home in Eugene, Oregon. May, 2002

That summer, rather than going to see Helen in Kansas, she and I met at the Denver airport. There our Colorado cousin, Margaret Shelley, picked us up and took us to her home in Broomfield. Margaret had arranged a reunion lunch with my childhood chum, Betty Kassel, and her mother, Jeanette Boehm, both of whom had moved to Broomfield. Jeanette, still sparkling, alert and attractive at ninety, had been my mentor, in whom I confided things it was too embarrassing to share with my mother. I hadn't seen Betty since our friendship in Altenburg, and neither of us would have recognized the other. She had married her childhood sweetheart, and after they moved to Broomfield became very involved in community affairs, including serving as the first woman on the chamber of commerce. After her husband retired, he established a successful real estate company, in which both were still involved. It was delightful to see both Betty and Jeanette again, and Betty and I kept in touch. During our visit, Margaret, Helen and I drove to Dillon, a resort town, where Margaret and her husband had a summer cottage. As we approached Dillon, we had spectacular views—snow-capped mountain peaks and rushing forest streams. The next day we went to Vail, a popular skiing resort, nestled among high mountains, and meandered among crowds of people in Vail Village. That evening in Dillon, I walked to Dillon Lake, a couple of miles from Margaret's cottage. On the way back, I witnessed a spectacular sunset—a panorama it would have been impossible to capture with my camera.

That fall I met with Rick Lazarro, handling public relations for the Science Museum, and together we selected about twenty slides to be shown at the Museum's annual fundraiser, the Galaxy Ball. The Museum also printed and enlarged a half dozen of the slides, which were exhibited at the Ball. After the fundraiser, those prints were brought back to the Museum and hung on several walls in the Cummings Room, a meeting room for groups. Needless to say, I took great pride in having my photos displayed there, and the Museum kept them there for several years before they replaced them with more timely exhibits.

In October, the New York State Chapter of the AIA met in Buffalo, and Bob attended most of the events. I went to the closing affair with Bob, the banquet held in Kleinhan's Mary Seaton Room. I wore my beautiful red formal gown—Bob's favorite as well as mine, feeling quite glamorous; and Bob introduced me all around. After dinner we danced, and as the banquet ended, walked across the hall to hear a special concert by Peter Nero and his orchestra, Nero playing the piano and conducting. The concert, with works by Bernstein, Gershwin, Copland and Morton Gould, was most entertaining. It was a great evening.

And then there were more photo opportunities. I had gone to an Open House at the Art Dialogue Gallery in February, 2002 and mingled with photographers exhibiting there. Following advice I received then, I submitted some of my photographs to the Gallery director, Don Siuta, and when he suggested I become a member of the Western New York Artists Group (WNYAG), I joined. I also took some of my photos to Michael Mulley at the College Street Gallery. After he said, "Why don't you join with several other artists and exhibit your works in the gallery during the Christmas season?" I followed his suggestion and was pleased when one of the photos I had in the show was sold. About the same time, another of my photos was sold at a fundraiser for the WNYAG.

As a member of the Olmsted Parks Conservancy, I had donated several of my Delaware Park photos to the Conservancy to use in their promotion, and they put several of them on their website. The Conservancy also used my "Footsteps in the Snow" photo for their holiday card, sent out to all members. I was delighted no end, and was thrilled when we received ours in the mail. That photo, taken on a crisp February day in Delaware Park had, I thought, been one of my best ever. But when I submitted it at the next month's print competition, it was given a poor score by one of the Camera Club judges in the monthly competition. Disappointed then, now I felt vindicated.

A note in my diary, on December 31: "Still looking for the real me, haven't found her yet. Would I ever?"

37

Ten Days in Germany

Seriously considering a trip to Germany in 2003, in October 2002 I bought a Berlitz course in German and began German lessons. Although I'd retained a basic familiarity with German, having spoken it as a child, I found the grammar difficult. I imagine Germans thought the same about learning English. A few months later, I read the book, *When in Germany*, heightening my interest in traveling there. In February, 2003, Elfriede wrote, saying her eyesight was getting worse, so I was surprised she was still writing to me. I thought, "I really should go, soon," and re-read the information I had on German history and geography. In April, having finally decided to go to Germany, I made plane reservations. Besides spending time with Elfriede, I planned to spend a few days in Hamburg with Ingrid and her teenage son, Michael, and also a few days in Berlin. As Michael had expressed a wish for an American T-shirt, I bought a "Just Buffalo" T-shirt for him.

I left Buffalo on May 29, flying to Frankfurt and landing at that huge airport. Bewildered when I first got there, I managed to find my way to the train ticket office where I had my Deutsche Bahn railway pass validated, and then boarded the ICE train to Hamburg. Passing through the countryside, I saw something altogether too familiar—graffiti on almost every building. In the little towns, the picturesque houses with their red-tiled roofs and churches looked distinctly German. But the landscape looked very similar to Western New York, with a lot of flat farmland and gently rolling hills. Unlike Western New York, though, there was a modern element: wind turbines, near Hamburg. Arriving at the Hauptbahnhof, the railroad station, I found my way out to the right street to get to my hotel, the Kieler Hof.

The hotel turned out to be a virtual hole-in-the wall, on the second floor of a three-story building. But the desk clerk was a friendly gentleman who spoke English. My room was sparse but clean, with a shower and WC just a few doors down the hall. I opened the window for air, and street noises drifted in. It was comfortable enough, considering I'd be out most of the time.

*Cousin Ingrid Schumacher and her son, Michael,
in Hamburg, Germany. June, 2003*

After getting settled, I explored the neighborhood and went as far as the beautiful Alster Lakes, in the heart of the city, with a bicycle and jogging path all along its periphery. I stopped to relax and enjoy the pleasant scene and the cooler air—it must have been well up in the 80s. On the way back, I found the Koppel Café, located in a building which also housed little art galleries. The café served vegetarian food and homemade bread, so I had a bunter Salat (a colorful salad), bread, and wine.

Back at the hotel, I took a shower and relaxed before going down to meet Karin, Irene Haupt's friend. Irene, a photographer friend of mine, originally from Germany, had asked me to bring back a precious piece of jewelry, a necklace of her mother's, which Karin had been safekeeping. Karin came to the hotel, right on schedule, leading a very large black dog, a furry, placid animal about the size of a pony. The dog attracted many stares as we went up the street to a sidewalk café for a glass of wine. There, Karin gave me Irene's necklace, securely wrapped, and then we talked. She was a friendly lady and spoke very good English. Being in a strange city, it was especially nice to meet someone with connections to a Buffalo friend.

Having dreamt I'd overslept and missed Ingrid and Michael, I woke up at 6:00 the next morning. Thankful that it was only a dream, I dressed and went down to the hotel's breakfast room. Breakfast turned out to be a generous spread—a pot of good strong coffee, two hard rolls, a slice of sour dark bread—very much like the kind my father used to order from Germany—butter, jam and cheese.

After breakfast I took my camera and went out, first back to the Alster Lakes where it was very quiet, no sailboats out yet. Then, consulting the *Lonely Planet Guide*, I went on a walking tour, beginning at the entrance to a delightful pedestrian mall, the Spitalerstrasse, with life-size Hummel figures, past the ornate Rathaus (city hall) and several churches, to the Trostbrücke, an historic bridge featuring a statue of St. Ansgar, Hamburg's first archbishop (801-65) and, finally, to St. Nikolas Church, bombed flat in World War II. The only remaining portion of the church is its unusual steeple, the ruins and surrounding space now a war memorial with a little garden dedicated to peace.

Back at the hotel, Ingrid and Michael, who had come early, were already in the hotel lobby inquiring for me. Ingrid and I hugged, and Michael smiled. I gave Michael the Buffalo T-shirt I'd brought him and Ingrid the little book I'd put together about the Meyn family, with pictures of my parents, Helen and Werner and their families, and mine. She was delighted to get the book and wanted to look at it right away, so we sat in the dining room and Ingrid paged through it while I identified the photos. She had a present for me too, a book about Hamburg, richly illustrated with photographs. Thanking her, I took a brief look through the book and then brought it to my room. Leaving the hotel, we walked to the train station where Ingrid bought fare cards good for an entire day for each of us.

Boarding the U-Bahn, we took the subway to a stop where we got on a double-decker bus for an hour-and-a-half tour of Hamburg. Aboard the bus, we sat on the upper deck where we had excellent views but were also positioned directly for sunburn. I was glad I'd put on sun screen before leaving the hotel. Although the tour guide spoke very rapidly and I didn't understand much, the tour seemed comprehensive, winding in and out of different sections of the city including the busy harbor—and around Alster Lakes. By this time, there were sailboats out on the water.

After the tour, it was lunch time, so Ingrid led us to one of the cafes along the Elbe River banks. There we had a nice meal – I had a plate of savory local fish and a frosty glass of beer while both Ingrid and Michael ate vegetarian dishes. We talked as we ate, Ingrid understanding most everything I said. "But speaking English for me is not so easy," she said. I told her I had the same difficulty with German.

Ingrid told me she worked half-days in an office and Michael attended a special school for the handicapped, training to become a cook or a handyman. She revealed that her husband had left her recently, after twenty-two years of marriage, for a girlfriend; and she suspected that part of the reason was the responsibility of looking after Michael, who needed special attention. She said she worked half days so she could be home when Michael returned from school.

After our meal, we took a tour on the "Louisiana Steamboat." We sat on the top deck, and again I had a fine view. The harbor was especially interesting, filled with ships, loading docks, huge containers, cranes, and the like. I thought about my father, boarding ship here in 1909 to come to America for the first time. Ingrid said that, after Rotterdam, Hamburg was the largest shipping port in the world. I could see many of the city's landmarks from the boat, including the spires of Hamburg's many churches. According to Ingrid, there were over one hundred.

After the tour, we walked back from the train station to the Alster Lakes so I could get a few pictures of the sailboats for Bob, and finally to the hotel. There Ingrid and then Michael and I embraced, said "Auf Wiedersehen," and promised to keep in touch. In my room, I took a shower and relaxed. After comparing what I'd budgeted and what I'd spent, I realized I couldn't afford to spend much more in Hamburg.

The next morning I took full advantage of what was set out for breakfast—a pot of tea, two hard rolls, a slice of sour black bread, butter, jam, cheese, and minced ham. Halfway through my meal, the cook brought a freshly-boiled egg, and I ate that too. I spread the minced ham on one of the rolls and saved that for my lunch.

Fortified with the hearty breakfast, I set out once more to my favorite spot, the Alster Lakes. I walked for a mile along the jogging/biking path, quite busy already, and got some nice photos of the lake and also interesting sculptures set along the path. I thought to myself, "This beats Buffalo's Hoyt Lake."

I walked to the Spitalerstrasse one last time and finished a roll of film. Seated on a bench and observing the crowd passing by, I noticed that Hamburg's population was mostly white. Ingrid had said that there was a 15% immigrant population, but that wasn't apparent. I did notice a black female clerk in the station bookstore, and a young black fellow among a group of students.

Finally, I checked out of the hotel, having paid the very reasonable 80 Euros, about $100 U.S., for two nights and breakfast. I boarded the train to Cuxhaven at 12:09, having inquired whether the train stopped in Cadenberge. I was assured it did, and one of the passengers said she was getting off there, too. I was very impressed with the efficient transportation system: It seemed you could go anywhere in the country—even villages—by rail, a very inexpensive way to travel.

As the train sped through the countryside, I was surprised to see graffiti everywhere, more prevalent than in the States. At the Cadenberge train station the other passenger and I got off. The train tracks ran right through the center of this historic town of about 4,000, which celebrated its 850th anniversary in 1998. It was Sunday and there weren't any other pedestrians about, but I found a map of the town near the train station and after a ten-minute walk reached my first destination, Eylman's Hotel.

The hotel manager was a friendly fellow; and when I asked whether I could stay three rather than the two nights I'd reserved, he agreed and even reduced the nightly rate. My room was luxurious compared to the Kieler-Hof, with a bedroom furnished with a TV and telephone, dressing room and bath. I called Elfriede and managed to communicate to her in my limited German that I would walk over to her house, on the other side of the train tracks.

Later, looking for her house at Querweg 2, I passed it and then noticed the little old lady standing in the yard at Querweg 4. It was Elfriede; she had forgotten to tell me her address had changed. We greeted each other with hugs, and then she ushered me into her house, part of a duplex she shared with her nephew and his family. She had just celebrated her 90th birthday, on May 30, and her living room was fragrant with the many bouquets of flowers she had received.

We sat and conversed, as best as we could with my limited German. She told me she had completely lost sight in the right eye and that her left eye was failing but that she could still see well enough to get around. I gave Elfriede my present to her, a handkerchief whose lace hem my mother had stitched and given me years ago. "Vielen Dank," she said, her face wreathed in smiles.

While we were conversing, Wilma, Elfriede's younger step-sister, burst in, all hot and sweaty from a Red Cross drill, still wearing her uniform. After greeting me effusively, she took me with her to her home to shower and change into something cooler. While she changed, I admired her many plants in the living room, including a half dozen orchids, pink, yellow and purple, blooming on the window sill. She showed me her lovely garden, and I photographed her there.

Cousins Elfriede Jagst and Wilma Steubner, in Cadenberge, Germany. June, 2003

Back at Elfriede's, she had coffee and a delicious apple cake with whipped cream set out for us. After that treat, I showed them my little book about the Meyn family. They were quite astonished when they saw Bob's photo: "Ah, ein Neger! Aber, ist er ein guter Mann?" (A Negro! But, is he a good man?) I assured them that, indeed, he was. Wilma, who knew quite a bit of English, helped me communicate with Elfriede.

Since I said I would like to see my father's home, Wilma drove us to the house, now owned by another cousin, Werner

Schumacher. Werner and his wife weren't home, so we walked around, Wilma showing me which was the original house and which were newer additions. She decided there was no point in waiting, so we got in the car and she drove to Wingst, the village next to Cadenberge, and stopped at the park there. Besides extensive woods, the park included a "baby zoo," fountains, plants and a hotel. This was a lovely place, and I was sorry later I hadn't taken pictures.

With me taking Elfriede's arm, we walked along the path through the park and then stopped for a drink at the hotel café. Sitting at a table on the hotel patio, we talked and enjoyed our drinks—Elfriede had a dark beer, I a light beer, and Wilma, half beer and half soda—because, she explained, "I'm driving." After leaving the park, we drove back to Wilma's house. By that time, her husband, Hans, who had been singing in a choral group that afternoon, had returned. Hans remembered some English, having spent two years in England living with a family there as a prisoner of war. He told me he fell in love with the young daughter and—under different circumstances—might have married her.

As I'd expressed a wish to meet Juergen Stelling, the gentleman who sent me the book on Cadenberge, Hans called him. Fortunately, he was home; so we drove to his house, where we were delighted to meet each other. Through Juergen, Wilma arranged a meeting with Burt Hitzegrad, minister of the Lutheran church, for the next morning.

After all that, I decided that was enough activity for the day. Wilma dropped Elfriede off at her house and then me at the hotel. I had a light meal of bread and salad and then turned on the TV in my room. An American comedy was showing, but since it was all in German, I turned it off, then read for a while before going to sleep.

The next morning I woke up at 6:40 a.m., still feeling tired. Nevertheless, I got dressed and was downstairs for breakfast as soon as the dining room opened, at 7:00. The cheery host, the hotel manager, brought me a generous breakfast of black bread, hard rolls, butter and jam, cheese, cold meat and a soft-boiled egg, orange juice and coffee. I had a bit of everything except the meat. After breakfast I set out for a walk around Cadenberge.

I was impressed with what an attractive little village it was, made especially so by the beautiful gardens everywhere. My first stop was at the watch and jewelry shop owned by Wolfgang Hesse. Elfriede's niece, Frauke, who lived on the other side of her duplex, worked in the shop and was expecting me. Wolfgang, who spoke very good English, remembered me as the person to whom he'd sent the brochures about Cadenberge's 850th celebration. He said he had been in Alabama just the year before to help a musician friend there make a recording. He'd also been in New York City.

After leaving the shop and continuing my walk around Cadenberge, I found myself at the Friedhof (cemetery), like a park, with each burial plot beautifully planted with flowers. There were a number of both men and women, busily gardening. I'd never seen a cemetery so lovingly taken care of. Today being Monday, shops were full, many shoppers parking their bicycles outside the shops. All the bicycles reminded me of Davis, the bicycle-friendly town where Darcy had lived.

At 11:00 I met Pastor Hitzegrad at the St. Nikolai Lutheran church, where my father had been a member. The exterior was striking, with a picturesque steeple; and the beautiful interior had retained many features of the original building, dating back to 1742. The first St. Nikolai congregation actually dated even further back, to 1319. Also striking were the ornate altar and organ. I told Pastor Hitzegrad how much I appreciated his showing me the church, and we had a pleasant conversation. He was fluent in English, having lived for a time in Seattle, serving as a supply pastor for a Lutheran congregation there.

At noon, Wilma dropped Elfriede off at the hotel with her Wagen, a walker with wheels, which enabled her to get around quite well. She and I sat in the cheery dining room near a window and ate Krabbensuppe (crab soup), quite tasty. We conversed as best we could, she telling me more about her family. When we finished, Elfriede paid the bill; I left a tip, hoping it was adequate. With her Wagen, both of us guiding it, Elfriede managed the walk from the hotel to her house surprisingly well. Once at her house, we both retired for a nap; I was really tired.

After our naps, Elfriede got out photo albums and shared pictures of her family, her husband—missing in action in World War II—and herself. At 4:00 Wilma arrived; and we sat down to enjoy a special "coffee," with numerous kinds of cakes and cookies. I helped myself to a luscious piece of cake that was mostly whipped cream and crust. Werner Schumacher and his wife arrived soon after.

Werner was the same age as I, just a few months older. His wife, Elsa, understood a bit of English. They looked through the Meyn family book while I identified the people pictured. In turn, Werner gave me a photograph showing their house in its earliest period, before any additions. He also showed me a list of names and birth dates of all the family—the five brothers and sisters in Bertha's family, and the second marriage of her husband after Bertha (my father's sister and Elfriede's mother) died. Uwe, Werner and Elsa's son, came in to meet me and have coffee.

After a while Wilma left, and we moved outside to sit in Uwe and Frauke's back yard. The yard was very pleasant, with a fountain and flowers and a little storage shed on one end of the yard, and a vegetable garden on the other. Frauke came home from work on her bicycle and gave me a road map including Cadenberge, showing all the streets. Elfriede brought out a bottle of wine, and we all raised our glasses high in celebration of the occasion. I finally excused myself, declining an invitation for dinner at Elfriede's, explaining I wasn't hungry. Then I walked back to the hotel. What a day it had been!

Wilma had planned a special treat for me for the following day—a catamaran cruise to the island of Helgoland, in the North Sea. She arrived about 9:00 a.m., and we drove to Cuxhaven, a port on the North Sea. There Wilma bought tickets for both of us, and we took a long walk along the harbor while we waited until cruise time. Once on board, we sat in numbered seats and Wilma bought us refreshing beers. Since it was foggy outside, there wasn't much to see.

Arriving at Helgoland, a tiny island, with a high hill affording an excellent view of the busy harbor, we went ashore with about two hundred other passengers. That day the harbor was crowded with cruise ships, and there were hundreds of tourists on land. Helgoland was bombed flat in World War II because of the presence of a German bunker. It had since been extensively developed and now was a favorite tourist destination.

Wilma and I passed scores of shops, some offering discount prices on liquor and cigarettes, and I bought a postcard. Now the sun was out, and Wilma and I climbed the many steps up the hill and then walked all around the flat periphery. There were many seagulls and other birds nesting in the cliffs. I took a couple of photos, including one of the Lange Alte, a picturesque eroded cliff. After circling the island, we descended down to street level, and I had Wilma take a picture of me, with the harbor in the background. After a tasty lunch of fish and potato salad, we headed back to the harbor for the return cruise. As we left, the fog moved in and the sky turned gray. We had been there at just the right time.

Back in Cadenberge, Wilma dropped me off at Elfriede's. She had a little spread of tiny open-faced sandwiches waiting for me, and I sampled everything. She gave me photos of herself as a young woman with her husband, and also recent photos. Then Elfriede, with her Wagen (automobile), and I went to the cemetery. There she led me to her parents' grave, nicely kept with flowers, shrubs and trees. Back at her house, she took me upstairs to show me her bedroom, with a bed big enough for two. Leaving, I told Elfriede, "Gute Nacht, schlaf gut." (Good night, sleep well.)

The next morning I got up a bit earlier, wrote postcards and took a photo of Eylman's Hotel—one of the remaining older buildings. This time at breakfast I took a roll, the ham, pepperoni and cheese, and made a sandwich for lunch. Then I checked out, and Wilma and her husband picked me up promptly at 9:00, stopping at the post office so I could mail my postcards. In a last stop at her house, Elfriede gave me more photos and a little packet of chocolate-covered fruit candies to snack on. Then Elfriede, Wilma and Hans took me to the train station and gave me a warm sendoff.

In Hamburg once again, I got on the train and arrived in Berlin around 3:30. In the station I looked for a place to buy a Welcome Card, recommended by the *Lonely Planet Guide*, good for a 72-hour discount on local and various attractions. While I was looking, a young man came up to me and asked whether I'd like to buy his card. He explained that he and his friend were leaving that afternoon, and said he'd sell it for ten Euros. That sounded like a bargain to me, and I bought it. It wasn't later that I noticed it was expiring that day. That was the one and only time I was "taken" in Germany. I had learned my lesson.

Walking out of the station, I found it surprisingly hot; it must have been eighty degrees or more. As I was wearing a long-sleeved T-shirt and scarf, Berliners could plainly mark me as a tourist. Eventually, I found the right bus to take me near my hotel; but finding the block in which the hotel was located was perplexing, even with a map, and it took a good half hour until I finally found the Pensione Curtis. There the agreeable proprietor changed my reservation from two nights to three, and handed me three keys— one for the room, one for the front door, and one for the Pensione door. Feeling half-baked, I took a shower, then went downstairs to the little café next door and enjoyed a very tall glass of good German beer. When I turned in that night, there were party noises next door, but they finally quieted, and I went to sleep.

All the next day, I managed to find my way around, taking the U-Bahn and walking. The scene at Potsdamer Platz was absolutely overwhelming, with enormous modern buildings everywhere, including the new Sony Center. Nearby, I walked up Eherstrasse, next to the Tiergarten Park (the zoo), passing by the site of the Holocaust Memorial, under construction. I went on to the historic Brandenburg Gate, and through it to the Pariser Platz and the lovely Unter den Linden Boulevard.

Leaving that site, I passed by the Memorial, with names and stories and a few photographs, dedicated to the hundred or more young people who died attempting to scale the Berlin Wall. I considered visiting the historic Reichstag, now with a new domed glass gallery in the center, but gave up that idea when I saw the long line of people waiting for admission. Then I walked by the new modern government buildings nearby, some still under construction, including the new Federal Chancellory.

Keeping in as much shade as possible I walked on to the New House of the Cultures of the World and took a look at the exhibits. Then a long walk up the John Foster Dulless Allee to the Martin Luther Bridge, down Spreeway to the Grosser Stern, and then Hofjagerallee and Klingerhoferstrasse to the Bauhaus. There I sat in the outdoor café and drank a refreshing cold beer. Inside the Bauhaus, I was fascinated with the display of a study by Lazio-Moholy Nagy illustrating the play of light and shadows from moving objects. Taking photographs was not permitted, but I bought postcards and a brochure.

Finally back at the hotel, I took a shower. I'd become acclimated to the hot weather , but my legs were covered with ugly red blotches—signaling I'd done too much walking that day. Soon after, a thundershower with drenching rain blew up, cooling everything down. After it stopped, I walked out to buy an apple to eat for supper. Watching TV and reading the Berlin paper, I learned that the big news of the day was the apparent suicide of former Minister Mollemann. I went to sleep that night with the many sights of the day swirling through my brain.

The next day my first destination was the Berlin Wall—or what remained of it. Taking the U-Bahn to the eastern part of the city, and then walking the rest of the way, I was thrilled to arrive at the East Side Gallery, at one end of a mile-long stretch of the Wall. Walking along the Wall, I took photos of parts of it, all now covered with graffiti. One section of the wall was decorated with an image of the two collaborators, the Russian Brezhnev and the German Honecker, embraced in a kiss. Other sections of the Wall dated back from its fall to the present day, including a few graffiti signed by Americans. I bought several small fragments of the Wall for souvenirs.

From the Wall I took the U-Bahn and then walked part of the way to the Lindenstrasse, leading to the new Jewish Museum designed by architect Daniel Liebeskind. I had expected something unique, and it certainly was a stunning work of architecture. Inside the museum, I spent about an hour and a half viewing the various exhibits and experiencing the memorial garden and empty tower, evoking the horrors of the Holocaust. The many exhibits documented the long, tragic history of the Jewish people in Germany and their persecution over the centuries.

Finally, I walked up Kochstrasse to Checkpoint Charlie, the only gateway for foreigners to the two Berlins during World War II. On the way I stopped at a sidewalk café, bought a bottle of citron water and sat outside to relax. With sips of the citron, I ate the sandwich I'd made that morning, hoping no one would notice it hadn't been bought in the café. After taking a few photographs at Checkpoint Charlie, I returned to my hotel, where I took a shower, read and relaxed.

That evening, considering it would be my last in Berlin, I put aside my pants, donned a skirt and top, and went out to find a place for dinner. I didn't have to go far, as I found a nice sidewalk café on the next block. There I had a tasty meal of salad, grilled chicken, a hot, crusty roll and a glass of red wine, served by a waitress with a tattooed back. Among people passing by, I noticed pretty young teenage girls, wearing pants or skirts barely hanging on their hips, and folks of all ages walking dogs of all breeds and sizes. Every person, it seemed, had a cellphone.

After a final walk around the neighborhood the next morning, I checked out of the hotel. Leaving, I told the friendly hotel proprietor that I had liked the hotel and that I thought Berlin was wunderbar. "Auf Wiedersehen," I said, and he answered, Kommen Sie zurück (come back)." As I left Berlin, I had the distinct satisfaction of having blended in well with Berliners, even being asked for directions several times. I hadn't completely learned how to navigate the transit system, however, as the bus I thought would take me to the train station turned out to be headed in the opposite direction. I wasted precious time taking a bus back, getting off, and then getting on the right one. I had just enough time to catch the train leaving for Frankfurt.

And then I made one other critical mistake. I boarded the train to Frankfurt, forgetting that there were two Frankfurts—one the Frankfurt am Main, and the other, Frankfurt an der Oder in East Germany, on the Polish border. As we arrived at the station, I got off the train and was bewildered: This didn't look like the Frankfurt I expected. It wasn't. Quickly consulting a train agent, I was told I had just minutes to catch a train going back to Berlin. I quickly bought a ticket and ran to get on that train. Back in Berlin, I barely had five minutes to catch the Frankfurt am Main train. Once aboard, I breathed a huge sigh of relief and stretched out, no one in the seat next to me.

When I arrived in Frankfurt, it was just getting dark, but still light enough for me to find the way to my hotel, only a few blocks from the train station. As the guidebook described it, the Pension Schneider turned out to be "a homely establishment in a sea of sleaze." The area near the train station was Frankfurt's red light district, with Eros clubs and bars everywhere, dubious characters standing in doorways and passing me on the sidewalks.

The Pension was a walk-up on the third floor, where I signed in. The proprietor, a friendly young woman, remarked that my German was quite good, and showed me the breakfast room (with service from 8 to 10 a.m.) and then up to the fourth floor, to my room. She gave me two keys—one for the room and the other to the fourth floor door, both of them tricky to work. Anyway, the room was quite nice—a little bathroom with a WC, and a TV besides the bed in the other room. I seemed to be the only guest on the floor.

After getting settled, I went out for a walk around. It was hot in Frankfurt, too, about the same temperature as in Berlin before it cooled off. As the guidebook stated, Frankfurt was packed with skyscrapers, and I kept craning my neck to take in the full view of several of them near the hotel. I had planned to go up to the observation deck of the Main Tower, one of the tallest skyscrapers and reportedly the best view of Frankfurt. But it was in an area deserted at that time of day, so I passed it up. Also, I wanted to eat a leisurely dinner and get back to the hotel before dark.

Near the hotel, I settled at a table in a sidewalk café, the Brassiere Kaiserstrasse. There I ordered what I considered to be the only authentically German meal of my trip—Wurst, Sauerkraut, mashed potatoes and beer; all delicious. Walking back to the hotel, I witnessed a spectacular sunset and captured it on film. In my room, too tired to do anything else, I watched an old movie, Jack Nicholson in "Wolf," and went to sleep.

On my last morning in Germany, I left the hotel before 7:00 to take a long walk to one of the bridges over the Main River and back, using up my last roll of film. In the hotel, I ate breakfast, showered, packed, and checked out. Having bought a Fahrkarte, I eventually made my way to the S-Bahn and to the airport. Once there, I passed through several security checkpoints, then bought a novel to read and sat in the lounge to wait for the flight to Pittsburgh and from there to Buffalo.

This trip had met all my expectations: meeting my father's relatives and establishing cordial relationships with them, tracing my father's roots in Cadenberge and experiencing the great cities of Hamburg, Berlin and Frankfurt. I was very glad I'd taken it.

38

Joy, then Sorrow

Two days in 2004 were exceptional: the first, one of the happiest in recent years, and the second, one of the saddest.

The first, a reconciliation with Marion on Mother's Day, was totally unexpected, particularly so because of the correspondence between Bob and Marion earlier that year. Attempting to end her long estrangement from him, Bob had sent her a book as a Christmas gift. Marion responded angrily with a photograph showing a broken doll, captioned "It was for my own good," and the message, "We have issues." Her accompanying letter explained that what she expected was a dialogue about her mistreatment as a child and teenager. Bob responded with a defensive letter, followed by her long letter listing the mistreatment she said she'd endured from both of us, some details so bizarre as to suggest that she had false memories of her childhood.

I was especially pained to read Marion's accusations directed towards me—all untrue—and I felt that Bob's having initiated a discussion with Marion was like opening a Pandora's box. Their brief correspondence ended when a letter from Bob in March went unanswered. With no hope of seeing Marion, I planned a trip to the West Coast for a visit with Darcy and also with Werner, and friends Jill and Richard in Big Sur. But before leaving on that trip, I made my usual visit to Helen, and then went to Indianapolis to attend the bat mitzvah of Dena, Faedra and Lou Weiss's youngest daughter. While in Indianapolis, I had breakfast with Jim and Monica.

On May 7, I flew to Oakland, then took BART to Pleasant Hill and checked in at a hotel. Darcy picked me up and drove to Berkeley, where we had dinner at an Indian restaurant. I gave Darcy a book from Bob, *Beautiful Buffalo*, recently published; and Darcy said he was sure it would be interesting reading. He said Bob had been correct in his "vision for Buffalo," which included locating the new University's campus in Buffalo. He remembered passing out pamphlets promoting the Committee for an Urban University's campaign while he attended summer school.

The next day, Saturday, we visited Martinez, on the Bay, an older city, parts of which Darcy said reminded him of Buffalo. We stopped at a marina to watch several men—one of them on roller blades—flying big, colorful kites. The roller blader let the kite, blown like a sail by a stiff breeze, propel him around the marina. It was a peaceful place—no traffic noise to mar the quiet. On the way back to Pleasant Hill, we passed by the John Muir National Historical Site, the seventeen-room Victorian house where naturalist Muir spent the last twenty-four years of his life. It was almost closing time, so we didn't take a tour, but I bought a postcard.

Sunday, Mother's Day, was like no other. Darcy had arranged a ferry trip to Angel Island, which promised spectacular views of the Bay, San Francisco, and the Golden Gate. The Island, a popular Sunday afternoon destination for picnickers, was originally used by the Coast Miwok Indians for hunting and fishing. Later, for almost one hundred years, the Island housed a variety of military installations. It also played a major role in the settlement of the west, opening as an immigration station in 1910 to accommodate the flood of immigrants arriving in California, closing in 1940.

Darcy arrived at my hotel the next morning, bearing a sweet Mother's Day gift, a platter of fresh fruit—strawberries, cantaloupe slices, and a banana. I ate some of the strawberries and melon while Darcy drove to Tiburon to catch the ferry to Angel Island. After the breezy 30-40 minute ferry ride across the Bay, we got off with the others, many carrying picnic baskets.

Once on shore, we consulted a map and decided to take one of the perimeter walks, about a two-hour hike. We were among the few hikers, most folks preferring to ride in the public vans. The weather was perfect for hiking, and the views, from high on the island, were panoramic. Darcy suggested we not attempt the trail to the summit of Mt. Carolina Livermore in order to return for the 1:20 ferry back to Tiburon. I'd learn the reason later.

Leaving Tiburon, we headed north on Sir Francis Drake Boulevard—a route leading to Point Reyes. Darcy explained, "We're taking this drive to bring back memories of the time you spent in Point Reyes three years ago." At Inverness, he turned up a side road up a hill where, he said, we'd have a good view of the countryside. Winding up a narrow road, we passed several artists' residences and studios. Finally, he stopped and parked in a space that appeared reserved for the owners of the house next it. To my question, Darcy said, "It's okay." He got out of the car, knocked on the door, and beckoned me to come. I was absolutely speechless when Marion opened the door, Michael next to her. After a moment, Marion and I embraced, and then Michael and I. All three were amused at how surprised I was; Darcy had managed to keep our meeting a secret.

I hardly recognized Marion and Michael, as they'd changed so much in appearance since I'd last seen them. They were both heavier as well as older (although Marion had retained some of her striking good looks). Marion poured us cold drinks, and Michael showed me around their house and yard. Their property, high up in the forest above the valley, included their contemporary home, a separate cabin, and a tool shed. Michael said that ever since a devastating fire in 1995 came near their house and burned some of the trees, he had kept the undergrowth cut, set new trees a safe distance from the house, and eliminated fast-burning shrubs. Retired from the railroad but now working on projects related to transportation, Michael used the cabin as his office.

Inside the house, I noticed three large photographs by Marion hung on the wall in the dining/seating area. One, a macro image, was of vividly red mushrooms against a black background, quite striking. Commenting on the photographs, Marion said, "These were done in a past phase; I'm very much into digital photography now." She and Michael had gone together to a number of photography workshops in the U.S. and Canada, Marion also on her own. She said that she was now taking a painting class; one of her recent paintings was hanging on another wall.

Over a dinner of grilled lamb, a salad made with vegetables from their garden, lemon tart, coffee and wine, Marion and Michael told us about their recent travels to New Zealand, which they prized highly, and Tuscany. Marion said Tuscany was nice but she wouldn't have wanted to stay more than a few days because "It was boring—nothing to do there." She liked Florence, Italy; Michael liked Milan. I told them about my trip to Germany and meeting relatives there, and she commented that her birthplace, Gelnhausen, was near Frankfurt.

Before we left, Marion, Michael and I embraced again, telling each other, "Take care." I thought several times of taking a photograph of Marion but didn't, fearing that it would be an invasion of privacy; I did take a photograph of the painting. Darcy had some difficulty finding his way back in the dark but eventually found the right road back, to San Francisco and then to Pleasant Hill. As he dropped me off at my hotel, we gave each other a fond embrace and said goodbye.

The next day I flew to Eugene, and Werner met me at the airport. At the hotel, he gave me a key to the guest room, where I'd stayed the last time I visited him. Werner fixed lunch—chili and quiche—and we retired for naps afterwards. We had dinner in the communal dining room that evening, Werner having brought his own bottle of wine. Werner had a light supper. He explained he got very little exercise and didn't want to gain weight.

After breakfast the next morning, I walked to the Farmers Market near the hotel and bought a bunch of the prized morel mushrooms, strawberries and eggs, with which Werner made a tasty omelet for lunch—a real treat for me. That afternoon he told me more about his life, and then played two short pieces for me. I was happy to hear that he still "had the touch." That evening we met his musician son, Richard, for dinner. Richard said he was very busy with musical engagements and would be playing bass in a concert in the Eugene Symphony Hall that night featuring renowned violinist Yo-Yo-Ma. Although I couldn't have foreseen it, that would be the last time I'd be with Werner.

Werner dropped me off at the airport the next morning, planning to play duo-piano that afternoon with his friend, Candyce. After flying first to Seattle, then Los Angeles, and finally to Monterey, I found my friends Jill and Richard Russo waiting for me at the airport. It was late by the time we arrived at their house, so I went right to bed. In the two days I was there, I took long walks each morning along the highway, noticing the many trees dying of an uncontrollable disease. The first day we had lunch at Nepenthe, the popular bar-restaurant sited 808 feet above sea level on the crest of a hill overlooking Big Sur. Browsing in the Phoenix gift shop, I was captivated by "the spinner," a copper mobile, and bought one, hanging it above our terrace when I returned home. There it spun whenever there was a breeze and was a continual reminder of beautiful Big Sur.

The second day I watched Jill as she planted flowers and vegetables and Richard went up on the roof to trim tree branches. Sitting out on the terrace, I enjoyed the view of the coast, listened to the crashing waves, and watched humming birds silently flitting to and from a nearby feeder. Jill told me more about herself—her early life, and how she'd always been interested in the arts, which is how she met Jack Solomon. She made a point of showing me her "music room" where she listens to classical music. Before dropping me off at the airport the next day, Jill and Richard treated me to a fine breakfast of vegetarian sausages and English muffins in historic Deetjen's Big Sur Inn, on the way to Monterey.

At the Oakland airport that evening, I walked through the airport to find the Jet Blue section. Imagine my surprise when I saw Darcy sitting in the arrival section, waiting for me! He said he'd re-read my letter and, seeing I had a several-hour layover, decided to come to the airport to meet me. We left the airport and he drove to

Berkeley, where we had dinner at a Thai restaurant, sitting at a table on the patio while a continual stream of people passed by. After conversation during dinner and a bit of a walk later, he took me back to the airport, and then we said a final "Goodbye." As I thought about this later, his wanting to see me again was a portent.

After the heart-warming visit I'd had with Darcy and Marion in May, I was completely unprepared for Darcy's call to us on August 23, the day before Bob's birthday. He blurted out, "I'm broke!" I couldn't believe it. Just a few months earlier, he seemed his usual self, spending money freely during my visit. He told us that he was out of work, had maxed out his credit card and was behind on both car and house payments. After a long discussion after the call, Bob and I agreed we would send him $10,000 as a loan to be repaid.

On October 4, I called Darcy. He said he'd gone for an interview but didn't think he'd get the job he was after. He had also been invited to sign a book contract, but hadn't. A week later I donated Darcy's precious baby clothes, many of which I'd sewn myself, to La Casa Vive, the center for refugees waiting to enter Canada. The Casa folks were happy to get them, and I was glad to know they'd be used rather than sitting in my closet. When I'd first opened the box in which I'd saved the clothes, I was sad to think they wouldn't be passed down to grandchildren. And when I looked at the family portrait of us taken when he and Marion were both here for their grandfather's funeral, it broke my heart. At age twenty-four he was a handsome young man, in a good position in San Francisco and a promising future.

In a long telephone call to him on his birthday, October 31, he said he needed more money, but Bob said we couldn't continue to send him funds. He had obviously been living beyond his means for some time. He said his consulting work had dried up after the 2001 attack: Federal monies for new transportation projects, on which his work depended, had become scarce. We did send another $3,000 in November. In a subsequent call soon after, Darcy, sounding very depressed, said that his closest friend had died unexpectedly. After the call, Bob said, "I might fly out to see Darcy during the Christmas holidays." I agreed that was a good idea.

The saddest news was yet to come. On the morning of my birthday, December 24, I received a phone call from Steve, followed by one from Helen, and then from Jim, all with the sad news that Richard, coming to check on Werner, had found him dead in his apartment. Werner had for years suffered from various health problems, which he largely kept to himself. Apparently one or a combination of problems had caused his death.

Later in the day, Darcy called, and we had a short chat, during which he said he was very sorry to hear about Werner. Later that evening, Steve called: On their way to Oregon, he, Heidi and Kieran were stranded in Buffalo by a storm. I invited them over for breakfast the next morning. Having Steve, Heidi and Kieran here Christmas morning was comforting, and it made the day less sad than it might have been. They stayed till afternoon, and we reminisced about Werner.

After they left, I unwrapped Bob's Christmas present—a beautiful wool boucle coat with a real fox fur collar and cuffs. It fit perfectly, and I felt elegant every time I wore it—the nicest present Bob ever gave me. Opening Werner's birthday gift to me sent tears to my eyes. The note with the box of Godiva chocolates read, "Happy Sweet Birthday." I was saddened to think that he was so thoughtful when he himself must have been feeling poorly. As Bob had planned, he flew out to Oakland after Christmas and spent two days there seeing Darcy.

In January, I flew to Eugene for Werner's memorial, held in the hotel where he lived, the auditorium filled with his many friends and relatives. Helen, Richard, Steve, Kieran and I all participated, Helen and I recounting fond memories. Twelve years younger than Werner, I had always been in awe of him, with his many accomplishments, but had loved him dearly. Steve, with his flute, Richard on bass, and Kieran on cello played some of Werner's favorite music; and Candyce played Clair De Lune. While he didn't participate in the program, Jim Allen, also there, had come to know Werner, as he would stay with Jim and Monica on the occasions he visited an old friend in Indianapolis. A reception followed the program, and afterwards Helen and I went to a private party held at the home of one of Werner's friends.

The previous afternoon, we had all gone to the country to the vineyard established by Werner and Faye, now under a new owner. In a grove of trees, we held a brief ceremony, Steve reading the Jewish prayer of committal. I wept as Steve and Heidi scattered Werner and Faye's ashes at the foot of their favorite tree, a fitting resting place. Faye had died years earlier, in 1990, in Eugene. Afterwards, I took a picture of us, including Susan Meyn, the widow of Werner's oldest son, David, who also lived in Indianapolis.

l-r: Helen Allen, Richard Meyn, Susan Meyn, Jim Allen, Steve, Heidi, and Kieran Meyn, together to remember Werner. January, 2005

Back in Buffalo, I decided to continue my new relationship with Marion, sending her a beautiful white, wool stole her mother had knit for me. In a letter accompanying the stole, Frances had explained that the stole was a gift to me for having adopted Marion. Marion wrote soon after, saying how moved she'd been to receive the stole, as she'd never had anything from her mother before. I also sent her a snapshot of her mother holding baby Marion, which Bob's mother had given us years before. I felt Marion should have that, too. Apparently, I'd made the right moves: Marion and I resumed a regular correspondence, and for my birthday that year she sent a lovely mohair scarf she had knit. It made my day.

Unfortunately, Darcy's situation had not improved. Bob tried to persuade him to come back to Buffalo, but Darcy was adamant about staying in California, his home, he said. He called me on Mother's Day, as he had faithfully for many years, and we had a bittersweet conversation—he reminiscing about the many pleasurable experiences we'd shared, dating way back to the days in Cambridge. We did not discuss his survival plans; he was still living in Pleasant Hill.

But soon after we talked he was forced out of his apartment and began living in his car. As might have been foreseen, he was robbed soon after, having his car broken into and both his birth certificate and driver's license stolen. Somehow, he was managing to survive; and as Christmas approached he sent us a card, with a "Happy Birthday" to me and a "Merry Christmas" to both Bob and me. He wrote that his phone had been disconnected but that otherwise he was fine. All Bob and I could do was hope for the best.

39

Christo's Gates, then a Plan

In January, the news that "The Gates," an installation by Artists Christo and Jean-Claude would open in Central Park in mid-February, captured my fancy. The project would consist of 7500 gates framing the Park's pathways, trailing swaths of bright, saffron-colored fabric, blowing in the breeze. Christo and Jean-Claude were famous for their various installations around the world including their most publicized, wrapping the Berlin Reichstag in silvery fabric, completed in 1995.

I figured this might be the only opportunity to see one of their installations. My good friend, Suzanne Taub, was also intrigued, and we spent the second weekend in February in New York. That Saturday afternoon, freezing cold but sunny and crystal clear, we went to see "The Gates," joined by Jack Miller, whom I'd met during the NYS convention in Cooperstown, New York several years ago, and his friend, John Sorrentino, a New York city architect who knew Bob. They picked us up at our hotel, and John found a parking place near one of the entrances to the Park.

As we'd imagined, walking through "The Gates" with crowds of others, young and old, was magical—the Park totally transformed by the brilliant orange flags—and Jack and I took photo after photo. After an hour's walk, thoroughly chilled, we left Central Park, ate a warming lunch in a restaurant near the park, and then stopped at the Museum of Modern Art to see some of the exhibits. Among the art, I spotted a large canvas by the rising young painter, Julie Mehretu, whose architecturally-themed paintings had also been exhibited at the Albright-Knox Gallery. When we left the Museum, John and Jack dropped us off at our hotel, thanking us for including them in our plan to see "The Gates".

During the weekend we also had dinner with Suzanne's youngest son, Michael, an attorney, and his partner, Alejandra. One night we dined at a Brazilian restaurant and the next at another popular ethnic restaurant. Sunday afternoon Suzanne and I managed to find our way back via bus and subway to the JFK Airport, and then back to Buffalo.

Still excited about seeing "The Gates," I decided to enter the best of my photos, together with a CD including Leonard Bernstein's "New York, New York" as a fitting musical accompaniment, in the

Camera Club's annual essay competition. The essays, six or seven of them, were shown at the annual banquet in May. My essay didn't fare well: The judge commented that these were only a series of photos without a theme. Of course I was disappointed, but I had to concede he had a point.

I don't recall when the idea first occurred to me, but by early 2005 I had become increasingly intrigued with the idea of travelling to Peru and seeing Machu Picchu—reputed to be one of the most spectacular archaeological sites in the world. I considered that such a trip might very well be the last big trip I'd ever take, as it meant cashing out the rest of my IRA account to cover it. In the downtown library, I had come across a fascinating book about Machu Picchu and had taken it home to read.

Besides numerous photographs of the site and color illustrations, the authors described what was once the royal estate built by an Incan emperor for himself and his guests as an escape from the pressures of the capital. Then I read another book, *Lost City of the Incas*. By then I was seriously considering joining a trip in late August sponsored by the Sierra Club. Travel within Peru included horseback riding in the Andes Mountains, hiking a section of the famous Inca Trail leading to Machu Picchu, experiencing Machu Picchu, and, finally, several days in the Amazon Rainforest. It sounded ideal. At my request, the Sierra Cub sent me a packet of information; and by March 31 I had signed on to the trip. During my visit with Helen in April (see photo next page), I told her about the trip. She agreed that it sounded like a great opportunity, and I made plane reservations then and there.

As Bob and I had a family membership at the Erie Community College's athletic center, I began regularly working out at the center, using the exercise machines to strengthen my leg and arm muscles, considering the strenuous hiking ahead in Peru. Having ordered appropriate camping clothes and equipment from Campmor, when the box arrived, it was like opening a Christmas present. I'd never used trekking poles, so I practiced using them, going up and down the hills at Tiffts Nature Preserve. Then I signed up for riding lessons at Greendale Farms in Orchard Park, a Buffalo suburb. Being mounted on a horse for the first time felt very strange indeed, but by the end of the first lesson I felt more at ease. By the fourth and final riding lesson, August 23, I felt fairly comfortable on a horse. Finally, I was ready to begin the trip.

Helen Allen, on her 85th birthday. April 29, 2005

40

My Last Big Trip

Bob dropped me off at the airport on August 27, and then I was on my way to Peru. First stop was in Lima, and at the airport—bewildered by the crowd meeting arriving passengers—I was relieved to meet my transport driver, who identified himself with a sign held up in the air and took me to my hotel. There I met Elizabeth (Liz) Asmis, who would be my roommate during the trip. Liz had come from Germany some years ago and was currently living in Chicago, teaching classics at the University of Chicago.

The next day we got on a plane for the short flight to Cusco, having a spectacular view of the Andes Mountains. Our trip guide, Edwin, met us at the airport there and accompanied us in the van to our hotel, the Hotel des Andes. In our shared room, on the lower floor, both Liz and I breathed a sigh of relief, finally at the end of each of our long trips to Cusco.

The beautiful city of Cusco, with a population of about 350,000, once the foremost city of the Inca Empire, was now the undisputed archaeological capital of the Americas, as well as the continent's oldest continuously inhabited city. Massive Inca-built walls lined the city's central streets and formed the foundations of both colonial and modern buildings. Many of the cobbled streets were stepped, narrow and thronged with Quechua-speaking descendants of the conquistadors. A wealth of colonial treasures could be found in the churches and mansions of the Spanish conquistadors; however, the city's economy now was almost totally at the whim of the international tourists coming to Peru and Cusco in increasing numbers.

A brief orientation in the hotel lobby by Edwin, himself from Cusco, was our introduction to this fair city; and we had our first taste of the coca tea, reputed to be good in warding off altitude sickness: Cusco is at about 11,000 feet. Edwin said, "Take it easy the first day; eat lightly, preferably fruit, soup and fish, and no alcohol. By tomorrow, you should have adjusted." I'd decided not to take any medication beforehand to prevent altitude sickness. Liz said she'd been taking Daimox but planned to stop, as she didn't think it was doing any good.

After getting settled in our room, Liz and I went for a short walk around, going as far as the Plaza de Armas, just a few blocks from our hotel. The Plaza is the main square in Cusco, with Cusco's most famous cathedral, La Catedral, on the northeastern end. As it had been chilly in Lima, we were glad to find it sunny and warm here, and sat down on a bench to take in the scene. We were instantly recognized as tourists, and we fended off several shoeshine boys. A little girl walking with her father stopped and stared at us until her father led her away. Later that afternoon, I took a long walk by myself and was completely charmed by the picturesque streets and beautiful plazas, historical buildings, and the colorful clothes worn by the Peruvian women and girls—the older women in their bright skirts and black top hats.

That evening we all gathered for a trip orientation by our trip leader, Rochelle Gerratt, from Oro Valley, Arizona. The orientation included introducing and telling a bit about ourselves and why we selected this trip. There were sixteen men and women, of all ages, in our group, from various places around the U.S., and we were all looking forward to a great adventure. Following our orientation, we walked out of the hotel to a nearby restaurant, where we all sat at a long table. During dinner we were nicely entertained by two separate groups of musicians, playing Peruvian music with traditional instruments. The first group of musicians played several sets for four dancers, two young men and women, dressed in Peruvian costumes. I should have had my camera with me to photograph them.

After breakfast the next day, Monday, I took my camera and went exploring. I stopped again in the Plaza de Armas, with its fine view of the hills above Cusco, and sat on one of the benches all around the square, enjoying the atmosphere. There I was approached by a young fellow, selling postcards, who engaged me in conversation. He said he would be finishing school in another year and then hoped to attend a university. He said he knew someone from Cusco who now lived in Sacramento, California and that he would also like to get to the States. I managed to put off buying any postcards and also refused any sales from other vendors.

Later I joined several in our group for a tour of the non-profit textile center. At the center, the director explained the various techniques and varieties of wool used by Peruvians through the ages, and we walked through a number of rooms where display cases held beautiful examples of weaving. We watched four Peruvians, three ladies and one gentleman, busily weaving in the main room. Of course, we were expected to buy something, so I did, but limited my purchase to a small piece of red and black wool, like a ribbon, that I planned to tie to one of my trekking poles.

Leaving the others at the center, I walked back to the hotel alone, along the main thoroughfare, the Avenue del Sol. Very long and wider than most in Cusco, the street was filled with cars, taxis and vans, as well as pedestrians. I had a fleeting moment of panic when I thought I was lost; but then I spied the familiar Catedral and found my way back.

That afternoon we all went with Edwin on an extensive tour to see two of the most famous cathedrals in Cusco: first, Santa Domingo, built on Coricancha, the Inca site that formed the base of the church. Coricancha, Quechuan for "golden courtyard," was the largest of the Inca temples. In Inca times it was literally covered with gold, as the temple walls were lined with some seven hundred solid gold sheets. There were also solid gold altars, life-size llamas and babies, as well as a replica of the sun. But all this incredible wealth was looted by the first conquistadores, melted down and used in their cathedrals and homes. Edwin said, "This site represents four levels of culture—Incan, medieval Catholicism, the recent monastery, and now a few modern buildings,"—and then led us on a brief tour through the cathedral.

Next we went to La Catedral, richly decorated. I marveled at the wealth represented by an entire altar of silver in one of the many richly-furnished chapels in the cathedral, its many wall-size paintings decorated with gold leaf, and gold and silver used profusely throughout. In one of the chapels, a black Jesus hung from the cross. Edwin told us the Spanish trained Peruvians to execute the paintings of Spanish noblemen and their families which hung on the walls. Everything was most impressive. But the Catedral was frigid; chilled to the bone, I was relieved when we left and I was back in the sun.

The next morning Liz and I packed up, and we all left Cusco, our destination Lares, where we would begin the mountain-riding segment of our trip. Our van stopped first at the Inca ruins at Sachsyhuaman, just outside of Cusco. We stayed there about an hour, walking around with Edwin as he explained details of the site. Sachsyhuaman, Quechan for "satisfied falcon," was built as a fortress by the Incans and was believed to have been occupied by as many as 5,000 Incan warriors. It was the scene of one of the most bitter battles of the Spanish conquest, when the Spaniards retook the fortress. They tore down the walls and used many of the massive blocks to build their own houses in Cusco, leaving only the largest, one of which was estimated to weigh over 300 tons. I took a picture of Rochelle and her partner, Roger, standing, dwarfed, in front of one of the blocks, which must have been twenty feet high and about as wide.

Opposite the ruins was the hill called Rodadero. The stone benches carved in the hillside were used for seating the Inca nobles, who watched the ceremonies that took place on the parade ground, the level area between the ruins and the hill. The parade ground was now used for the annual ceremonies on June 24, marking the winter solstice, with the participants dressed as Incan warriors. The colorful celebration, Inti Raymi, was a popular tourist attraction.

Leaving Sachsyhuaman, we continued on our way to Lares, to meet our trekking crew and horses. Our experienced driver maneuvered the seemingly endless breathtaking hairpin curves and switchbacks skillfully. I watched from my window seat as one panoramic view after another swept past my eyes. We stopped once, at a high pass of about 15,500 feet, an opportunity for us to get out our cameras for photographs. But without a panoramic camera, it was impossible to capture the majestic view.

Finally arriving at Lares, we met our crew, composed of the wranglers, who would take care of the horses and equipment, and the cooks who would prepare the meals. We each had a brief introduction to our respective horses, selected for us according to our sex, size and experience, and then tried mounting and dismounting. Edwin took me to my horse, Suffa, who proved to be very gentle, sure-footed, and not easily spooked. When I made the mistake of walking behind Suffa, Edwin warned, "Don't ever do that again; it frightens the horse and you may get kicked."

After a lunch of sandwiches and cold drinks, we set off, all of us mounted on our horses and Edwin on the lead horse, on the trail out of camp. As we rode out and began winding up a steep mountain trail, I was incredulous. I couldn't believe that, after only four brief riding lessons back in Buffalo I could be risking my life, riding on steep trails barely wider than my horse and no protective barrier on the right hand side. I didn't dare look off to the right but imagined the abyss below. Others with limited riding experience must have been having the same thought—nothing for it but to trust the sure-footedness of one's horse.

After an hour or so of riding, my initial sense of panic had subsided; and by late afternoon I began to feel fairly comfortable riding. But then a disquieting incident occurred. Our pack of horses, with Edwin in the lead, had been descending a mountain trail and were about to cross a narrow bridge over a ravine to continue on the trail along the mountain on the other side. All of a sudden there was a commotion ahead. A small landslide had deposited loose soil on the trail, and Edwin's horse had slipped and lost its footing, sliding all the way, fifty or more feet down into the ravine.

Luckily, quick-thinking Edwin had jumped off the horse as soon as he felt it slipping. Those of us well behind Edwin saw the horse—still upright—down in the ravine but didn't know what had happened. Meanwhile, some of the wranglers cleared the trail, and we all passed safely, crossing the bridge and continuing up the trail on the opposite side. Two of the wranglers descended the ravine and somehow brought the horse back up. Not too long afterwards, we reached our camp, and I was thankful to have arrived safely.

Our crew had already set up tents, and Liz and I put our belongings in one of them. It was good to stretch our legs after riding all afternoon; and we both wandered off—in different directions—for brief walks around the campsite. All of us, I'm sure, were totally ready for "happy hour" at about 7:00. As if to reward us for our mountain riding initiation, Edwin treated us with martinis, topped off with green olives. To offset the alcohol, we also had a choice of hot coffee, hot chocolate, or hot tea, and piles of popcorn. Dinner followed soon after: a delicious hot soup and then a main course of chicken, carrots and rice, with strawberries and cream for dessert. Soon after, Liz and I said, "Good night." I felt snug and warm in my North Face down sleeping bag.

The next morning broke with a beautiful sunrise, the sun ascending over the mountains and bathing our camp in sunshine. We packed up after a hearty breakfast of French toast and syrup, sausages and coffee. I had planned to hike with Rochelle and a few others, but after only fifteen minutes felt completely enervated. I joined a half dozen other hikers feeling the same way, and we walked downhill to the place where we would have lunch. I was amazed to discover how much energy it took for even downhill hiking at this high altitude. We were then at probably between 12,000-14,000 feet. With hearty appetites, we were all most appreciative of the delicious hot soup, followed by rice and vegetables, with plenty of good Peruvian bread on the side.

After lunch we had a long break, and some of us napped or otherwise relaxed. We set out again at 2:30. The last part of the trail was quite easy, and we reached camp at 4:00. Here, in a valley it felt much colder, and I immediately put on warm layers. We had all been advised to bring winter clothes, and I had brought a wool sweater, fleece vest, fleece jacket, mittens and a wool cap.

In camp, we exchanged notes about the day's ride. Mary, one of the less experienced riders, said that her horse had suddenly gone off the trail and lain on its side; "I got off just in time!" Laura, in the tent next to ours, said her horse, apparently spooked by something, had pushed her right leg against a rock, and the leg had swollen. She had, of course, brought antiseptic and bandages and was sitting in the tent, nursing her leg. I thought how lucky I was to have Suffa as my horse.

During happy hour, we imbibed more martinis and hot chocolate. Then we dined on good hot soup, followed by trout served in a sauce. Soon after dinner, Liz and I settled in our sleeping bags. That night, to make sure I wouldn't wake up freezing, I kept on all my clothes and even pulled my fleece coat into the sleeping bag as an extra layer.

The pancakes served for breakfast the next morning cooled quickly, and we ate them hurriedly. On the trail that morning, Brian, the youngest of our group and one of the few hikers, broke into a run as the trail sloped downhill. Unfortunately, he slipped and fell flat on his face. We stopped and watched while Edwin, assisted by Pepe, another guide who joined us at Lares, quickly administered first aid. We could see that Brian was bleeding profusely. Edwin thought at first his nose might be broken, but then decided it wasn't. After Brian was well bandaged and helped onto his horse, we continued on our way.

The trek today continued upward, ascending into the higher altitudes. I abandoned my plan of hiking and rode all morning instead. We stopped for lunch in a little valley, just below the 15,200 ft. pass to which we would climb. It was cloudy and cold, and I was glad I'd worn enough warm clothes. As we were eating a most delicious vegetable soup, it suddenly started to hail... right in our soup! It was so bizarre we all laughed while pea-sized bits of hail continued to fall. Nevertheless, we finished the rest of our lunch. As we said to each other, hail is better than snow; it would have been messier. I wished later I'd gotten my camera and recorded this odd event; the landscape was all white, covered with hail. It continued hailing for about fifteen minutes more and then stopped as the sun broke through.

After lunch we climbed to the pass—way up in the clouds. When we stopped to give the horses a break, I saw in my mind's eye what promised to be a most unusual photograph. I quickly got my camera, climbed a little hill above the horses and people, and photographed the group, set against a backdrop of mountains and sky. Back on the trail, it was all downhill.

In the valley below lay a beautiful blue lake, and I wondered whether we would be camping near it. I decided to walk the remaining trail to our camp below—about an hour and a half's hiking. I managed it, overcoming feelings of tiredness and forcing myself on. The trail down through pine forests and scrub reminded me of the landscape at Point Reyes, in California. We finally reached camp at 4:00, and I was very glad to relax.

Happy hour that night featured red wine. Pepe called for anyone with a corkscrew so he could open the bottles. I came to the rescue—I had one in my Swiss knife. The cooks had done our dinner outdoors, heating stones in the fire pit and then placing lamb, fish and potatoes, wrapped in parcels, to roast on the stones. While we waited for dinner, Edwin took us outside the tent to see the panorama in the crystal clear skies. He pointed out the Southern Cross—which I'd never seen before—the Milky Way, and other constellations. When dinner was finally served to our hungry group, it was, indeed, a feast—with chocolate pudding for dessert. Liz and I went to bed almost immediately after dinner, and I slept soundly.

The next morning it didn't seem that cold, but I realized it must have gone down to freezing, as there was a thin layer of ice on the water in the wash basins, set outside our tent. It seemed to take forever, but when it was finally served, the breakfast of omelettes and bread was delicious. As this would be our last horseback riding day, a little ceremony was held after breakfast. With our trusty crew gathered together, Rochelle thanked each of the wranglers and cooks and also presented them a generous tip to show our appreciation. Besides getting a photograph of the group, I used the occasion to photograph my faithful horse and the young wrangler who took care of Suffa and was always attentive, there to lend his assistance whenever I needed it. He always helped me mount and dismount: I couldn't do that myself.

Then we had about a two-hour trail ride down towards Urabamba, in the Sacred Valley of the Incas, all downhill on a rocky trail, no problems. We stopped for lunch about noon and then walked down to a point near Urabamba, a town with a population of about 8,000 and a convenient base from which tourists could explore nearby historic sites. As we walked down the trail, we passed the homes of people living on the outskirts. Judging by their houses, these urban folk seemed to be far better off than those in the mountains.

Before we left camp that morning, Edwin had taken us to see the dwelling of a family living near our campsite. The cramped house had a thatched roof covering several small rooms, one of which, the kitchen, had a fire burning when we were there. It was smoky and dark inside; and we guessed that its inhabitants spent as much time as they could outdoors during the day. The family lived off what produce they could raise and the woven items they succeeded in selling to groups like ours. Edwin told us, "Last year, many people died because the weather was unusually bitter and cold."

We had become accustomed to having Peruvian women, sometimes with their young children, bring blankets, rugs and other colorful woven things near our campsites to sell, always sitting a discreet distance away. Usually one or more in our group would buy things—if for no other reason, as a contribution to them. On the last day in the mountains, I gave away some candy to a Peruvian woman and her two daughters sitting near our campsite. Rewarded by bright smiles, I took their picture.

As we neared Urabamba, several of us chose to ride in the van to our hotel rather than walk the remaining miles. At the very attractive, modern hotel, with a beautiful, 360-degree view of the Andes, we were assigned to our motel-like cabins. Our room seemed absolutely luxurious to me after having spent the past several days "roughing it" in the mountains. As it turned out, Liz had a long walk and did not get to the hotel until a couple of hours later—completely exhausted—so I had the room all to myself.

When I saw myself in the mirror for the first time since leaving Cusco, I was shocked. I looked a fright! But after a long hot shower and shampoo, I felt halfway decent again. The mirror revealed the lingering effects of edema, a condition I first noticed the second day in the mountains. The high altitude affects blood pressure, causing body tissues to retain water. As a result, one's hands, feet and legs especially become swollen. I could see that even my face was puffy. That puffiness, in fact, did not completely subside until the last few days of the trip. But, I told myself, it was a small price to pay. At least I didn't experience the severe headaches or nausea that most of the people in our group experienced at one time or another in Peru.

Before dinner, several of us went to a Peruvian textile outlet, which had many beautiful items made of alpaca wool on display and for sale. Thinking it was time for me to buy a gift for Bob, I selected a pair of soft black socks for him. I also bought a gorgeous fringed, red winter scarf for Helen. Both were very reasonably priced—certainly much less than one would pay for goods exported to the U.S.

Dinner that evening was special. We celebrated with Georgia, from Salt Lake City, as she observed her sixty-third birthday. Ecstatic, she said, "This was the best possible way to spend my birthday." Rochelle had even arranged a birthday cake. While we dined, Peruvian musicians played for the enjoyment of our group as well as other diners. We were amused when they played a few Beattles numbers, I suppose thinking the Americans among the hotel guests would appreciate hearing them. Soon after dinner, Liz and I went to bed, delighting in the prospect of sleeping in a comfortable bed, with clean linens, and in a nice, warm room.

This was truly a day I'd never forget. After a fine breakfast in the hotel, we packed and got on a bus for a short ride to the train that took tourists from Cusco to Machu Picchu and also stopped at Urubamba. We would ride the train as far as the Inca Trail connector, a point seven miles from Machu Picchu itself. On the train we were treated to views of the beautiful countryside along the Urubamba River. The river rapids were awesome; we heard that some of the rapids were navigable and that riding the river was one of the various activities tourists engage in while in the area.

Getting off the train, we set forth with backpacks and trekking poles. The young woman who accompanied us as our guide informed us that hiking this seven-mile section would probably take most of the day. She said that the first three hours would be the most grueling, the trail continuing steadily uphill on a stony path. We would have a break at Wiñay Wayna, the site of other Inca ruins, and eat lunch there.

Unused to this kind of hiking, I found it exhausting. Paul, a veteran mountain hiker, told me that establishing a steady pace with rhythmic breathing would help. I did adapt a pace comfortable for me, but I doubt I could have finished the trail—the most difficult of any I'd ever hiked—without the aid of my trekking poles. The poles served both as a support on the narrow trail and a great help in boosting myself up the many steep steps. Fortunately, we had frequent stops along the trail as our guide pointed out one beautiful orchid after another among those that grew profusely in this area— the Peruvian cloud forest. We also stopped along the way at the sheltered rest stops built to accommodate the many tourists who walk the Inca Trail.

It was during one of those stops that someone remarked, "If Sylvia can do it, so can I." Someone had asked Rochelle what the group's age range was. Brian was clearly the youngest, and I think everyone had already identified me as the oldest. Roger was the only retiree; the others, in various occupations were mostly middle-aged, a few older. When several of the other women said they were inspired by my example, I felt better about having my age revealed.

Relieved to arrive at Wiñay Wayna, we ate lunch, sitting on one of the many terraces cascading down the hillside. Wiñay Wayna was the site of one of a number of ceremonial centers erected by the Incas. The name means "everlasting youth," and I loved being there right then and there, because I felt that being able to hike a portion of the Inca Trail surely was a sign of everlasting youth. After we ate, we followed our guide through the remains of the buildings, marveling at the intricate stonework seen among the ruins. This was a great place for photos, and I, like everyone else, took advantage of the opportunity.

Continuing on, we met a number of hikers along the trail. Some had walked the entire 30-kilometer trail (about twenty miles), tent camping at the hostel we passed. In late afternoon we reached the Sun Gate, the dramatic entrance to the Machu Picchu ruins. Soon we were rewarded with our first glimpse of Machu Picchu. Although I'd seen many pictures of Machu Picchu, I was overwhelmed by the actual sight, absolutely breath-taking. I imagine that approaching Machu Picchu from above, as we did, is much more dramatic than approaching from below. Immediately, we all busied ourselves photographing this fabulous sight. Rochelle graciously took a picture of me with Machu Picchu in the background.

Sylvia at Machu Picchu, Peru. September, 2005

Machu Picchu is considered one of the best known and most spectacular archaeological sites in the world. What makes it so is its setting, carefully located and landscaped by the Incas, in perfect alignment with mountain peaks and constellations. While not religious, I felt a profound spiritual presence here. The ruins are located on a ridge which ends in the magnificent peak of Huayna Picchu. There are precipices on both sides and many terraces descending down into the valley.

Until its discovery by the American explorer, Hiram Bingham, in 1911, it remained unknown to scholars and travelers, just as it had Spanish chroniclers. Situated in the isolated Urabamba region of southern Peru, it was hidden by dense vegetation and familiar only to the farmers who grew subsistence crops on the grounds of the ancient site. Since Bingham's discovery, continuing excavations have revealed ever more information.

Having had a glimpse of Machu Picchu, to which we would return the next day, we were content to walk down to the tourist center, where we took a bus down a dizzying route of switchbacks to the town of Machu Picchu below. Once in town, we checked into our hotel. At dinner that evening, in one of the restaurants near our hotel, I joined others in our group celebrating with a pisco sour, a popular local drink, rather like the American whiskey sour. I had hoped to find a local delicacy such as roast guinea pig on the menu, but, disappointed, settled for a Quiche Lorraine.

The next morning we took the bus to Machu Picchu and then spent the morning touring the ruins, Edwin as our guide. He led us through the extensive ruins, up and down the stairways made of blocks of granite, pausing often to explain the particular temple or dwelling we visited. We passed through the Watchtower, a building on top of the ridge serving the Incas as a lookout for spotting any approaching enemies. We visited temple after temple and passed through the Sacred Plaza, with its altar. Near the altar was a wall which was believed to confer energy on those who pressed their palms on the stones. Several of us, including me, tried it; I suppose if you believed the wall conferred energy, it did.

I remember vividly the acrophobic climb to the highest hill, site of one of the temples. Looking up at the temple and the people gathered there, I wondered whether I could overcome my tendency to acrophobia, expecting our group would also make the climb. Determined to do it, and climbing up the steep, narrow steps, I kept my eyes on the step in front of me—never daring a look to the side. My trekking poles, planted on either side as I ascended, added support. Successfully achieving the climb, I also managed the climb back down. Georgia had opted out and met us at the foot of the hill.

Having achieved that climb, there was no way I was going to attempt the climb to the top of Huayna Picchu and I was secretly relieved it was not included in our schedule. But daring Liz did it anyway. She'd gone off by herself that morning, taken an earlier bus, and was at the ruins before us. There she noticed the passage leading to the peak and decided to attempt the steep ascent. She managed the vertiginous climb up, but once reaching the top had to struggle for a place among the other climbers who crowded the very small area.

As we toured the ruins, we marveled at the superb craftsmanship of the Incas. The stones from which the buildings were constructed—some weighing tons—were cut so perfectly that, without mortar or other material, they fit together like pieces in a puzzle. We passed by a place which Edwin said might have been a quarry and saw some stones, partially cut, still in the rock. How the Incas cut the stones and transported them is still open to speculation.

At the end of our tour, we took the bus back to our hotel. After we were treated to a 3-course lunch at a nearby restaurant, we returned to the hotel, packed up, and took the train back to Cusco. During the train ride, perfectly geared to tourists, a young woman and man strutted down the aisles showing off the latest in Peruvian styles. Back in our hotel in Cusco, we bid an affectionate farewell to Edwin. He had been not only an excellent guide but a friend and companion. I myself felt he had always looked out for us—and several times paid special attention to "Sylvie," as he called me. I gave him a hug and kiss.

We ate dinner that night in a restaurant known for its curry, and I chose a dish of vegetable curry and naan, unleavened bread, freshly-baked right in the restaurant's oven. During dinner, we listened to an environmentalist, currently living in Peru, who spoke about the challenging environmental issues facing Peru, as well as all of South America. The planned construction of the Peru-Brazil transcontinental highway was part of a 40-year old plan to connect the Atlantic to the Pacific. The highway, expected to cross areas of Peru now relatively isolated, promised new development and jobs. But environmentalists were concerned because the highway's route, cutting through a large piece of the Amazon cloud forest, would hasten the destruction of natural habitat in the area and alter patterns of human settlement. In the last leg of our trip, we would be traveling through the cloud forest into the rain forest, the very areas slated for change.

Back at the hotel that night, Liz and I packed, leaving behind whatever we wouldn't need in the rainforest. The next morning, we met David and Arturo, the guides who would accompany us on the next part of our trip. With David and Arturo joining us in the bus, we began the descent towards Manu National Park: From an elevation of 10,600 in Cusco, we would gradually descend to an elevation of about 250 in the Park. On the way, we stopped to view a distant mountain, Ausangate, at 6356 meters or a little under 21,000 feet, one of the highest mountains in Peru.

We stopped again at a place where about a dozen ancient funeraries still stood on a hill overlooking the valley. These funeral towers, reserved for the elite, were believed to have been created in the 8th or 9th century by people who lived there before the Incas. Each tower was just large enough to contain a mummy.

Arriving at the village of Paucartambo, we had a twenty-minute break, just long enough to get off the bus and take a short walk around. In the village, a picturesque stone bridge spanned a mountain street, with views of the Andes and the high Amazon Basin beyond. Then we went on to the cloud forest and the entrance to Manu National Forest. At the park center, we ate a picnic lunch and then had time to wander around taking note of the plants and trees typical of the cloud forest.

On the way again, we passed through the cloud forest, with its low hanging clouds, and finally across the mountain into the rain forest. The change was visibly noticeable—the beginning of luxurious green foliage and tropical plants. At one point, the driver stopped the van suddenly. As we were wondering what had happened, he motioned us to step quietly outside, which we did. A beautiful green snake, motionless, was paused right in the middle of the highway; after several minutes it stirred and slithered over to the opposite side, and we got back in the bus. As we neared our destination for the evening, we stopped several times to walk down the road, Arturo and David pointing out beautiful orchids and other native plants.

Near the Cock-of-the-Rock Lodge, where we would spend the night, we began seeing birds high in the dense trees. My binoculars were in my duffle bag on the bus, so I missed a closer look. But within walking distance of the lodge, we stopped at a bird blind, where I was entranced as we watched several of the brightly-colored cock-of-the-rock males performing their elaborate communal mating dances.

We arrived at the lodge just before a rain shower. Liz and I were delighted to find our lodging a comfortable cabin, complete with mosquito netting above the beds to ward off insects. Although there was no electricity, we had enough candles for light. We also had a shower with hot water and a flush toilet. After a delicious dinner in the lodge dining hall, Liz and I went to bed, pulling the mosquito netting down around us, a novelty for us both.

Liz and I were among those of us who rose at 5:30 and had a quick cup of hot coffee before walking to the bird blind. There we stayed about an hour to watch the beautiful cocks perform their mating dances, displaying their plumage as they flew in and out of the trees. The males, in brilliant red plumage, did their best to attract a mate, as the plainer females watched. It was exciting to see a few aerial matings.

Later, at breakfast, we were given a list by our guides of some hundred or more species of birds we could expect to see while in the rainforest. After breakfast we got in the van for a four-hour long ride deeper into the heart of the jungle, stopping once in a village for a half-hour break. There we found a general store which sold everything from car batteries to bottled water and snacks.

Getting back on the van, we continued on to a camp near the Madre de Dios River. There the guides divided our group into two, each group boarding one of the two eight-passenger riverboats, David with one group and Arturo with the other. Our belongings were stored on board, and we put on lifejackets and settled in our seats for our first cruise down the river. Underway, it was exciting to actually see some of the birds on the list. Rochelle and Terry both had guides to the birds of Peru; and they and our guides helped us identify individual birds as they were spotted. It was quite late when we returned to camp, ate dinner, and went to bed.

The next morning we were up for an early breakfast and then, leaving camp, got in our boats to head up to the Manu River and our next camp. There was dense fog that early, shrouding the river and river banks. Eventually the fog cleared, but the weather that day was a combination of intermittent rain and clouds, quite chilly. Our guides had told us that we could expect cooler than normal weather conditions, as a cold front was passing through. Having expected high heat and humidity in the rainforest, this was a surprise, and one we were not exactly prepared for.

With the rain and splashes of water as our boat motored along the river, the two persons sitting in the front seats huddled under tarpaulins to keep dry. Laura, in one of the front seats, was taken with chills and started shivering violently. "Laura," David said, "please move back and let someone else take your place." She did, but felt ill the rest of the day.

There were a great many birds to be seen along the river banks, as well as a few white caiman, South American crocodiles resembling alligators, lying on the sandbars along the riverbanks. We also spotted two separate families of capybaras, largely aquatic rodents, feeding on the foliage along the banks. Those we saw were about the size of large pigs. At lunch time, the cooks, with us on the boats, prepared a delicious lunch of vegetable and chicken salad.

After a rewarding morning of bird-watching, we reached our safari camp near the lake of Cocha Salvador about 2:00 p.m. After getting settled in our cabins, we gathered in the lodge at 3:00 for what David said would be a two-hour walk. At the lodge, we had seen several monkeys in the trees nearby. On the walk, with the aid of binoculars, we spotted more monkeys, of several different species, and birds, high up in the trees. David pointed out various species of trees as we passed under them. Sugar ants were trailing up and down one of the trees; and David warned us to be careful not to disturb them, as their bite could be quite painful.

Our "two-hour walk" turned into three hours; and it was dark by the time we returned to camp. Dinner followed at 7:00. Arturo treated us to a taste of rum from a bottle he'd brought, then we enjoyed a tasty dinner of soup followed by the main course of beef and vegetables. Liz and I went to bed soon after.

The following morning we got up a bit later. Then Liz and I and several others walked down to the lake, from where we took a catamaran to cruise silently around the lake. During our cruise, we saw a family of giant otters, fishing. We also saw a white egret, a heron and a large black caiman, half immersed at the water's edge. The black caiman are hard to spot because, with their coloring, they're hard to distinguish from logs. Caimans, jaguars, and humans—who prize the pelt—are the otters' primary predators. After our two-hour cruise, we were ravenous and enjoyed a big breakfast including eggs, prepared sunny-side up, and plantains.

We had time before lunch to sit back and relax, and then a long siesta after lunch. At 3:30, I joined others to go with Arturo and David back along the path to the lookout, to look for peccaries, monkeys and other wildlife. We didn't see any peccaries, but, standing on the viewing platform overlooking the lake, we did see several spider monkeys climbing down trees and another family of otters. We watched incredulously as the otters, not noticing us—swam by so close we could almost touch them. Then it was back to camp, dinner and bed.

We woke up early, aroused by a really strange noise, one I'd never heard before. "Liz," I said, "it sounds mechanical, like a pump. I wonder what it is."

"I have no idea," Liz said. We found out later that these were calls from howler monkeys, passing through camp and establishing their territory.

After breakfast, we motored up to another lake, Coca Otorongo, to see ore birds and monkeys. We saw another group of giant otters, more birds, tiny bats the color of bark, clinging to a tree limb, and some woolly monkeys up in the trees. We also saw a pair of hoatzins, with their unusual spiky crest, bizarre-looking birds. At one point we climbed up a fifty-foot observation tower. At this height we were above the lower tree canopy and had a better view.

Back on the trail, we stopped, amazed, at an enormous tree. A kapok tree, this was of a stupendous size, at least as wide and tall as some of the giant California redwoods. This was too good a photo opportunity to pass up, so we had Arturo take a group photo of all sixteen of us, dwarfed, in front of the tree. He said the tree was about 300 years old and about 175 feet tall.

After the walk, we set off in our boats for a 5-hour trip down the Manu River to our last camp, near Boca Mona. On the way, we stopped to visit the Mattiguena camp. This small habitat, provided by the park service, houses one or more indigenous families. The people, who stay here for an indefinite period, raise crops for food and also sell woven items and small crafts to tourists who visit the camp. I took a picture of a plant with a beautiful red flower, the Aphelandra. One of the families, the mother, father, and several children, stood for a photograph. I gave away a Nestles candy bar to one of the children, but then I wondered whether he would eat it, candy not being part of the family's diet.

When we reached our camp, the heat and humidity hit us. Now we knew what we had missed, and we were thankful for the cloudy, cool weather we'd had. Liz and I took showers as soon as we settled in our cabin. I felt tired and a bit out of sorts. While Liz went exploring, I stayed in the cabin and rested.

At dinner, I bought a beer but drank only half. After I ate the hot soup and took a few bites of chicken, I felt slightly nauseous, and left the rest of the meal on my plate. Not wanting to leave, as it would be our last dinner together with Arturo and David, I endured sitting through the lengthy meal. Although bottles of celebratory wine were passed around, I managed only a few sips. As we lingered over the wine, David and Arturo explained the plans for the next day. Since the eight-passenger plane that would take us back to

Cusco would hold only half of us, Rochelle assigned us to two separate flights. I was glad to be among those on the first flight, leaving at 11:00 a.m. I was relieved when the party finally broke up and I could get back to our cabin and to bed.

I woke up the next morning feeling better. At breakfast, Rochelle thanked Arturo, David, and all the crew and gave them a combined tip from all of us. After Liz and I packed, she went out to do more exploring while I stayed put. Soon those of us on the first plane were called down to the lake for the short cruise to the Boca Mona landing strip. At the airport, our luggage was weighed to ensure that the small plane's load wouldn't exceed a safe limit. As our plane rolled onto the landing strip, we said goodbye to David and Arturo.

It was chilly in Cusco—quite a contrast from the hot weather in the rainforest, and I put on several layers of clothes to get warm. In mid-afternoon I stopped at a café to have a cappuccino; it was delicious and warming. I took advantage of a free afternoon in Cusco, walking around the familiar plazas and then visiting the Inca Museum. It was filled with a fine collection of metal and gold work, jewelry, pottery, textiles, mummies and more. It held the world's largest collection of Incan wooden drinking vessels, 450 in all. At our last dinner in Cusco, again at the Curry House, my appetite was back, and I relished the vegetable fritters, vegetable curry and naan. A glass of red wine was just the right accompaniment.

Before we left Cusco the next morning, I went for a short walk after breakfast and stopped in the Plaza de Armas, my favorite spot in Cusco. It was a lovely morning, sunny and warm. As I saw people going in and out of La Catedral, I went to have a look. Going in, I saw there was a mass in progress. Engrossed by the ceremony in progress in this beautiful, sacred place, I stood in the back and listened for about ten minutes. As I left through one of the cathedral doors, an old lady standing in the doorway pressed a little medallion on me, quickly pinning it to my sweater. As she entreated me to contribute some money, "por La Catedral," I gave her two soles.

After leaving La Catedral, I sat down on a park bench to soak up the sun. While there, the young fellow selling postcards came over. Again, I resisted buying any, but we did have a conversation, during which we exchanged e-mail addresses, and he promised to send an e-mail the next week. As I got up to leave, we wished each other well. It was a nice encounter, in fact, the only conversation I had had with a Peruvian other than with the guides.

When I got back to the hotel, everyone was packed up and ready to go. At the airport, I was surprised by the hefty airport tax,

$28.00; fortunately, I had enough money left to pay it. We boarded our plane on schedule but then sat on the runway for four hours, due to adverse weather conditions. To lighten the plane load and increase the possibility of getting airborne, passengers were asked to volunteer to take another flight, with the offer of a free trip. About half the passengers disembarked.

My seatmates, a young man and older woman travelling together, were reading a book about the Inca Trail; they'd just finished four days of hiking the entire trail. The woman said it was pretty tough, and she'd never do it again. Finally we took off, to cheers from the passengers. In Lima, we had just enough time for dinner at a restaurant before returning to the airport for our flight to the States. I was on the same plane with Ann, both headed to Atlanta in an overnight flight.

As day broke and it turned light, I woke up and was dismayed to find that the little ring I wore on the fifth finger of my right hand was missing. I loved that ring, and could have cried. It must have slipped off at some point the day before or earlier that morning without my noticing it. Anyway, the flight arrived in Atlanta on schedule; and I proceeded through customs and retrieved my baggage, ready for the flight to Buffalo. What extraordinary experiences I'd had; I couldn't wait to tell my stories!

41

Focus on Photography

And tell my stories, I did. In Peru I'd taken several rolls of film; now back in Buffalo, I selected the best images to use in slide shows. I delighted in reliving my Peruvian experiences during the slide shows I presented—at home to friends, to the Women's Society at the U.U. Church, to a book club in Niagara Falls, and as a travel talk at the Buffalo Science Museum.

Jesse Kregal, a timpanist with the Buffalo Philharmonic Orchestra and who had hiked the entire Inca Trail, heard about my Peruvian travels and said he'd like to see my slides. So I invited him over one evening, and he brought along his eight-year old daughter. She was so excited by several of the images, she burst out with "Wow!" each time. Soon after, Jesse's own photos of Peru were on exhibit at WNED's radio/television studio in downtown Buffalo. I went to see the exhibit and was impressed by the beautiful photographs, several of them portraits of Peruvians.

In June, 2006, I printed and framed three of my Peru photographs and showed them in the Member's Exhibit at Art Dialogue. There they elicited several favorable comments; and one, "At the Top," sold on opening night. This was the photograph I'd taken while horseback riding in the Andes, when we'd stopped for a break at the summit of a mountain pass. In October, 2007, I used the same three photographs in my submission for admission as a member of the Buffalo Society of Artists. Part of the application process was to have the jurying committee review my photographs. Having been rejected twice before, this time I'd hit upon a winning combination: On October 17, I received a congratulatory letter from the Society.

The Buffalo Society of Artists (BSA) was established in 1891, by local artists, with the mission of educating the public as to the value of local American art. In 1912, the gala opening of the BSA's Second Catalog Exhibition attracted hundreds of Buffalo socialites, with President Grover Cleveland's wife in attendance. The Society abandoned shows during the Depression, but in 1935 resumed annual exhibitions, continuing the Society's commitment of promoting the work of Buffalo artists. Now the Society regularly held two exhibits each year, in the spring and in the fall. I was elated to become a member of this prestigious group, which included painters, photographers, sculptors, and mixed media artists.

After my acceptance, I went to my first meeting with BSA members, attending their annual dinner and business meeting. There I met several members, including one of the jurors, who congratulated me and said that the voting in my favor had been unanimous. A month later I went to the reception for new members and, as one of eight presenters, showed a dozen of my Peru slides, receiving favorable comments. As I attempted an answer to the question of the "why" of my photographs, one member suggested that they were "intuitive." I guess they were.

A diary entry dated January 4, 2004, posed the question, "During twenty years of photography, did I improve in the process?" When, in 2007, I sorted through my many prints and slides, discarding half, I realized how much of my leisure time had been spent photographing. Now, having my photographs regularly exhibited at Art Dialogue and selling several, along with becoming a member of the BSA, seemed to indicate that I had, indeed, progressed.

In December, 2007, Ted Pietrzak, the Burchfield Penney Art Center Director, invited those members who were also artists to show selected works in a special exhibit on December 14, the last exhibit the Center would hold in their present location, in Rockwell Hall: a new building was scheduled to be completed and opened in early 2009. I entered one photo, of a tree in Delaware Park, its black trunk and bare limbs silhouetted against a sky colored pink and lavender by the winter sunset. On opening night I mingled with the crowd and was pleased to see my work hung among the works of over a hundred artists, including Priscilla Bowen, an artist friend. Priscilla, Beth Abgott and I posed happily for a photo, taken by Priscilla's friend, Jackie Brooks.

Beth Abgott, Priscilla Bowen and Sylvia, at the opening for the Burchfield Exhibit, "Artists Among Us". December, 2007

     Besides landscapes, I found other aspects of Buffalo, "a rust belt city," interesting. In 2004, I did a series of photographs showing some of the graffiti drawn not only on abandoned but also occupied buildings, inciting the wrath of owners. I found much of the graffiti artistic, but most Buffalonians hated it. The mayor himself ordered a widespread cleaning and eradication and fined several of the graffiti artists. One of my subjects was the wall of a vacant brick building near Main Street and Ferry. Though gradually deteriorating, its windows broken and doors boarded up, the textures and the bold, colorful graffiti made it an irresistible subject. I placed a 10 x 12 framed print of that photograph, which I called "Vacant," in one of Art Dialogue's regular exhibits.

     Michael Gillis, a personal friend and also the co-owner of Elmwood Framing and Interiors, where I had all my photographs framed, was intrigued by "Vacant," to the extent of experimenting with re-printing the photo, heightening the colors and the graphics. The result pleased us both, and Michael made a much larger print of it and framed it, figuring that he would find a buyer. I agreed to the sale, and soon after, it was sold and put on hold for the buyers. I was stunned when Michael told me the buyers, interested in industrial photos of Buffalo, were JoAnn Foletta, the Buffalo

Philharmonic's conductor, and her husband. What an honor it was to have them as collectors of one of my photographs!

I included the Buffalo Olmsted Parks Conservancy as collectors, as I had gifted them two of my Delaware Park photographs, framed, in March, 2004. The Conservancy welcomed them as "a wonderful addition" to their collection, stating that, of all the photographs contributed, mine best captured the spirit of Delaware Park.

Now, active in both the Western New York Artists Group, whose members showed regularly at Art Dialogue Gallery, and the Buffalo Society of Artists, whose members exhibited regularly at various venues, I became friends with several artists in both groups, expanding my social network. By then I had dropped my membership in the Science Museum Camera Club, which I no longer found satisfying.

Many photographers were abandoning film for digital photography, but I was one of the holdouts still using film. There were others, and in July, 2008, I joined a group that called itself the "Still Film Photographers." The group met regularly at the Locust Street Art Center, on Buffalo's east side, and several members used the facilities at the Center to process their black and white photographs. In November, I joined a half dozen other members in experimenting with night photography, something new for me.

One night I returned from photographing buildings in Buffalo and saw an intriguing subject in the house next door. A brightly illuminated lamp in the neighbor's living room window was perfectly framed in the space between the drapes pulled to either side. I set up my tripod on the neighbor's lawn and shot the last two frames in that roll of film. The result was a striking image of a glowing white lamp centered in the black window frames, against a red background. The BSA included "Night Light" in their Spring 2009 exhibit at the Kenan Center in Lockport, and in their catalogue for the show. I also used "Night Light" as my entry for the Still Film Photographers show at the CEPA Gallery that May.

Not all my leisure time was spent in photography. In 2003, I had begun volunteering as an ESL (English as a Second Language) tutor for Literacy Volunteers, and had for two years tutored a young Chinese woman, whose husband attended U.B. and then found a job in the Buffalo area. She and I became friends and remained so until they moved away. Then I acquired another student, a young South Korean woman; but she ended the sessions after several months because of a health problem. I decided then to try another volunteer activity, this time with Compeer, an organization dedicated to improving the lives of adults and children receiving mental health treatment and striving towards good mental health.

As a Compeer friend, I met every two weeks with my friend, a pleasant woman in her fifties with a lovely smile that lit up her face. She was divorced, had two adult daughters, one living with her, and a teenage son who had problems of his own. My visits with "Jackie" (not her real name) served as a relief to whatever problems she was experiencing at home; and since she didn't have a car, she was very appreciative of my taking her places.

Together we went for walks in Delaware Park and at the Erie Basin Marina; visited the Buffalo and Erie County Botanical Garden, strolling through the beautiful floral displays; saw exhibits depicting Buffalo's early history at the Historical Society; and spent hours at both the Albright-Knox Art Gallery and the Burchfield Penney Art Center. Jackie always enjoyed seeing the art on exhibit there, as she had been a bit of an artist herself in her younger days. I also brought her to Art Dialogue when I had one or more of my photos on display, and encouraged her to resume her artistic bent. We discovered that we had both been exhibitors in one of the first Allentown Festivals, Buffalo's annual event, including artists in all media and from all over the United States. She had exhibited some of her sketches; I exhibited some of the pottery I was making then.

Besides volunteering for Compeer, I reluctantly agreed to serve as Interim Treasurer for the U.U. Church. It was a position of considerable responsibility, and I was relieved when another person became the full-time Treasurer several months later. Managing the business end of Bob's office, I was not willing to involve myself further in financial matters.

42

Bob's World

From the time we married, I had spent a good part of my life in Bob's world of architecture. Now I continued to assist him in his office and also as his companion on occasions which interested us both. Bob was not a movie fan and rarely went to see a movie, but we both saw two documentary movies about architects, the first about Louis Kahn, the second, about Frank Gehry. The Oscar-nominated biographical documentary about Louis Kahn, a world-renowned American of Estonian and Jewish descent, was made by his son. Many of Kahn's masterpieces were shown, among them his first significant commission, the Yale University Art Gallery in New Haven, Connecticut; the Salk Institute in La Jolla, California; and, near Buffalo, the First Unitarian Church in Rochester, named "one of the greatest religious structures of the 20th century" by architectural critic Paul Goldberger.

The movie also revealed the little-known secrets of Kahn's personal life. He had been involved with three different women: his wife, Esther, whom he married in 1930; Anne Tyng, who began her working collaboration and personal relationship with Kahn in 1945; and Harriet Pattison. His wife apparently was unaware of the other women and families until after Kahn died of a heart attack in 1974. The women all met at his funeral. It must have been awkward for all.

The documentary, "Sketches of Frank Gehry," provided the viewer insights into Gehry's ideas and how he implemented them through creative partners and staff. The movie was especially interesting to Bob, since he had known Gehry from the time when they both, as young graduate architects beginning their careers, worked in a Boston firm. Since then, they'd travelled separate paths, Gehry's spiraling into fame. When they met at AIA affairs, Gehry acknowledged Bob, but consistently ignored his overtures suggesting a collaboration.

The life of Frank Lloyd Wright inspired books, both fiction and non-fiction, and even an opera. Suzanne Taub gave us tickets for the Buffalo Philharmonic Orchestra's performance in November, 2007, of the opera, "Shining Brow," based on episodes in Wright's life. Married to Catherine Lee Tobin and the father of three children with her, Wright met and fell in love with Mamah Cheney.

Sometime later he left his practice and his family and travelled with Mamah to Europe. When they returned, he designed a new home for Mamah and studio near Spring Green, Wisconsin. Wright called the complex Taliesin, Welch for "Shining Brow," reflecting his ancestry. Mamah met a tragic end a few years later when Julian Carlston, a deranged caretaker, killed her and six others and set fire to Taliesin, destroying it. Wright built a second Taliesin, which also burned; finally, a third, much larger, complex still stands.

In January, 2004, the Albright-Knox Gallery featured the work of rising young black artist Julie Mehretu, and Bob and I went to the opening. Mehretu was born in Ethiopia, her father an Ethiopian college professor and her mother a white American teacher. They moved to America when she was six years old. Mehretu's distinctive, large paintings reflected her interest in geography, architecture, history and urban life, using architectural drawings as part of the layering process. Bob was enthralled, because she was black, young and pretty, as well as artistic. He didn't learn until later that she was gay and travelling with her partner.

Meeting her at the opening reception, Bob introduced himself to Mehretu and—on the spur of the moment—suggested he could have a reception in our home the next evening to meet Buffalo's black artists. I was negative to the idea: I didn't appreciate Bob's spontaneity and figured that she most likely had the weekend's activities all arranged for her anyway. As it turned out, she did not respond to Bob's invitation, and soon left for New York with her partner, Jessica Rankin, a transplanted Australian artist. After her work was exhibited in Buffalo, Mehretu became known as a highly original artist, pushing abstract art in a new direction by opening it up to social and political content.

In August, we went to Ithaca for the New York State Chapter of the AIA's annual convention, during which Bob was presented with an award. I drove my car, with Bob and Linda Sichel, who was working with Bob at the time, as passengers. It was a pleasant, scenic drive, but as I drove into the city and stopped at a red light, my car was rear-ended by the vehicle behind me. When the police arrived and took a report, the driver, a young woman, admitted she wasn't paying attention. Fortunately, the car was drivable, so we continued on to our hotel. That evening we went to the awards dinner, when Bob was presented the William James Kideney Gold Medal for his contributions to the profession and the community. Bob was very pleased to receive that prestigious honor, and I was happy for him.

Of all his projects, Bob was most proud of the new Frank J. Merriweather Library, which opened on April 1, 2006. Located on Buffalo's east side and serving a mostly black population, Bob designed the library to reflect an African village. The design meshed six open circular rooms—symbolic of village huts—nestled against a stunning central circle with a towering, light-filled, colored glass dome. As Bob and I entered the library for the opening that afternoon, we saw a crowd gathered in the central circulation area, listening to African drummers.

Bob and Sylvia, after the Merriweather Library Opening.
April, 2005

Mayor Byron Brown and several other dignitaries celebrated the library's opening; and Bob gave a five-minute presentation, acknowledging all who had contributed to the project, also mentioning me. We had extended an open invitation for a reception afterwards at our house, and forty people came, enjoying the party food I'd prepared, soft drinks and wine. Charles Rush, Bob's first intern architect, and his wife, Marge, now living near Albany, lingered to talk and were the last to leave.

In a Buffalo News article, the library was called "a signature building on Buffalo's eastside and a beacon of hope for the community." With a richly-decorated interior using African motifs, and one room devoted to the largest collection of African-American history and research materials outside of New York City, the library was expected to be, not only an invaluable resource center but, with an attractive, well-equipped auditorium, also a major community gathering spot. An article in the July/August 2006 *Buffalo Spree* magazine about Bob included a photo of the library and a nice one of us, both looking pleased.

In October, 2007, I accompanied Bob to New York for a party given by our friends Nancy and Charles Wolf in their Soho loft apartment. The occasion was to celebrate the start of a new medical center in Kigutu, Burundi, about seventy miles south of the capital, Bujumburu, as envisioned by Deogratias (Deo) Niyizonkiza, a native of Burundi. Bob had met Deo several months earlier at a fundraiser held in the Wolf's apartment. He'd brought with him photographs of the new Merriweather Library. After one look at the photographs, Deo said to Bob, "Can you design a clinic building along the same lines as the Library?" Bob assured him he could. Then, "out of a clear blue sky," Bob said, Deo invited Bob to travel with him to Burundi in September to visit the site, paying his travel expenses.

Bob did go and spent eighteen days, experiencing "another world." Staying at a nearby hotel, Bob visited the site, sizing up the proposed clinic's location and deciding what type of plan would be feasible. On his return to the States, Bob drew up five different master plans and presented them to Deo. The project would be funded by the non-profit organization, Village Health Works, founded by Deo, working with the Burundian government.

At the party, Deo greeted me warmly, pleased that I'd come. Circulating among the guests, I met author Tracy Kidder, who was writing a book about Deo, an unusual twenty-two-year-old. Originally from Burundi, Deo had fled ethnic violence there and come to New York. Nancy and Charles Wolf found him, homeless, in Central Park, and took him under their wing, financing his education. Deo was taking a year's leave from his medical studies at Dartmouth College to drum up funding for the clinic. Bob and I headed back to Buffalo the day after the party, Bob expecting to be given a major role in the project.

The Burundi project became more complicated than anticipated. After some additional work refining parts of his initial design, Bob's continued involvement became problematic, partly because of Burundian building requirements and restrictions, and partly due to the lack of communication on the part of Deo. By December, it was clear that Deo had turned to other sources for designing the clinic facilities rather than pay the fees Bob anticipated. It was a disappointing end to Bob's expectations regarding his role in that potentially exciting project.

But there was cause to celebrate. Marshall Purnell, the Washington architect who, with his partner, Paul Devrouax, had worked with Bob on the Municipal Office Building years ago, was elected as the new President of the American Institute of Architects, the first African-American to achieve that position. It was an occasion not to be missed, so in mid-December Bob and I went to Washington for the inauguration.

Bob had sent out notices to all the African-American architects, hoping for a good representation at the ceremony, and he handed out noisemakers to those who came, contributing to the applause following Purnell's address to the assembled guests. I managed to get a photo of Bob with Purnell, Bob beaming with pride. Feeling glamorous in my favorite red gown, I enjoyed the evening, mingling with AIA people I'd met years ago and others I'd known while Bob had an office in Washington.

The next day Tony Diamond and his wife, Irene, picked us up at our hotel and took us to brunch at the elegant Fort Myers Clubhouse, resplendent with Christmas decorations, where Tony, retired from military service, was a member. Tony, of Greek ancestry, and Bob had been best friends in high school, both being cross-country runners. But when he heard about our interracial marriage, Tony abruptly broke off their friendship, and Bob did not hear from him again. Bob had told me the story of Tony's rejection and how hurt he'd been.

So it came as a complete surprise when Tony called Bob about a year earlier, telling him that he and his wife were in Buffalo for a visit with friends and inviting us out for dinner at the Anchor Bar. Although not yet ready for a reconciliation, Bob did accept the invitation, and we met them for dinner. During the evening's conversation, it was clear that Tony was doing his best to repair the rift he'd caused; and we ended the evening on a cordial note. Since then, Tony had made more overtures, through telephone calls and e-mails, and Bob gradually warmed up to Tony. Whenever Bob was in Washington, he and Tony would get together.

In Buffalo, the new Burchfield Penney Art Center, designed by Gwathmey Siegel and Associates, opened on September 5, 2008, and Bob and I went to the opening, hearing speeches by Director Ted Pietrzak, Mayor Byron Brown, and other officials. I thought the new museum was splendid and was especially impressed by the vastness of the attractive main gallery, designed to accommodate huge paintings and sculptures. Bob, critical as usual, found fault with the design of the main floor: "You have to walk past the coffee shop, the admissions desk, and the gift shop, all the way down the lobby before you get to the main gallery." He thought it should have been placed near the entrance.

Later that month, I flew to Indianapolis to see Monica and Jim Allen. The weekend I was there, we drove to Valparaiso to celebrate the confirmation of one of our Bunge cousins' son, Isaac. Isaac and his mother, Marcia Bunge, lived in Valparaiso, where Marcia taught at the University. After the confirmation in a Lutheran church on that Sunday, a reception was held at the University, and we met other Bunge cousins and Marcia's mother in a mini-reunion. Later that afternoon, we drove back to Indianapolis; and the next day I left for Buffalo.

On November 19, 2009, Bob was honored by the Buffalo Chapter of the AIA with the Louise Bethune Award, for his significant contributions to Buffalo architecture. I accompanied Bob to the affair, held downtown, dressed in a black cocktail dress and over it a pink velvet vest with a fur collar, and wearing my mother's amber beads. "You look lovely," commented a young woman, who told me she owned a vintage shop in suburban Orchard Park. Bob received many congratulations, and I was gratified when Bob acknowledged my continuing support in his acceptance speech. We sat at a table with the chapter president and his wife. I was happy to be there, but it was cold in the room, and I couldn't stop shivering. I could hardly wait to get home and warm up with a hot cup of coffee.

Monica and Jim Allen, Marcia Bunge at Valparaiso, Indiana.
September, 2008

43

Changing Times

During her visit back to Buffalo early in 2007, Bob and I had cocktails with writer Diana Dillaway and her partner, David Olsen. Diana, formerly from Buffalo, wrote about the city's decline in *Power Failure*, citing the failure of people in power to invest in the city, which might have prevented its decline. Bob had been one of the many Buffalonians Diana interviewed for the book. Diana invited me to visit them in their home in Ventura, California, suggesting that I take Amtrak from Oakland as an inexpensive way to travel.

I followed up on her suggestion, and that summer went to Ventura and spent several days there with Diana and David. I thoroughly enjoyed staying in their comfortable cottage, just steps away from the beach and ocean. Since I'd brought my swim suit, I even ventured a brief swim one afternoon; diving into the surf, I swam out for a few minutes and then let the waves carry me back. As I was not a strong swimmer, that was enough. Ventura, however, was a favorite among surfers. On my morning walks, as I passed the beach near their house, I would see a number of surfers, parked along the road, heading out in their wetsuits and carrying their surfboards.

Diana and I took long walks along the beach; and one afternoon we drove to the Santa Barbara Mountains and took a 2-1/2 hour hike along the Romero Trail. While I was in Ventura, she and I took a side trip to Calabasas, invited to visit Tammy—Frank Evans and Lydia Wright's daughter—and her husband, Kevin, and son, Alex. Diana gave Tammy a copy of her book, and Tammy said she was sure she'd find it interesting, having grown up in Buffalo.

During the same trip I spent two days with Marion and Michael in their home in Inverness, near the entrance to Point Reyes. One afternoon Marion and I went for a walk along Limatour Beach, familiar to me from my experience with the Sierra Club, and then hiked the upper trail. As I walked along the beach, I kept my eye open for interesting shells, but didn't find any. I did pick up a small, bleached white, V-shaped piece that reminded me of a similar object in one of Georgia O'Keefe's paintings, and mounted it on one of the walls in my study next to a postcard picturing that painting. Marion and I had a good visit; and as she dropped me off at the airport, I told her how much I loved her and that I hoped to see her more often.

I saw her again two years later, on another trip to San Francisco, in August, 2009. This time both Marion and Darcy came to the hotel where I stayed, and we had lunch at Sinbads, a seafood restaurant with a view of the Bay Bridge. Marion said she had turned to making jewelry and painting, having given up photography. She'd been suffering from back pain and sciatica, and could no longer carry around the tripod and other equipment she used for her beautiful landscape photographs. I said I was sorry to hear about the back pain. She had corresponded with me in the last few years with note cards made with her photographs, and I treasured those. I asked her once whether she'd ever considered publishing her photographs. "No," she said, "I do those photographs for myself."

Marion, obviously hurting, left right after lunch to beat the late afternoon traffic, but not before I took a photograph of her and Darcy, and then Darcy one of Marion and me. He and I spent the rest of the afternoon and the next couple of days together. The following day, we went back to Angel Island and hiked the perimeter trail again. Returning to the city, we stopped at Pacific Beach. There I was finally close enough to the Pacific Ocean to touch the water, as I'd hoped. While Darcy waited for me on a bench along the boardwalk, I went down to the water's edge to watch the tide roll in and took a few photos, hoping that they would capture the moment. Then I joined Darcy, and we talked as the sun set, barely visible in a cloudy sky.

On my last afternoon there, we went first to Pier 39 to see the noisy sea lions, crowding each other for position on the pier where they get fed, then walked around the many shops and restaurants on Fisherman's Wharf. From there we took a bus to Coit Tower, on Telegraph Hill, where we had a panoramic view. From the hill, we walked all the way back to my hotel, passing through the North Beach area and Chinatown. When I left the hotel that evening, Darcy accompanied me to the airport and we said a fond farewell. Who knew when I'd be back in San Francisco.

Bob had loved the prestigious Ellicott Square location, but early in 2008, with no staff , facing an uncertain future and lacking the financial resources necessary to continue leasing the downtown office, he decided it was time to move back to Humboldt Parkway. After selling a few of the file cabinets, discarding materials including reference books, drafting equipment and supplies, and packing the remainder into countless storage boxes, we had a closing-the-office party on May 2, with food and drinks set out on tables in the hallway.

Bob's sailor friend, Lou Brehm, played his keyboard while about twenty-five people showed up to wish us well. Our friend David Gordon took photographs, including one picturing Bob and me in the office doorway. I had David make a larger print of that photo and gave it to Bob that Christmas.

With help from two teenagers, Bob had cleared out the front studio to squeeze in work stations for himself and me, a cubicle for each of the two computers, a place for the printer, fax machine, copier and typewriter, four file cabinets and a supply closet, to fit with the existing storage cabinets, tables and models. This left a narrow passage just large enough for one person at a time to move from one end of the studio to the other.

After a few weeks, the office was functioning efficiently; and Bob liked the convenience of having the office right at home. As he jokingly told friends, "I can walk into my studio in my pajamas, whenever I please." I was fine with having the office at home, as long as I could separate office work from my other activities. I had my own study downstairs in what used to be one of the children's bedrooms.

Just as Bob and I were getting older, so were our friends, and several had health problems. Our long-time musician friend, Harry Taub, died on October 15, after a long illness. Bob and I went to his memorial service held in the contemporary Unitarian-Universalist Church in Amherst, filled with Harry's friends and family. A trio played some of Harry's own compositions, evoking the fine musician he was. Ruth Ellen Bunis, another friend of ours, officiated as rabbi; and Harry's son Michael gave a moving tribute to his father. Bob and I went to the reception afterwards held at Harry's Harborside Restaurant.

Two years ago, we had invited Suzanne and Harry to dinner at our house with Trudy and Andy Anderson, who were in Buffalo visiting Trudy's son, Adam Perry, an attorney. Suzanne and Trudy had known each other years before, when Trudy was living in Buffalo, but hadn't seen each other for years, so they enjoyed getting together again.

Suzanne and Harry Taub, Andy and Trudy Anderson, with Bob at our home in Buffalo, New York. 2006

In September, 2009, we went to the funeral of another long-time friend, Frank Evans, who died after a long illness. Bob had regularly gone to visit Frank, confined to his bed at the Niagara Lutheran Nursing Home, bringing him the Sunday New York Times and sometimes a bottle of wine. Frank, obviously enjoying Bob's visits, always kept up a lively conversation. Bob and I went to the funeral service at the church Frank and his wife, Lydia, who'd died previously, had attended.

Both Will Clarkson, another of Frank's long-time friends, and Bob participated in the service, reading passages from the Bible. Frank Jr., Frank and Lydia's son, delivered the eulogy, barely holding back the tears. At the reception afterwards, we talked with Tammy, Kevin and Alex, who'd come from California. "We'll be back in Buffalo now and then, and we'll call you," Tammy said. With both her parents gone, we wondered whether they would.

44

On a Par with Bob

One of the artists I met when I joined the BSA was George Grace, a published writer in addition to being a fine painter. I'd always liked to write, and when I told George I was interested in becoming a more creative writer, he suggested joining a writer's group, which met regularly at his home. In February, 2008, I began attending the bi-weekly sessions. There were usually a half-dozen writers and poets at each session, reading a poem or short story to be critiqued. At one of my first sessions, I read a poem I'd written about traveling by bus to Kansas. Air travel to Kansas had become increasingly expensive, and that year I'd decided to try taking Greyhound.

The scenery, the folks riding the buses, and the stations were a whole different experience. In the dirty, littered St. Louis bus station, crowded with passengers, I heard the unmistakable strains of the "X-files" theme, evoking memories of that TV show, one of the few I watched regularly. While on the 36-hour trip to Hays, I wrote "Thoughts during a Long Bus Trip to Kansas." Everyone liked it, and George said, "It shows your sense of humor." Thus encouraged, I kept writing, sometimes even submitting short articles to *The Sun Magazine*, hoping that one of mine would be accepted and published in their column, "Readers Write." I also started subscribing to *The Writers Magazine*, which contained many helpful writing tips.

Every two months I went to Diva Studios for a haircut, and my hair stylist, Susan Morrow, enjoyed hearing about my trips and various activities. One afternoon she said, "You should write a book." I thought about it, and said to myself, why not? I began writing an autobiography based on the diary I'd been keeping for years, including fairly detailed accounts of the Africa, Papua New Guinea, and Peru trips. When the autobiography took up increasing amounts of time, I dropped out of the writers group to focus on it.

In February, 2011, I read an article published in the *Buffalo News* written by a writer friend of mine. The article appeared in a new column, "Women's Voices," and it was the story of how the writer, Veronica Hogle, originally from Ireland, came to America on a one-way ticket and eventually moved to Buffalo with her husband. After they divorced, she managed to make a living for herself and her three small children. I called Veronica to tell her how much I enjoyed reading her article, and she said, "Why don't you write one?"

It seemed like a good opportunity and a challenge as well. I decided to write about how Bob and I happened to come to Buffalo, what my experience had been as the wife of an architect, and how I had created new roles for myself. With Veronica as my critic, I wrote and re-wrote the article. Finally I arrived at a version both she and I were happy with, passed it by Bob, who suggested just a few changes, made the changes, and submitted it. A few days later, the column editor called to tell me she liked the article and that they'd like to publish it. I was ecstatic! Several days later, a *News* photographer came to take photos. The *News* would select one for the article.

The article was published in the Saturday, April 9th *Buffalo News*. I was overwhelmed by the positive response that followed: It seemed just about everyone I knew, including people at church, artist friends, the ladies in my tennis group, and others read the article and said they loved it. Some sent the original article so I'd have extras to give away. I'd wondered whether men read the column and discovered that, in fact, they did. I happened to have some minor car repair done at Nirelli's Collision the following Monday; and as I walked in the office, the manager said, "Can I have your autograph?" Other men also congratulated me, and I was especially pleased to receive a nice note from Don Siuta, Director of the Art Dialogue Gallery, and also from independent writer and art critic Gerald Mead.

Bob, too, was happy about the publicity. I had portrayed him favorably in the column, mentioning his many achievements and awards; and he e-mailed the article to numerous people. In those euphoric moments, I felt on a par with Bob for the first time in our married life, no longer just "the architect's wife" but with an identity of my own. With renewed confidence, I felt ready to meet new and unexpected challenges. And it was time to close this book.

List of Photographs

Bob and Sylvia, Minneapolis, Summer, 1952 (page 9)

Bob and Sylvia, Baalbek, Syria, 1965 (page 40)

Bob and Sylvia, with children Darcy and Marion, and their dog Duke posing in their home. Buffalo, 1968 (page 44)

Bob and Sylvia, at the Minneapolis AIA Convention. May, 1981 (page 69)

Marion and Michael Ongerth at home. Berkeley, California. Summer, 1988 (page 76)

John Hembree, Paluka, and Sylvia, preparing to motor down the Semliki River. Zaire, Africa. September, 1989 (page 96)

Bob and Sylvia, in San Antonio, Texas, for the College of Fellows Board Meeting. April, 1993 (page 122)

Bob with Randy Vosbeck and Kathryn Prigmore at the College of Fellows Dinner. December, 1994 (page 128)

Bob and Sylvia at Bob's Burchfield Penney Exhibit. May, 1996 (page 135)

Bob and Sylvia, after receiving her Master of Science Degree, SUNY at Buffalo. May, 1997 (page 139)

Heidi and Steve Meyn celebrating Christmas with the Coles. December, 2009. (page 144)

Sylvia with Huli wigmen, in Papua New Guinea. September, 1999 (page 151)

Darcy Coles at summit of Mt. Diablo, California. May, 2001 (page 171)

Werner and Candyce, duo pianists, at her home in Eugene, Oregon. May, 2002 (page 178)

Cousin Ingrid Schumacher and her son, Michael, in Hamburg, Germany. June, 2003 (page 182)

Cousins Elfriede Jagst and Wilma Steubner in Cadenberge, Germany. June, 2003 (page 186)

Helen Allen, Richard Meyn, Susan Meyn, Jim Allen, Steve, Heidi, and Kieran Meyn, together to remember Werner. January, 2005 (page 201)

Helen Allen, on her 85th birthday. April 29, 2005 (page 205)

Sylvia at Machu Picchu, Peru. September, 2005 (page 215)

Beth Abgott, Priscilla Bowen and Sylvia, at the opening for the Burchfield Exhibit, "Artists Among Us". December, 2007 (page 226)

Bob and Sylvia, after the Merriweather Library Opening. April, 2005 (page 231)

Monica and Jim Allen, Marcia Bunge at Valparaiso, Indiana. September, 2008 (page 235)

Suzanne and Harry Taub, Andy and Trudy Anderson, with Bob at our home in Buffalo, New York. 2006 (page 239)

www.ingramcontent.com/pod-product-compliance
Lightning Source LLC
Chambersburg PA
CBHW052034090426
42739CB00010B/1905